They Started in MGs

They Started in MGs
*Profiles of Sports Car
Racers of the 1950s*

CARL GOODWIN
Foreword by John Fitch

McFarland & Company, Inc., Publishers
Jefferson, North Carolina, and London

Library of Congress Cataloguing-in-Publication Data

Goodwin, Carl.
They started in MGs : profiles of sports car racers of the 1950s / Carl Goodwin ; foreword by John Fitch.
    p.   cm.

ISBN 978-0-7864-6052-6
softcover : 50# alkaline paper ∞

1. Automobile racing drivers — United States — Biography.
2. Automobiles, Racing — United States — History.
3. M.G. automobile — History.
I. Title.
GV1032.A1G65   2011
796.72092'2—dc23   [B]   2011022541

British Library cataloguing data are available

©2011 Carl Goodwin. All rights reserved

No part of this book may be reproduced or transmitted in any form or by any means, electronic or mechanical, including photocopying or recording, or by any information storage and retrieval system, without permission in writing from the publisher.

On the cover: *inset* Ken Miles driving his MG Special (photograph by Bob Canaan); George Valentine driving a black MGA, 1958 (collection of Bill Victor)

Manufactured in the United States of America

McFarland & Company, Inc., Publishers
Box 611, Jefferson, North Carolina 28640
www.mcfarlandpub.com

This book is dedicated to my wife Nancy,
who woke up in a tent with me to hear the engines at Mid-Ohio,
who put up with so many troublesome old sports cars in the garage,
and, oh yes, I almost forgot about the racing.

To my son Brian, who happily drove the Speedster
to his summer job with the construction company.

To my son Douglas, who stepped on the throttle of the Siata
as soon as he was out of sight of the house.

To grandsons William and Benjamin,
who might do the same things.

Acknowledgments

An effort was made to compose this book of first-person stories from drivers, photographers, mechanics and race officials, so thanks to them all. With apologies to those missed, the book could also not have been written without Fred Egloff, former editor of the Chicago Region SCCA newsletter; Tom Saal, Joe and Georgia Brown, Alix and Pat Lafontant, Don Snelbaker, Hemp Oliver, Rollin LaFrance, Bob Karol, Chris Kintner, Jim Sitz; Bob Canaan, Jack Campbell, George Ivanyi, Stanley Rosenthal, Fred Vytal, Stewarts Photo, Artemis Images, Bill Green, Mark Steigerwald and the International Motor Racing Research Center at Watkins Glen; Larry Berman, Mickey Mishne, Matt Stone, Chad McQueen, Michael Lynch, Art and Dutch Brow, Ralph Cadwallader, David Gardner, Pete Vack of *Veloce Today*, Beth Lunney of *Classic MG*, Randy Riggs of *Vintage Motorsport*, *Vintage Racecar*, *Classic Motorsports*, 356 Registry, the National Automotive History Collection of the Detroit Public Library, the Bridgehampton Historical Society, *Road & Track*, Tony Carroll VSCCA, Jim Donick VSCCA, Philippe Defechereux, Ken Breslauer, Society of Automotive Historians, Sports Car Club of America, the Cleveland Sport Car Club, MG Car Club, Shipley's Office Supplies, and Eric and Shelley at Our Photo Lab. Also Bill Ellis, Griff Davies, Jim Raymond, Tom Blanchard, and Dwight Davis.

Table of Contents

Acknowledgments vi
Foreword: Adventures in MGs by John Fitch 1
Preface 5

THE DRIVERS

Fred Allen 7	Fred Egloff 91
Cameron Argetsinger 9	Gus Ehrman 96
S.H. Arnolt 13	Charlie Ellmers 100
David Ash 16	Bob Fergus 103
Bob Ballenger 19	John Fitch 105
Hank Becker 25	The Funny Face Auto Racing Team 108
John Gordon Benett 31	Richie Ginther 111
John Bentley 33	Cal Gleason 113
Art and Dutch Brow 37	Isabelle Haskell 117
Hubert Brundage 39	Chuck Hassan 121
Ralph Cadwallader 42	Chuck Henry 126
Jim and Sally Carroll 43	Phil Hill 130
Sam Collier, Miles Collier 46	Bob Holbert 133
Harry Constant 49	Ed Hugus 137
Denver Cornett 52	Dick Irish 140
Tom Countryman 54	Rowland Keith 145
Briggs Cunningham 59	LeRoy Kramer Jr. 148
David E. Davis Jr. 65	Haig Ksayian 150
Bob Dickens 71	Bob Larson 153
Chuck Dietrich 73	Ed Licht 158
Suzy Dietrich 76	Otto Linton 163
Frank Dominianni 80	Bill Lloyd 167
Bob Donner 83	Bob Lossman 168
Ralph Durbin 87	Karl Ludvigsen 171

Ebby Lunken	177	Bill Staufer	232
Sandy MacArthur	184	Bruce Stevenson	235
Henry Manney III	188	Chuck Stoddard	238
Don Marsh	190	John Tame	241
Jack McAfee	192	Dick Thompson	244
Steve McQueen	195	Lake Underwood	247
Ken Miles	199	George Valentine	249
Bill Milliken	202	Bill Victor	252
Charles Moran	206	John von Neumann	254
Al Moss	209	Fred Wacker	257
Alan Patterson	211	Harley Watts	260
Bill Pollack	213	Herb Whiting	264
Bob Said	217	Bill Wonder	266
Art Seyler	220	Doc and Peggy Wyllie	270
Bob Shea	222	Sherrie Zuckert	273
Carroll Shelby	229		

Bibliography 275
Index 279

Foreword: Adventures in MGs

by John Fitch

At twenty-one, with a year at Lehigh University behind me, and having inherited a small trust fund, I started out to see the world. I booked passage on a Dutch freighter, the *Beemsterdyke*, for England. It was incredibly slow and took a full three weeks to arrive.

Once in London I fell in with a lovely little ballet dancer whose friend, Ham Johnson, owned a wheat barge on the Thames. Ham insisted I stay on the barge with him while I was in town, which seemed like a fine idea to me. We talked of all the places we'd like to go—and Ham suggested a trip through the British Isles, Scotland and Wales, which also seemed like a fine idea to me. (The Continent would have been my choice, but the war on Poland had started and visas were unobtainable.)

Pooling our resources, we bought a used MG Magnette sedan for $700 and took off on our journey. Now this car was not in the best of shape. The engine and gearbox were fine, but the steering and suspension were horrible, and it leaked oil at an alarming rate. Also, the starter was inoperative, and we were forced to push-start the car all through our trip. After several thousand miles this became routine. At a thousand yards our educated eyes could spot the slightest incline on which to park for a coasting restart.

On a particularly twisty stretch through Wales we overtook a brightly painted Model 328 BMW (a phenomenal road car of its day) being driven with enterprise and obvious skill. The driver saw us approaching and accelerated away. I was at the wheel of our MG and set out after him, sliding in the turns and using up all of the road to keep him in sight. Johnson was literally green on the seat beside me, and thinking back on the condition of the Magnette's suspension, I can well understand why. But I was having a grand time in my first all-out "dice," too enthralled to be discouraged by Ham's discomfort.

John Fitch prepares to race, in the 1953 G.P. Italia, at Monza (courtesy Bernard Cahier).

Finally, however, the BMW simply outdistanced us and we resumed our trip at a more sedate speed. (Before I am branded an outlaw and mad dog of society I must point out that these roads were deserted and that no speed limit existed on the open roads on the British Isles. Citizens, and even foreigners, are assumed to possess sufficient judgment to regulate their speed according to their abilities, without resort to a stifling edict based on the presumption that all cars are of uniformly poor design and bad construction and that all their drivers are equally incompetent.)

I'd seen formal road racing (in which cars must compete over real or simulated roads, with sharp turns, high-speed bends and straightaways, testing engines, brakes and suspension to the fullest) for the first time in my life at Brooklands that year and my motoring appetite was whetted by the sight of Prince Bira flying around the high bankings in an E.R.A. Pushing the crippled Magnette at speed was the closest I had come to realizing my growing ambition to race at the time, but I had already determined to possess a responsive, nimble sports car of my own someday.

However, the war intervened, and I was not to achieve this until 1948, three full years after I was liberated from the Nazi POW camp.*

John Fitch was shot down while strafing a German supply train. After parachuting from his burning P-51, he was captured and spent three months in a prison camp, becoming the leader of its 200 occupants near Nuremberg, and an active member of the Radio Club, in which each man had a different part of the radio and all would meet, assemble the radio and listen for news of the American Army getting closer. Among Fitch's group was the son-in-law of General Patton, and it was Patton who sent the Seventh Army in to liberate the camp.

I bought my first sports car — on a loan from the National City Bank — early in 1948: a spry, lemon-yellow British MG-TC. And I was so enthusiastic that I immediately set up shop as an automobile dealer, beginning with a few square feet of space in a sporting goods store in White Plains, New York. The TC sat in the middle of the floor, surrounded by outboard motors, fishing rods and bicycles. MGs were then selling for $2395 — and to the average American motorist it seemed ridiculous to put out this kind of money for a little wire-wheeled "toy" automobile.

When I told Elizabeth that I intended to enter a sports car race at Bridgehampton in June she wanted to come along. She'd never seen one and I'd never competed in one, so this made us even. Road racing was being revived in the States after many years, Watkins Glen, New York, having held the initial event the previous fall, and not since the era of Barney Oldfield had sports cars raced on public roads.

In an MG-TC borrowed from one of my customers (I'd sold out my stock of new TCs by then), I lined up with the other drivers, many of whom also drove MGs. I was well to the rear of the starting grid, but soon found to my amazement that I was moving up car by car through the pack as I grew accustomed to the speed and the road. I write this calmly, but I was anything but calm in the dizzy whirl of initial impressions in my first race.

Preface

This book, about the early sports car racers who started in MGs, was first a series of articles for *Classic MG* magazine. I had written a piece for them titled "MGs at Put-in-Bay." Of course it was about the classic island race in which I supposed that 90% of the starting field was comprised of MG-TDs owned by engineers who worked at TRW (that's Thompson Ramo Woolridge, a major automotive parts supplier). While not completely true, it was close enough.

After it ran in the magazine, editor Beth Lunney said, "Our readers just loved that article. Can you do something else about early MG racing?" I was in the middle of a long feature article for *Vintage Motorsport* about the Cunningham team at Le Mans in 1960, the year they took the Corvettes over. Naturally, it was titled "24 Hours Without Brakes." I told Beth, "Let me think about it — I'm sure I'll come up with something."

Later, the idea came to me to have a short series about early drivers and call it "They Started in MGs." I was going to write about ten driver profiles and send it in. But it was like eating potato chips: it was hard to stop. When I stopped writing, there were 54 drivers. I sent it in to Beth and it was obvious the only way to feature them was as a series. They were in alphabetical order with Cameron Argetsinger, the father of road racing in America and a good driver as well, near the head of the list.

As *Classic MG* began to run these, the idea came to do a book. The book at that point was made up of sports car pilots from the Midwest to the east, from the well-known to the little-known, but all of them interesting characters. They didn't all have to race an MG, just own one and be led into racing by the spirit of the car. Without the MG, an inexpensive machine capable of racing safely, sports car racing would never have started in this country. Of course, many of these drivers went on to other cars including Alfa, Porsche, Triumph, Healey, Jaguar, Fiat, Ferrari, Maserati, Mercedes, Cooper, Lola, Lotus, Elva, Mustang, Corvette, and the list goes on. Most of the drivers are from the era of the '50s and '60s, and most are amateurs.

As a longtime writer of radio and television commercials, I very much like the conversational tonality that you can only get with a verbatim interview. This has the added advantage of originality. Readers enjoy this style of storytelling and other automotive writers have been influenced to copy it. It is my trademark, in the six or so magazines I write for on a regular basis.

As a person in the sport since 1953, I knew many of the drivers I was going to call. I worked with Carroll Shelby at Chrysler's advertising agency, I worked with John Fitch on promoting his energy-absorbing safety barriers for racing circuits, and I knew many of the drivers from Cleveland, Detroit, Pittsburgh and Columbus. When I found myself getting short of interview subjects, I would call other people I knew, including Fred Egloff of the Chicago Region of the Sports Car Club of America and Jim Sitz, a racing photographer in California. In the case of drivers who were deceased, I would interview their friends—Sitz for Richie Ginther and John von Neumann; Egloff for Wacky Arnolt and Roy Kramer, et cetera. I tried to paint these people with a broad brush—not only their racing exploits but a little about what they did for a living and other interests they had, such as sailing in the case of racing driver and race official Charlie Ellmers. Many, including Ellmers, were in service to our country and I tried to note that. As always, I got quite a lot of help from Bill Green and Mark Steigerwald of the International Motor Racing Research Center at Watkins Glen. This is the best research resource anywhere for this kind of material. They were particularly helpful with racing records for certain of the drivers.

Most of the photographs you will see are from the drivers themselves. As they go from race to race, they accumulate them. It's about the best way to get them, although I do have access to the collections of three racing photographers: the great Alix Lafontant—he and his wife Pat were friends of ours when Nancy and I and our retriever Cooper lived in the Southwest; Joe Brown—he was a deacon at my mother's church, Calvary Presbyterian in Cleveland, and Joe's wife Georgia worked for our dentist; and then Rollin LaFrance, a gifted amateur photographer who makes his living as an architect. Some of the photographs are from the talented Jim Sitz, some from Don Snelbaker.

Chuck Dietrich, a factory driver for the Elva team, competing against the best English drivers (and that includes Jim Clark) calls the sport "our little foolishness." Maybe it is. But in this sport are the finest of the human species. People who will stop while out on the course and dive into a burning car to save a total stranger. People who will give their last spare clutch to a competitor. People who will make daring passes during the race and then go out and have dinner with those they raced against. And there's no need to detail the millions of dollars that sports car racing has donated to worthy charitable causes. These are the folks who put a Make a Wish child in their racing car, for a couple of fast laps the kid will never forget. These are the people who started in MGs.

The Drivers

In the fifties, nearly all the well-known racers started at the wheel of an MG. It was the car that started the sports car scene. It was the car that started racing in America. With apologies to those I've missed, here are just a few of the drivers, in alphabetical order.

∾ Fred Allen ∾

A well-known Rochester, New York, driver and import car dealer, Allen owned and drove MGs including a TC that he ran at Watkins Glen, September 20, 1952, and a sleek Motto-bodied MG before moving up to Austin-Healeys the same year. In fact, he raced the Healey 100S owned by movie star Jackie Cooper. Fred co-drove the Motto MG at the '54 Sebring with Gus Ehrman to an 11th-place finish, and raced the MG Special at Edenvale, Ontario, in 1954. He not only won the one-hour handicap, but placed 2nd overall in the Motto MG to the powerful 4.5 Ferrari of overall winner Erwin Goldschmidt. Allen finished ahead of all the Jaguars, Healeys and Triumphs in the race. Then, in the second race for cars up to 1500cc, Allen placed first, with a speed of 62.8 mph. By 1955 he was the regional executive of the Finger Lakes Region, SCCA, newly founded by himself, Joe Cerino, John von Hold and Alix Lafontant, the famous racing photographer. In 1956, Fred was on the MG factory team at Sebring, co-driving an MGA with John Van Driel and finishing 6th in class.

The region's newsletter carried an ad for "Sports Car Sales" at a dealership in Pittsford, New York, owned by Fred Allen and Charlie Kirby. "Authorized dealers for all imported cars," it asserted. The Motto MG again went into competition at the July 4 race at Beverly, Massachusetts. Later in '56 Allen turned the Finger Lakes region over to Alix Lafontant and hit the rally trail. Fred and his wife Penny ran the "Experts Road Trial," a tough 12-hour high-speed rally, finishing 2nd, then on to the Great American Mountain Rally, finishing 8th in their Porsche. At season's end, they were 6th in the region's rally standings.

This beautiful Motto-bodied MG was driven by Rochester, New York, MG dealer Fred Allen at Thompson Raceway in 1953. Driving against OSCA, Bandini and Porsche competitors, the best he could do was 7th place (courtesy Alix Lafontant).

Fred Allen (right) smiles with his racing friends at the 1955 Beverly, Massachusetts, sports car races. At left is Jaguar driver Charlie Wallace; in the middle is movie star Jackie Cooper. Allen drove the #75 Austin-Healey 100S at Beverly (courtesy Alix Lafontant).

In a Volkswagen rally car, Fred Allen stops at a checkpoint for the Western New Yorker Rally in 1953 (courtesy Alix Lafontant).

In 1957, Fred became active on the region's Contest Board. Late in '57, he and Penny went to the Nassau Speed Week. In a report for the newsletter of the Finger Lakes Region, he noted that, in four short years, the race week had gone "Miami Beach." Summer hotel rates were no longer given consistently and everyone seemed out for the buck. He also noted the poor safety communications on the track: they didn't even know that Rod Carveth had put his new Aston Martin through the fence. By the '58 season, the Interregional Northeast Council—a group of several area sports car clubs that Allen had helped to organize—was active in putting on races and rallies from Dunkirk to New York City. In 1959, the region had another good year for the Lake Erie Invitational Race at Dunkirk, New York.

❦ Cameron Argetsinger ❦

Cam Argetsinger is the Father of Road Racing in America. In addition to being the founder of U.S. racing at Watkins Glen, he was an active racing driver for many years, and he owned a number of interesting race cars that were street-driven. Among these were a Healey Silverstone, a black Jaguar XK-120M with beige interior ("just like Phil Hill's," Cam noted), a Cadillac Allard with its suspension set up by a top Indy

Above: The father of road racing in America, Cameron Argetsinger, drives his MG-TC in his own race, Watkins Glen, October 2, 1948 (courtesy The International Motor Racing Research Center/William Green Motor Racing Library). *Below:* Recipient of the 2007 Bob Akin Award from the Road Racing Driver's Club is Cameron Argetsinger, pictured here in his Watkins Glen home (courtesy Road Racing Drivers Club).

mechanic, and the ex–Paul O'Shea 300SL Mercedes, the fastest SL in the world. As his race organizing was crowned with success, however, his early racing met with a few mechanical problems.

His first competition was in the red #2 MG TC at his own race, Watkins Glen, October 2, 1948. His son Michael fills in some of the details: "My father drove the TC in the 'Junior Prix,' a four-lap warm-up race, but he had a flat tire on the third lap. In 1949 at Watkins Glen, he drove Bill Milliken's Bugatti Type 35 in the GP, but there was a problem with the fuel system and he DNF'd." Also in '49, he was entered at Bridgehampton in the #45 MG but he sold the car just before the event. "In 1950," Michael Argetsinger continues, "he drove the Silverstone Healey at the 'Glen and was doing well, in 8th place, until a valve stem broke. In 1953, he drove a Jaguar XK-120M in the Seneca Cup. He was running 3rd until he lost his brakes and finished 5th. He did not race again until Sebring in 1960 when he entered his Alfa Romeo Veloce (#48) with co-driver Bill Milliken. It was the last race for both of them and the car finished 4th in Class and 27th overall. He intended to race the Targa Florio in 1965 with Carel de Beaufort and von Hanstein had offered them a Porsche 904. But when de Beaufort was killed at the German Grand Prix in August of 1964, he lost interest in doing the race."

Argetsinger initiated sports car racing in the post-

In the middle of festivities at the end of the 1963 Watkins Glen Grand Prix is Cameron Argetsinger, center, next to race-winner Graham Hill, as a spectator congratulates Hill (courtesy Alix Lafontant).

war era. Prewar, ARCA put on sporadic events, not well attended. In providing a venue to SCCA and other clubs, Argetsinger created a phenomenon. He guided development of racing at the 'Glen from the original 6.6-mile course through town to the beautiful 4.6-mile interim course on the hill in Dix Township, to the permanent course that debuted in 1956. Then he influenced other events. In '48, Bruce Stevenson came from Sagaponack, New York, to observe the way that races were organized. In '49, Bruce and his MG Car Club had their own race, at Bridgehampton. In 1950, the racing started at Elkhart Lake. Then it was George Weaver's Thompson Raceway, in 1952 the first permanent course, and West Coast events too. There was an appetite for racing in America and Argetsinger showed them the way.

In 1961, he realized his dream of bringing a World Championship Formula 1 United States Grand Prix to Watkins Glen. It featured Dan Gurney, Stirling Moss, Jack Brabham, Graham Hill and race-winner Innes Ireland. Cam was active with racing at Watkins Glen up until 1970. Then he became executive vice-president of Chaparral in

As Cameron Argetsinger looks on, Miss Gold Seal begins to pour the traditional Gold Seal victory champagne for Walt Hansgen, winner of the 1957 feature race, in a Cunningham team D-Type Jaguar (courtesy Alix Lafontant).

Midland, Texas, and then executive director of the SCCA until 1977. Later he became commissioner of IMSA, a post he held until the mid–1990s.

During roughly 60 years in the sport, he has owned a number of interesting machines—those noted above and a Ford GT40 that he got in 1967. "He had 14 new Packards," his son adds, "including a 1940 Darrin convertible—only 30 were built that year. He also owned two vintage Packards—a 1917 Twin 6 roadster and a 1930 twin cowl Phaeton. In 1961, he had one of the first E-Type Jaguars in America—delivered to him by Walt Hansgen. He owned the Ardent Alligator and had entered it at Sebring in '52 but had to cancel because of an exam at law school."

In recent years, Cameron Argetsinger, an attorney by profession, has been devoted to the International Motor Racing Research Center at Watkins Glen, as president for the last five years. This is the premier racing history center in the world. It is where knowledgeable sportsmen donate their collections of racing photographs and memorabilia; it is where they give their financial support. This is where racing writers and historians know they can get accurate information from people who know sports car racing.

S.H. Arnolt

During World War II, S.H. Arnolt made a fortune manufacturing small gasoline-powered engines for the military. His company eventually produced other items including aluminum lawn furniture. A more divergent pair of product lines cannot be imagined. His factory and home were in Warsaw, Indiana, but, according to Fred Egloff, he maintained an office in Chicago. As president of the Arnolt Corporation, he was among the pioneers during the immediate postwar years in introducing British and Continental sports cars into the U.S.

Through his affiliated company, S.H. Arnolt, he started importing the MG and Morris Minor cars, becoming their Midwest distributor. He eventually added Riley, Daimler, Bentley, Rolls-Royce, Aston Martin and Bristol.

"His office, showroom and shop was on East Erie Street in Chicago," notes Fred Egloff, longtime editor of the Chicago Region SCCA publication *Piston Patter*, "just off the Outer Drive and Lake Michigan. This location also served as the headquarters for the Midwestern Overseas Centre of the MG Car Club, which he sponsored."

Mr. Arnolt early realized the American sports car owners needed quality accessories

Arnolt MG #72, here at Put-in-Bay in 1956, is ready to race, with a number on the side and headlights taped up. These Arnolt coupes, with their Italian Bertone bodies, were beautiful cars but not often seen in competition because they were heavier than the MG TD that they were based on (courtesy Joe Brown).

for their vehicles and established Accessories Ltd. to produce or procure them. They were primarily designed for use on MG. The line included Shorrock superchargers, Vokes filters, Borrani wire wheels, dash assist grips, mirrors, ashtrays, Arno-Lite driving lamps, racing radiator caps, aluminum valve covers, etc. MG owners appreciated the Arnolt sports car heaters (with 12-volt fan and hose connection to the radiator).

"Arnolt joined the Chicago Region of SCCA in October 1951, listing an MG TD as his personal car. He liked MGs but preferred Italian styling to the prewar British style of the MG with clam shell fenders. Hearing that Bertone was in a financial crisis," Egloff notes, "he contacted them proposing that they design and built a new body for the MG-TD. This led to the styling exercise that led to the more dynamic flair that Bertone had used on the Alfa Romeo 'Bats.' Using the 'TD chassis a convertible and a coupe were introduced to the market and on display near the bank corner in downtown Elkhart Lake during the 1952 round-the-lake races. Mr. Arnolt and his wife participated in the Monte Carlo style National Elkhart Lake Rally. They cancelled a fishing trip, flew down from Canada at the committee's request running a 'landcruiser' bus in the event, providing a mobile press quarters and rally headquarters. They received an award as 'The Best Rally Enthusiasts and Sports.'"

Arnolt began driving in races in 1953 at the wheel of a Nardi at Chanute Field and Janesville, Wisconsin. He place 2nd at Janesville. He already had plans for a more competitive car, having commissioned Bertone to create a new design — the 2-liter Arnolt

A shiny new Arnolt Bristol drives into Thompson Raceway, Thompson, Connecticut, driven by importer S.H. Arnolt (courtesy Don Snelbaker).

The Arnolt Bristol team at Sebring in 1956. The drivers of two cars from Wacky Arnolt's team open the doors at the same time during their Le Mans start in the 1956 Sebring 12-hour race. Car #40 is the Ted Boynton/Jim Peterson entry and car #39 is the Bob Ballenger/Phil Stewart car (courtesy Lefty Dobbins, Bob Ballenger collection).

Bristol. He began to race the Arnolt Bristol in 1954. It was initially classified as a modified car.

S.H. Arnolt found a number of ways to earn the nickname "Wacky," a friendly, endearing kind of name in the sports car club. At one race, the Offutt Field SAC event, Arnolt was racing his car in E-Modified class against entries including Bob Larson and Suzy Dietrich, both in supercharged MGs, plus Ted Boynton's Le Mans Replica Frazer Nash. As Fred Egloff recalls, "Arnolt was well ahead and thought he had the race sewn up. So he pulled into the pits where a table was set up and had tea and crumpets as he relaxed in an Arnolt lawn chair. He enjoyed the respite so much that he failed to notice when Larson and Dietrich passed him, which cost him the race."

In another adventure, "a bunch of us in Chicago," says Egloff, "decided to attend the SCCA Convention in Detroit. We took the train together. When we pulled into the Detroit railway station, Wacky was asleep in the overhead luggage compartment. Bob Goldich was one of the Arnolt drivers from Chicago and proved to be the life of the party at the Convention, just before losing his life at Sebring."

The Arnolt Bristol was by now accepted by the SCCA as an E-Production car. It was at the top of the hierarchy in that class, which included the Triumph TR3 and Morgan Plus 4, running successfully for many years. They were popular from the Midwest to the East and were first seen at the Put-in-Bay road races in 1955, as driven by

Tom Payne of Ypsilanti, Michigan. These cars were also raced at the 'Bay in 1956, 1957, 1958 and 1959.

As race-wins built for the Arnolt Bristol, Wacky decided to enter a team at the 12-hour Sebring event, fielding three cars in 1955, 1956, and 1957. In 1955, his drivers included Rene Dreyfus and Bob Grier; John Parks and Ernie Erickson; and Arnolt himself with Bob Goldich. The team was supported with transportation, and a crew led by LeRoy Kramer as team chief. The team finished first, second and fourth in class, and they also won the team prize.

In 1956, the three-factory-car team returned to Sebring with Juan Lopez as crew chief. Bob Ballenger and Phil Stewart finished 2nd in Class E and 13th overall. One car dropped out and another finished 18th.

The 1957 race was to prove a disaster. Bob Goldich, who was sharing a car with Arnolt, crashed and was killed. The team withdrew in honor of Goldich. A long-held rumor said that "Wacky" had the fatal car returned to Warsaw, Indiana, where it was buried in an unknown spot at the Arnolt factory.

Soon thereafter there was a fire at the East Erie Street facilities, destroying and damaging a large number of Arnolt Bristols. Arnolt withdrew from racing for the 1958 and 1959 seasons. In 1960 he returned to Sebring with his three-car team. At least one of the cars had an aluminum body in place of steel. These race-prepared cars were called "Bolides" (flaming meteors). Max Goldman and Ralph Durbin took a class victory with a 14th overall finish, followed by another team car with a 4th in class, with the other car capturing 10th. They were the only team to finish intact and took a team victory. During 1960 the team captured 6 class victories in SCCA races before disbanding as Arnolt began to lose interest.

He served on the board of directors at Road America for years, remaining there to guide the premier racing course of the Midwest. He passed away in 1963. He left quite a legacy, beginning with an MG.

✦ DAVID ASH ✦

Mister MG, as he was known, worked for J.S. Inskip and drove a variety of MG-powered machines from a TC to an aluminum-bodied Special to the factory-sponsored streamliner at Bonneville. While living in Glenbrook, Connecticut, he started racing at Linden Field, New Jersey, in 1950, in an MG TD borrowed from Boris Said, who was 18 years old, too young to race. His second race was Watkins Glen, September 23, 1950, also in a 'TD. And here Gus Ehrman tells the story of the Inskip Motto MGs: "David wrecked his MG TD at Watkins Glen and it was too expensive to fix. So he decided to have Motto in Italy put a body on it. This turned out to be a good car so they had two more made. One was cycle fendered and the other two were envelope-bodied. John Thornley got Sid Enever to make up the engines. They were EXPs, 1500cc engines with different heads—the heads and the blocks had their own cooling systems."

And this is the story of how he got into the car business: "David was quite a sales-

Top: The #4 aluminum-bodied MG driven by Dave Ash leads the #1 Irish/Fergus Siata through a corner at Sebring in 1952. The Special was one of three built by J.S. Inskip, the MG importers (Bill Foster collection). *Bottom:* David Ash waits to race, in the #44 Motto-bodied MG special, talking things over with his racing crew (Don Snelbaker collection).

man," says Ehrman. "I brought him into the business. He was unhappy working with his brother and I hired him to sell MGs. Then he went to Inskip as the sales manager and later started a magazine. He was the best man at my wedding. Later on, David got divorced and I went to California and we got out of touch. The last time I drove with him was Sebring in 1957." David Ash organized the MG team for Sebring in 1956 and 1957 and it was entered by Hambro Automotive. Active in the MG Car Club, he was chairman of the Race Committee for the 1952 Convair Trophy Races, as well as assistant editor of the club magazine.

As noted by MG enthusiast Michael Eaton, "Ash drove in 5 of the Sebring 12-hour races, from 1952 to 1957. In 3 of those years, he was the top MG finisher and in 1952, he finished 6th overall in his 1500cc MG special. David's final racing accomplishment occurred in 1957, when he was selected by the British Motor Corporation (BMC) to drive in record attempts at the Bonneville Salt Flats with American champion Phil Hill and England's Tommy Wisdom in the EX-179 record car. David's vast endurance experience served him well as he helped the team establish 56 American and 9 International Land Speed Records in both 12-hour and 6-hour trials averaging over 118 mph and 132 mph respectively."

The David Ash/J.S. Inskip aluminum-bodied MG Special brakes for a corner at what appears to be the 8.5-mile Callicoon, New York, race course in 1953 (Don Snelbaker collection).

Ash was also head of the MGCC Trophy Committee and active in all club activities, many of which he attended with his Great Dane. MGCC was very active in the East and Midwest, in sanctioning races with the full range of competition cars, not only MG. If the Sports Car Club of America had not been formed to sanction races, MGCC could have taken over that function. Benefits to charitable causes were common to both organizations, and donations of gate receipts to health care, child care and community service groups were routine.

✑ BOB BALLENGER ✑

Bob Ballenger is one of the Chicago drivers of the fifties. Starting with an MG TD, he drove Porsches, including the rare high-tail Spyder, during the early part of the decade, then went to Sebring to drive for the Arnolt Bristol team, collecting a first-in-class in the process. He wound up his driving career in an RSK before shifting over to the sailing scene. And he was the one who influenced Masten Gregory to get into sports car racing. But let's let Bob tell us in his own words:

"Early in 1951 I bought a used MG TD. I went to the Elkhart Lake race when they raced around the Lake on back roads. I bought a round of drinks at the hotel bar and became a member of the Chicago Region SCCA. Then I drove in some hill climbs. I was president to the Chicago MG car club and did some rallying.

"I married my wife Toni in 1951. Her maiden name was Simpson. Her sister was Luella Simpson, who had married Masten Gregory, and they came to our wedding in July of 1951. When he saw the MG, he became very interested. He had never driven an MG or a sports car of any kind, so I took him out in it, which he liked very much. Then he went home to Kansas and bought a Jaguar XK-120 to race and, after that, a C-Type Jaguar, which really brought him to the attention of people. Another sister of Toni's, Betty, married Dale Duncan, who was also in sports car racing for several years, well-known when he raced a 4.5 Ferrari.

"After the MG, I bought a used 1952 Porsche Cabriolet. It was black and I painted it white with black tear drops over the front fenders and went racing in the SCCA club events in 1954. At the Iowa City race I won the Porsche production race in the Cabrio and was given a 1955 Speedster that belonged to Phil Stewart's wife to drive in the 1500cc modified race. [Phil Stewart, in turn, was one of the Chicago OSCA owners, very successful in an Mt-4.] It was pouring rain and I won that over a Porsche Spyder and the Glocker Porsche as they were aquaplaning and the Speedster was not.

"Ed Trego, the Porsche dealer from Hoopston, Illinois, who sold me the Cabrio, asked if I wanted the blue Speedster that he had on the floor and I said 'you bet.' I painted white tear drops over the fenders and did some more racing. I had a company car, so the Speedster was the only car that we owned. We drove it shopping and to the races and then put on the straight pipes, raced it, and drove it home. I used #14, as it was easy to put on with white tape and remove it before we drove home.

"I went to Sebring '56 and '57 with the Arnolt Bristol team and drove in the 6

Bob Ballenger (at the wheel) and Phil Stewart position their #39 Arnolt-Bristol in front of the team pits at the 1956 Sebring. The #39 car finished 13th overall and 2nd in class (Lefty Dobbins, Bob Ballenger collection).

hour race at Road America in '56 in a Ferrari. Here's how that happened. I was 27 years old when I got a call from Mr. Stanley 'Wacky' Arnolt and was asked to be a team driver for his 3-car assault on the 12 hours of Sebring in 1956. I had been racing my 1955 Porsche Speedster and a friend's 1954 Mexico Porsche 550 around the Midwest and was lucky to win a couple of 1955 National SCCA races at Kansas City and the 1st race at Road America in my Speedster.

"I was teamed with Phil Stewart from Lake Forest, Illinois, while the other two cars were to be driven by Ted Boynton from Highland Park, Illinois, and Jim Peterson from California, while the boss Wacky shared his ride with Bob Goldich from Glen Ellen, Illinois. The Arnolt Bristol was the brain child of Wacky's when he mated the Bristol 404 BMW-derived engine and chassis to a beautiful Italian Bertone body and shipped them to the U.S. to be raced in the 2-liter production category in SCCA events.

"Who did we race against? Here are just a few but you can go to '*1956 Sebring 12 Hours* http://www.teamdan.com/archive/wsc/1956/56seb.html' and get the complete list and finishing order: Juan Manuel Fangio, Eugenio Castelloti, Luigi Musso, Harry Schell, Hans Hermann, Wolfgang von Trips, Phil Hill, Masten Gregory, Sterling Moss, Peter Collins, Carroll Shelby and on and on, as the best were there.

"Our cars came from the Arnolt headquarters in Warsaw, Indiana, on a transporter with 3 race cars and one spare. Each car had 2 mechanics assigned and a group from the Chicago Region SCCA to run the pits, timing and scoring. When the transporter

Top: Bob Ballenger exits the #7 Ferrari at a pit stop in the 1956 Road America 6 hour race. The crew opens the trunk to fuel the car while a pit steward watches carefully. *Bottom:* The #7 Ted Boynton/Bob Ballenger car takes a fast sweeper at Road America during the 1956 6-hour race. Boynton had purchased the car from Cincinnati driver Jim Johnston, who ran it as a red car with the #15 on the side (courtesy Leo Cummins, Bob Ballenger collection).

Speeding down the front straight under the start/finish banner, Bob Ballenger takes the checkered flag at Road America in his #14 Porsche Speedster (courtesy Bob Ballenger).

left Indiana it was still winter and having no antifreeze in the radiators each block on all 4 cars showed a long crack at the base of the block. Not a very good way to prepare for a 12-hour race but it was an oversight. Some little back alley shop in the small town of Sebring got out his welder and closed the cracks and we went racing.

"We split the racing into 3-hour shifts and I started our car #39. We were aligned across the track from our cars and there was a countdown from 10, 9, 8 seconds and at 1 we were to sprint across the track, jump into our cars, start the engine and go race for the next 3 hours.

"About lap two you had a chance to fasten your seat belt.

"No roll bars, no shoulder straps, no fireproof clothing, and helmets not much better than the old leather hats of the '30s. But hell it was fun. I got a great start and got our car in first in class and kept it there for 3 hours. Phil took over and as cars started to fall by the wayside we kept our production Arnolt running and moved up the ladder. Driving into the sun as it was setting during my second stint was something I do NOT want to ever do again. It was actually painful and took some of the fun out of what we were doing. Phil drove the last 3 hours without a mistake and our car #39 ended 13th over all, first in the 2-liter production SCCA category and 2nd OA in the racing car class, which was won by a Ferrari Mondial race car.

"Wacky's car retired with water pouring out of the cracked block and Ted Boynton's car finished 17th with water leaking all over the pit lane and running on 5 of the 6 cylinders. We had a great time and I thought I would do it again if Wacky would ask me to drive for him in 1957."

Bob Ballenger in the Porsche Speedster makes an inside pass on the high-tail Spyder owned by Fred Vetter, during a race at Milwaukee Mile, the road course on the infield (courtesy Bob Ballenger).

In the fall of 1956, September 9 to be exact, Ballenger got a ride in the Ferrari 500TR of Ted Boynton for the 6-Hour Enduro at Road America. It was the first weekend of enduros ever seen at Elkhart — track builder Clif Tufte was a big fan of endurance racing and he wanted to establish it at RA, which he did. Big-name entrants included John Fitch and Briggs Cunningham in a D-Type Jaguar, John Kilborn and Howard Hively in a 4.5 Ferrari, Ernie Erickson and Frank Bott in a D-Type and Jack Ensley and John Gordon Bennett in another D. Part of the race was a battle between ex–World War II fighter pilots, Fitch (P-51) and Hively (ex-P51 and P-47). The race finished with the Kilborn/Hively car in the lead, then Fitch/Cunningham, Erickson/Bott, Ensley/Bennett and Boynton/Ballenger.

"Wacky Arnolt asked me to drive for him again in '57," Ballenger continues, "and I said I would, and there I was back in Sebring for the March 23rd race. There were some changes in the lineup for drivers as I was paired with Jim Peterson from California in car #39 while John Weitz and Bob Gary were in car 38 and Wacky was again paired with Bob Goldich in car #37. Ted Boynton and Phil Stewart had gone on to different teams. My wife Toni was with me this year and it was nice to have her along so she could take photos and see how the team functioned.

"Both my brothers-in-law were there this year. Masten and Lou Brero were driving a factory Ferrari 290S car #15 and Dale Duncan was driving for the Chevrolet Corvette team with John Kilborn in car #31. We were pitted next to the Corvette team and got to watch their new and untried Corvette SS driven by John Fitch and Piero Taruffi, car #1. This was a very radical car designed by Arkus Duntov.

"During practice they had invited Juan Manuel Fangio to test the new SS and see what he thought about the car. His mount was a Maserati 450S that he was to co-drive with Jean Behra, car #19. After one lap he came in and asked for a pillow as he had a hard time reaching the pedals. He then roared off and after a couple more laps he broke the Sebring record. The Corvette guys were jumping up and down and WOW they had a great new car. Fangio thanked everyone and went back to the Maserati pit, climbed into the 450S and went about 10 seconds faster after just one lap. So much for GM and their new car which retired on lap 23 with suspension failure during the race.

"All the big names were there again: Sterling Moss/Harry Schell, Maserati 300S; Mike Hawthorn/Ivor Bueb, Jaguar D Type; Peter Collins/Maurice Trintignant, Ferrari 315S; Alfonso de Portago/Luigi Musso, Ferrari 315S; Colin Chapman/Joe Sheppard, Lotus-Climax; Jack McAfee/Hans Herman, Porsche 550RS; Phil Hill/Wolfgang von Trips, Ferrari 290 MM; Roy Salvadori/Carroll Shelby, Maserati 250S; Briggs Cunningham/Bill Lloyd, Jaguar D Type and on and on. The best in the world.

"Jim Peterson and I were given the title of being the 'rabbit,' had the high revs and were to go as fast as we could and if the car broke, so what, as Wacky wanted us to run away from our competition. I, again, was to start, and the day finally arrived.

"I was standing next to Lance Reventlow who was driving a Maserati 200SL and we agreed that Sterling Moss always started to run at 7 of the countdown and we were going to do the same thing. Seven came, and Lance and I and a bunch of guys were on our way across the track to our awaiting cars. Again I got a super start and only wished the Arnolt Bristol had 200 more horsepower and I would be battling among all those red machines. Needless to say the car was much faster than the car I drove in '56 and I was really enjoying myself. My 3 hours went rather quickly and I built up a lap over Wacky in car 37 before I turned the car over to Jim.

"The stop went without a hitch and Jim was off and running before Wacky came in to turn the car over to Bob Goldich. Bob got in and was away and within minutes we heard an ambulance was on the track and a full course yellow was out. Masten came flying in the pit lane and stopped in front of our pit and saw me and hollered, 'Thank God, I thought you were in that car.' That's when an official came over and said our car #37 was in an accident. Bob Goldich never made the first lap and as he approached the esses he was a bit too fast, hit the curbing and the car flipped. He was killed instantly. This could not be. This was for fun. These things don't happen to a team like ours. This was not possible.

"I stood there hugging my wife and all we could think about was Bob's wife back home expecting their second child. I turned to Toni and said, 'This is it. I'm done and will never race again.' I turned to Wacky, who was in shock, and I asked him if I could pull in the other two cars and he said, 'Yes please.' Hours later after many phone calls and arrangements that were made, Wacky sat us all down and said Bob would want us to go to the banquet that night. We all did not want to, but he insisted.

"We were all at our table and there was not much conversation amongst us when a short stocky man came over and stopped right in front of me and asked if he could join us for dinner. We said of course and he sat down across from me. In broken English he said, 'I have lost many good friends during my racing career and today you have lost one and I would like to sit with you this evening as I know how you all are feeling.' That man sat with us and helped us to understand that racing can be very dreadful at times like this. That man was the winner of the 1957 Sebring—Juan Manuel Fangio.

"I didn't go near a track for a year and a half. Then I wandered back and became a race official. I worked at Wilmot Hills and Road America. I was a course marshal. I organized the South Bend course workers. I met them all in Midwestern towns—I traveled a lot for business.

"Through SCCA I knew Ernie Erickson and, in 1959, he asked me to co-drive his new Porsche RSK in the now 500-mile race at Road America. I missed racing and decided to do it. I never got to start that race as during a gas check in practice with me in the car I made a mistake going down into corner 5. I had just passed a car on the left side of the road, hit the brakes hard and one front brake locked up and the car spun and I hit a boulder on the inside of the hill and the car got launched in the air. I don't remember how many times I saw gravel, sky, gravel, sky and it finally stopped. I have been told by Emmett Stains, who pulled me out of the wreck, that it had been 20 feet in the air. I have lunch with Emmett often and we talk about what happened 49 years ago.

"I was a lucky guy as the car went into the woods and came to rest upside down over a tree stump that was in the passenger seat and that's what I leaned up against and kicked the door out as the three gas tanks were broken open and fuel was everywhere but did not catch on fire. Emmett reached in and pulled me out and I got a free ride to the Plymouth, Wisconsin Hospital. [I got] 104 stitches in my face and chin and went back to the track and rested. My wife came up the next day and drove me home and I never raced again.

"Then I just dropped out of sports cars. We got a sailboat, an 18-foot catamaran. We took it around to sailboat races. We once sunk it in 30 feet of water but we recovered it. After that we got a series of Erickson keel boats—23, 27, 30 and 35-foot boats. We had a huge jenny on the 35. We named it *Casa de Lago* or house on the lake. We kept our boat at Monroe Harbor for just one year, then Montrose, and then we were the first sailboat in Waukegan when it was built. A boat from Chicago is the biggest yacht I've been on, Dick Jennings' *Pied Piper*, a 70-foot maxi-boat.

"I had a sequence of Audis—an A4, an RS4—I sold that before I got arrested—and today I have an Avant wagon. It's a 4-banger and I get 35–36 miles per gallon. Now the only racing I do is not in sport cars but $1/24$ slot cars, radio controlled $1/8$ scale sports cars, and now Sim racing in the computer."

✑ Hank Becker ✑

Hank Becker grew up in Shaker Heights and went to University School, a private school from which most graduates went to Ivy League colleges. At his first sports car race, he was a mechanic with Dick Irish and Jim Carroll of Sports Cars Ltd., a Cleveland business at 7070 Euclid Avenue.

Hank's job was to drive a Siata 1400 from the dealership to Lockbourne Air Force Base in Columbus, Ohio, for the 1953 race there. This was the very car that had won its class in the 1952 Sebring. It took 2nd on Index and was 3rd overall, too, as driven by Dick Irish and Bob Fergus. Dick Irish drove it in the race. He beat David Ash in the aluminum-bodied factory MG and David complained. The car was white with blue trim at Sebring. Stan Blumenthal, the owner, had it painted blue with gold trim, for some peculiar reason.

"The car had a racing screen and a straight pipe. Somebody said, 'You'll get a ticket for sure. We'd better make a muffler for it.' So we took an oil can and punched some holes in it, and fitted it to the end of the pipe. It drove without problems on the way to Columbus."

Then Hank drove the Siata back to Cleveland. "The pit car was following me and all of a sudden I went off the road," Hank says. "I had been driving harder on the way back, and the exhaust gasket blew out. There were not enough holes in the muffler to let out the gas so it accumulated in the cockpit, under the tonneau cover. It put me to sleep and I went off the road. The damn thing nearly killed me," Hank complains.

"Other than that, it drove OK! Actually that was a great handling car, maybe the best of the era."

"One of the more interesting cars, then, was the MG of Cleveland disc jockey Bill Randle. Bill did a lot to make rock & roll famous. Then Bill decided he wanted to go racing. John Moncur was a Brit who worked for Jaguar Cleveland. Bill had John set up an MG TD for him. This was going to be a state-of-the-art, stand-back! racing car. God knows what it cost. It had bike fenders, headlights mounted low and lots of engine modifications." The most notable result of this car was the classic Joe Brown photo from Put-in-Bay, of Randle's car up on two wheels— it was a miracle it didn't roll that day. Later Bill got a Keift MG, with an aluminum body and MG engine, made by the same English company that produced the highly successful Keift Formula III car driven to many race wins by Dick Irish.

At Put-in-Bay in 1952 — the year of the first race — Hank was up there with Dick's brother Chuck Irish and Bob Fergus. Bob had just bought a Type 35 Bugatti. They were downtown when they all decided to go back to the hotel, the Bayshore Hotel, which was beyond turn 1 on the other side of town. "How will we get there?" someone asked. "We'll drive," Fergus announced. He piled in the driver's seat, Chuck Irish got in the passenger's, and Becker had to sit on the rear deck with his feet dangling dangerously close to the spoked wheels. "With the engine turning over, Fergus got on the gas, upshifted, accelerated, braked for the corner, downshifted and managed to make the corner. I'm still hanging on," says Becker. "We made it out to the hotel without mangling my feet in the spokes but I don't know how."

In the very early days of the sport, MG-powered racing cars fielded Classes F and E. But that was in 1954. "One year later," says Becker, "Terrible Tom Payne came in with his Porsche Spyder, then it was the Holder brothers with theirs. Then we had an OSCA at the Akron races. We took 2nd in the Keift. Jimmy Carroll went to the Canadian

Top: Hank Becker in the #7 MG-TD gets his car tech'ed by inspector Joe Kovach at Put-in-Bay in 1953. Waiting its turn behind Becker's is a white TD, one of 35 MGs racing there that year, including an Arnolt MG (Hank Becker collection). *Bottom:* Speeding through town at the Put-in-Bay race in 1954 is Clevelander Hank Becker. His MG-TD is supercharged, lightened and modified, and runs in Class EM. Note no roll bar — those were to come later (Tomi Thompson, Hank Becker collection).

It's Hank Becker, at the wheel of the Keift MG at the 1954 Akron Airport sports car race. He drove the Keift in the 1500cc modified race and Joe Bodner's stock TD in the production race. Behind the 1954 Ford tow car is the front fender of Hank's Allard, with a fender-mounted spare. The Allard was a thin-gauge aluminum K2 body on a J2 frame with a Cadillac engine installed by Bill Frick (Hank Becker collection).

races and saw the so-called production classes. They put an Alfa engine in a TC. Some highly-modified MGs were seen at the Dunkirk hillclimb, as well as a Volkswagen with a Porsche Spyder engine.

"The boys who were running superchargers used Castrol R — it covered the smell of alcohol or AvGas, which was illegal for racing and which they had to use to avoid cooking the cylinder head. They would mix it with the fuel and it had a very distinctive smell. Bob Shea was looking for some AvGas, but the little airport at Put-in-Bay didn't have it. Bob ran 12 to 1 compression in his MG and blew his engine without the AvGas.

"There was a Healey Silverstone in Cleveland — bike-fendered with a Riley 2.5-liter engine. It had been bought by a beer company for a promotion. It was later sold to Jim Garin of the Automobile Club. He couldn't race it because it would be in the same class with a Ferrari." He later went to Put-in-Bay and, while driving around the island, hit a tree hard enough to make the headlights point towards each other.

Hank Becker volunteered to work a flag station at the 1954 Put-in-Bay race and they put him in the one at Cemetery Corner. "The whole area was solid poison ivy. It didn't bother me because I was wearing long pants and shoes with socks. We taped off the area and waited for the races to start. Up comes a character and his girlfriend, with

Race worker Hank Becker is out on the course at the Hagerstown, Maryland, airport in 1956, carrying a clipboard with the names and car numbers of entrants. Hank worked with the famous Fred German, founder of Race Communications Association, a pioneer group in racing (Hank Becker collection).

shorts and no shoes, and they sit right down next to the flag station. We asked them to leave and told them about the poison ivy. They absolutely refused and finally we said, 'OK, have it your way.' I can only imagine what they were like the next day, covered from head to foot in poison ivy."

At a later Put-in-Bay race, about 1956, he drove a Volkswagen. His employer, Jaguar Cleveland, wanted to get some exposure for VW. "We want you to drive it," they said. "Sure," replied Becker. So they took a new car and mechanic John Moncur began the process of loosening it up. He told the parts gofer to drive it and never use 4th gear. He drove it home to Akron. But it was still way too tight. "You really want to make it run?" asked mechanic George Clark. "Then ask the owner if I can make it run." "Then George put the car on the chassis dyno," says Becker, "and he takes off the air cleaner. He poured most of a can of Boraxo drain cleaner into the engine. That really loosened up the engine." Hank and another driver, both sandbaggers, went to the starting grid, Becker in his Pirelli suit with the Allard badge and the other man in a Dunlop suit with a Triumph badge. They were first and second in the race. Invited to run in the feature race, they both declined.

Beginning in 1951, Becker attended Cornell University at Ithaca, New York. He had an interest in aviation and worked at the local airport in exchange for flying lessons. His instructor was a Navy man with a pilot's license so early it only had two digits. He had flown off the first aircraft carrier and lived to tell about it. The airport was near Lake Cayuga, which occasionally played host to a Grumman Widgeon amphibious plane owned by the son of the owner of Johnson's Wax Company. He once greeted Hank with "Here, boy, fuel the plane." Becker graduated from Cornell in 1955, with a degree in engineering. After competing in his own MG TC and a Cadillac-Allard, Hank also drove a TD, Joe Bodner's supercharged TC, a TR3 and a 120 Jag, driven for Jaguar Cleveland.

Becker's Cad-Allard had a Jaguar Mark 7 transmission that would not stay in first gear while accelerating. Once, at a race at Dunkirk Airport, Hank found himself on the grid next to Jim Kimberly's Ferrari. They were gridded by displacement. Shortly after the start was a 120-degree right and then an S-bend. Becker knew he could not get the transmission to stay in gear at the start so he asked Starter Jesse Coleman to put him at the back. He was there with an E-Production Triumph whose driver was surprised to see the big-bore car that far back. "I will go by you on the right," Hank told him. At the start, Becker rocketed past eight rows of cars just in time to see a startled Coleman back-flip off a hay bale.

Becker also drove two C-Type Jaguars, but not in competition. Actually, there were three of these wonderful cars in Cleveland. One was a silver car, owned by Doug Meyer. It had been used as a pace car in the Put-in-Bay races. Later it languished in the parking lot of a Lincoln-Mercury dealer and then it was bought by Pat Black. Pat owned a marine hardware manufacturing company called Merriman-Holbrook and was a longtime sailor on Lake Erie at Mentor Harbor Yachting Club. The other two were the navy blue C-Type of Joe Blaser and the dark green car of Art Seyler. Art is a good friend of Hank Becker's. Cleveland had no D-Types, but there was one in Akron; in fact, it was an ex–Ecurie Ecosse machine. It had a headrest and a fin, and was metallic silver in color. The cylinder head had brass plugs between the spark plug holes, to fill in where the fuel injection nozzles had been. Lucas had taken their FI system back. Hank can't remember whether that was before or after the car went to Nassau and had an accident. The owner of Jaguar Cleveland, Vince Pinote, had a XKSS, the street version of a D-Type, in medium metallic blue.

A favorite car of Becker's, to say nothing of the rest of the world, was the Porsche Spyder. He spent considerable time tracking these cars in and around northern Ohio. One of them was for sale at Bo Miske's place, Foreign Cars of Akron. But unfortunately, the four-cam engine had been ruined by people at the dealership. It was a sad tale. The rear bodywork had been removed and the cam covers likewise. There was snow all over everything, the crank was no doubt ruined, and a roller-bearing crank cost $2000 at the time, a big chunk of change. Out on the West Coast, there were a few Corvair-engined Porsche Spyders and you could find pushrod Porsche Spyders when a rebuild of the original engine was not affordable. As most people recall, there were only three Spyders in Cleveland: the Holder brothers', Chuck Stoddard's, and the 4-cam-engined Spyder that Judge Herb Whiting drove to his office every day in nice weather.

～ John Gordon Bennett ～

Gordon Bennett, born 1913, immigrated to the United States from the Isle of Jersey, in England. He was an executive at the Jaguar distributing organization and he started in MGs September 15, 1951, at Watkins Glen. He soon drove a very special MG, described by Ferrari mechanic George Jasberg: "It was an MG TD that was highly modified and was built at J.S. Inskip. It had a completely aluminum body. The block and cylinder head had separate cooling systems, to avoid overheating. I saw it while I was getting parts at Inskip's. The engine was full-race. Three of them were made — I believe Charles Moran had one of them. He used to come over to Momo's after work, driving an old 1941 Plymouth — he had a Ferrari and the MG at home."

Benett drove his MG against Phil Walters in the Porsche America at Brynfan Tyddyn in 1952. "Supercharged cars overheat when pressed," Walters explained. "When that happened, I was able to get by him." Benett later drove a variety of machinery, from the 750 Stanguellini to the mighty Cunningham C-4R; the C6R, Maserati 300S

John Gordon Bennett sits in his MG-TD before the start of the Lockbourne AFB race, August 9, 1953. His car is lightened by removal of the fenders ... and even the driver's door! (courtesy Alix Lafontant).

Top: Here it is again — the car without a door. John Gordon Bennett, MG TD #4, obviously thought his chances of winning the race would be improved without the weight and bulk of the door on his car. This is at the 1953 Lockbourne race. *Bottom:* At Thompson Raceway in 1954, John Gordon Bennett drives the Stanguellini 750 to a 2nd in class, 3rd overall in the H- and G-Modified race. The car was entered by Briggs Cunningham and imported by Tony Pompeo (courtesy Alix Lafontant).

and D-Jaguar too — eleven races in all for the Cunningham team, according to historian Larry Berman. At Le Mans in 1954, he placed 5th overall and 2nd in class with co-driver Briggs Cunningham. He had 5th OA and 2nd CL at the Road America 500 in 1957, co-driving a D-Type Jaguar with Charlie Wallace, and 3rd overall there in 1956.

⁐ JOHN BENTLEY ⁐

John Bentley was a Chicago Region SCCA driver and a well-known racing author in the fifties. Auto writer Pete Vack remembers a technical article on the Tucker car that Bentley wrote for *Road & Track*; he also wrote for *Sports Car*, the SCCA magazine. He is most closely associated with the number 77 G-Modified 1100cc Siata, a car he drove to many first-place finishes.

But he started in an MG. According to Bill Green at IMRRC, he drove an MG TC in the 1949 Watkins Glen Grand Prix. It was car #14 and it finished 4th in class, 10th overall in the Grand Prix. He only raced the MG a year and then moved into a Healey Silverstone, which he drove in the 1950 race at Watkins Glen, as car #59. That year, he finished 3rd in class and 9th overall. The following year he had yet another car, a Jaguar XK-120. This he raced at the Mt. Equinox Hill Climb, going up the 5.35-mile ascent in 8:11.0 minutes. Also in 1951, the MG was brought back out and participated in a time trials at Thompson Speedway. The MG was also raced at Bridgehampton in 1949, '50 and '51. In '52, Bentley drove a Porsche to 2nd overall in the Sagaponack Trophy race.

Bentley competed at Elkhart Lake in 1951 and '52 in the Jag and he also raced the MG there in 1952. The Porsche coupe was also raced at the Vero Beach 12-hour event in 1952. With co-driver Karl Brocken, car #57 took a 7th overall.

The Porsche was driven through 1953, and in '54 Bentley got the Siata. These cars, made in Turin by Georgio Ambrosini and his son Renato, were reasonably light, fairly powerful and unequaled for handling. Renato had been in the Italian Resistance during World War II and shortly after the war won the Italian National Championship in the 750 class. Bentley's Siata Spider was the smallest of the model range, which included a 1400 and a 2-liter car. It had a Siata-tuned, Weber carbureted version of the Fiat 1100 engine.

Bentley drove a lot of the airport courses with the Siata — it was just before the era of the purpose-built racing circuits. He drove a Cumberland, Westover AFB (Massachusetts), Chanute AFB, Lockbourne AFB and Atterbury AFB, in addition to the Brynfan Tyddyn race on public roads near Wilkes-Barre, Pennsylvania, and the Giants Despair Hill Climb. Nearly all of these races resulted in 1st-place finishes. He backed these up with a very heavy schedule of racing that included Andrews AFB, Mt. Equinox Hill Climb, Watkins Glen and Hagerstown, Maryland. With Bentley's driving skill, it would have given him a national championship except for one thing: the OSCA 1100 of Rees Makins. This was the first OSCA in the country, purchased from Edgardo Fronteras by Frank Bott, who also race- prepared and sometimes drove the car. These are all Chicago people.

Leading a Porsche Cabriolet in the F-Production/G-Modified race at Westover AFB, Chicopee, Massachusetts, in 1954 is John Bentley in his Siata Spyder. He finished second in national points after an OSCA 1100 (courtesy Don Snelbaker).

The OSCA 1100, like the later 1340 and 1491cc cars that followed, were built by the Maserati brothers in Bologna. They had state-of-the-art overhead camshaft engines that were tremendously powerful. So none of Bentley's driving skills, nor the Siata's handling prowess, could help them get the championship. Up to that time, the G-Modified class had been dominated by Italian cars including OSCA, Siata, Cisitalia and Moretti. In 1954, the first of the lightweight British cars was seen, the 3rd-place Lotus Mk6 of Gunnard Rubini. In 1955, Skip Swartley's OSCA Special won the championship, but a Lotus Mk9 and a Lester MG were high in the standings. Unable to win the championship in '54, Bentley sold the Siata and raced a Mercedes-Benz 300SL in '55 as well as one of the razor-edge Abarths that he ran at Watkins Glen. By '57, he had shifted over to an Ace Bristol and an Alfa Giulietta.

John Bentley drove at Sebring 14 times and at Le Mans 3 times. He ran the very first Sebring in 1950—when it was only 6 hours—in a Simca 8 with co-driver Paul O'Shea, who would later become famous for giving Mercedes-Benz their only SCCA championships—three of them: 1955, 1956 and 1957. The Simca was not particularly fast but it did go the distance and got a 5th in class F and a 21st overall. In a might-have-been effort, Bentley teamed with Ed Hugus in a Cooper Bobtail for the 1956 12-Hour race. In the #56 car they were running well up in the field until a mechanical failure put them permanently out of the race. Later in 1956 Hugus and Bentley drove the Cooper at Le Mans. They managed to work out the bugs and lasted the whole 24 hours, finishing a very fine 8th overall in the little 1100cc car that didn't have to slow

John Bentley of Port Washington, New York, in the #77 Abarth leads the #35 Porsche Speedster of Bud Fehnel from Nazareth, Pennsylvania, at Watkins Glen in 1955. Fehnel finished 10th and Bentley was 14th in the somewhat underpowered Abarth 1100. Also in the Queen Catharine Cup: Bandini, Siata, Moretti, Alfa and OSCA (courtesy Alix Lafontant).

down for the corners! Three more Sebring DNFs followed, including one in 1958 with the well-known Detroit driver Bill Bradley, who was later the distributor for the Merlyn racing cars. The pair drove an Elva Mk III but went out on the 71st lap. But that's why they call it an endurance race.

OSCA driver John Gordon, later a co-driver with Bentley, remembers: "I first met Mr. B in December 1957. He lived in Northport, New York. He had been driving a Porsche Carrera Speedster and had accumulated a couple bushel baskets of fouled spark plugs with that engine. He had remarried, a lovely gracious lady from Orange County, Virginia, named Fran. He was working as a movie producer for the U.S. Navy at their training devices center in Port Washington. A few years later, the Defense Department consolidated them with the Army training command in Orlando, so he had to move to Florida.

"His 1957 model Giulietta Veloce Spider was surplus at the time, and I decided to buy it for use in driver schools. When he had taken delivery from Max Hoffman, he had the axle ratio changed to 4.56 — the factory shipped them with 4.1. In schools I found I had an advantage over the others because 4.1 is too tall for the average club track. In 1958 I was in his pit crew with the Elva — with Bradley as co-driver. The factory had not prepared the car very well, a rush job."

Bentley's second-highest finish at Sebring came in 1960 when he co-drove with Jack Gordon in an OSCA 187N, a little 746cc car, to a 12th overall, finishing ahead of his 1954 nemesis Rees Makins, in an OSCA twice its displacement at 1491cc, in 13th place. The Bentley/Gordon car was 1st in its class.

Co-driver Jack Gordon says, "John placed an order for the car at the end of 1959. It was delivered in February of 1960 at Kennedy Airport. We had a little time before Sebring for some preparation. We added two extra driving lights and checked to make sure everything on the car was tight. Ours was one of the last with the improved 187N engine. It had the new oversquare block and the new cylinder head with the carburetors on the left side, and a different model Weber carburetor. It was very reliable because the Maserati brothers had been building basically the same engine since 1923. We drove 3-hour shifts and I did the night driving. We had one near miss— some guy in a Ferrari came out of the pits and almost hit me. I had to get on the brakes and stop the car. Then I had no brakes left. The reason we finished ahead of Rees was that he spent a lot of time digging out of the sand. Otherwise, his lap times were a lot faster than ours.

"In 1961, John was talked into driving a Beach sports racer," says Gordon. "It had a Saab two-stroke engine. I told him a Saab would never last twelve hours." Bentley drove with Eugene Beach and Henry Grady. They went out before the 100th lap. "It was an embarrassment," adds Gordon.

The OSCA 750 was driven at Sebring again, in 1962, to another first in class, ahead of a factory team of Deutsche-Bonnet cars with Howard Hanna as the most prominent driver. "We won our class," Jack Gordon notes, "but we weren't as fast as we were in 1960—finished about ten fewer laps."

In those two years, '60 and '62, John Bentley and Jack Gordon also drove at Le Mans. In 1960, they were 18th overall, quite a good finish in the little 750 car, but not good enough for a class first. "When we got to Le Mans we couldn't keep up with the DBs. Chinetti owned the car—it was from the factory—but his crew didn't seem to do a good job of preparing it. It rained a lot. Bentley did not like driving in the rain, but I did. We finished ahead of just one of the DBs."

Then, in '62, Gordon had a new OSCA, the 1600 model, but unfortunately they DNF'd with engine failure. "It was a Zagato-bodied car," Gordon observes. "I think it was serial number 006. It was a large car, like a boulevard car, and slower than the 1300 Abarth GT coupes."

The following year at Sebring (1963), Bentley and Gordon drove a Lotus Elite 1200cc all-fiberglass coupe to a solid 38th overall finish. But it looks like they switched out of Italian cars a year too soon, as they were beaten by a Simca-Abarth and an Alfa Romeo. "The last time I saw Mr. B," Says Jack Gordon, "was at Daytona in 1965. He was driving a Sunbeam Tiger—absolutely god-awful beast of a car."

Bentley's final year at the Sebring, Florida, enduro was 1966, when he moved out of the small-displacement mode and drove a Shelby Cobra, car #7. His co-drivers were Henry Byrne and Arthur Latta and the entrant was the Space Science Service of Orlando, Florida. They placed 22nd overall, which is not bad, but put them behind the Cobra of Tom Payne (15th OA) and the one entered by Scuderia Bear of Pittsburgh—that would be the colorful Ed Lowther and his co-driver Bob Grossman, usually seen in a Ferrari GT. They finished 10th overall.

As a racing driver from 1949 to 1966, we see that John Bentley had a good 17 years of racing with lots of interesting cars, some good finishes, challenging racing circuits and friends in racing. It was a rich life.

∽ Art and Dutch Brow ∽

Art is a longtime SCCA racer whose 38-year career went from MGs to formula cars and V8 sedans. Before getting into racing himself, Art crewed for Jack Uhr at Put-in-Bay in 1955. They made an E-Modified car out of a 1953 Porsche coupe by supercharging it. Then they fabricated aluminum doors, hood and rear deck, just as the GT would later have. They found this car would accelerate with a Porsche Spyder, "but it couldn't stop or corner like one," Art notes. Then Art borrowed an MG TC from racer Bob Shea and raced it at Put-in-Bay in 1956. "We also ran that TC in hill climbs at Sewickley, Pennsylvania, Mansfield and Youngstown, at time trials, and drag races. The drags were at Derby Downs in Akron. We got a Shorrock supercharger for the car and ran it on alcohol. We changed the wheels to 15-inch wires with Englebert tires. When

An exciting moment at the Put-in-Bay road races is immortalized in this George Ivanyi watercolor: Art Brow gets the #3 MG-TD out-of-sorts at Cemetery Curve on the 3.1-mile course, recovering shortly afterward. This was the incident where the heater shook loose and fell down on Art's feet so he couldn't brake for the corner (George Ivanyi, Art Brow collection).

Top: At the 1959 Put-in-Bay race, Art Brow in his Turner leads Bob Shea in a Sprite (Art Brow collection). *Bottom:* Art and Dutch Brow pose with their MG TD in 2010. Art drove the car in the 1957 Put-in-Bay race, when it was owned by Bill Staufer. In the 1980s, both Art and Dutch raced Formula Vee open wheel cars at road courses in the Midwest (courtesy Nancy Goodwin).

we got to the drag races, the Olds 88 drivers laughed at us. But we went through the quarter mile at 90 miles an hour and later did 100 with the TC."

The next year Art borrowed Bill Staufer's MG TD and raced it in 1957, the same year that he joined SCCA. "I'm number 1926," he quips. Then he bought a Turner and raced at the 'Bay in 1958 and '59. Following that he raced his 1951 Porsche coupe in a couple of events at Nelson Ledges and then stopped racing for awhile. He picked it up again in the late '60s, with a Formula Vee that was built by a man on the east side of Cleveland. "We finally got it to the point where it would handle," Art says, "but it was really too heavy. I won my first race with it at Watkins Glen in about 1969."

Then he bought a Caldwell D-13 FV, noting, "We went out to Marblehead to pick it up." In the middle of all this, Art was offered a seat in a showroom stock Camaro in the "Longest Day" 24-hour race at Nelson Ledges. Then, in 1989, his wife Dutch decided she would like to race so they towed two FVs to the races, Art's D-13 and her C4 Zink. Art and Dutch drove their FVs, at racing venues including Nelson Ledges, Mid-Ohio, Watkins Glen, Cumberland, Marlboro, Akron Airport and many more. Art gave up racing in 1994, at the age of 70. But he still builds an engine now and then just to stay in the sport, and he's gradually restoring a rotary-engined NSU convertible.

◈ Hubert Brundage ◈

While the first race he drove was in an MG TD (Watkins Glen, car #31, September 23, 1950), the first race he entered was at Palm Beach Shores, January 3, 1950. George Huntoon drove his Duesenberg-engined Ford to a win, followed by another at Bridgehampton, June 10, 1950, in the same car, #41. Hubert Brundage is best known as the creator of the Formula Vee class and as founder of Brumos Porsche in Jacksonville, Florida. He was originally a commercial pilot from Hammondsport, New York. After flying for twelve years, he opened a Volkswagen agency as a part of his family's Brundage Hardware Store. Shortly afterward, he moved to Florida, remaining a VW dealer. Hubert raced the MG and then a VW Special of his own design. After costs of the Formula Junior class got out of hand, Brundage believed there was a demand for a budget open-wheel road racer with stable technology.

One of Hubert's employees was Bill Bencker, then active in SCCA's Florida Region as a driver and race official. Bencker co-drove a Porsche 904 in the 1965 Sebring 12-Hour race with Briggs Cunningham and John Fitch, finishing 4th in class. When Bencker went to Europe in 1960, Brundage asked him to arrange construction of a VW racing car with Enrico Nardi, who made several small-displacement racing cars in addition to the well-known steering wheels. The specifications were left intentionally vague to see what Nardi would come up with. The result was a single-seat racer very close to its present form. The basic VW suspension was used, but with the addition of transverse leaf springs. The engine was brought inboard for balance and a simple aluminum body covered the car.

In 1962, George Smith, an SCCA racing driver and official, formed a company

Top: Profile view of FV early version with high back section. Hubert Brundage commissioned a car from Nardi in Italy and this is the prototype in Miami just after it arrived. *Bottom:* Rear view of Hubert Brundage's FV built by constructor Enrico Nardi (courtesy Paul Schiemer).

Top: Another view of the Brundage Formula Vee (courtesy Paul Schiemer). *Bottom:* Hubert Brundage (#10) starts the 1952 Sebring in his Volkswagen Special. He would finish 11th overall (courtesy Jan Brundage).

with Bill Duckworth, an Orlando garage owner, to build Formula Vees at a company called Formcar. FV is still a great way to go racing. And Brumos Porsche is a longtime sponsor of racing cars, notably more than one car that won the Sebring 12-hour race.

∽ Ralph Cadwallader ∽

Not exactly a household word in racing, Ralph was a Cleveland club racer who loved his MG and loved the Put-in-Bay races. As racer Art Brow recalls, Ralph was the general manager of MG Motor Sales on Madison Avenue in Lakewood, Ohio, during the 1950s and '60s. The MG store was first owned by George Weber in partnership with Bob Lossman, who later bought him out. One day, a customer who owned a Jeepster came in looking for a sports car. He was Bob Shea, who was operating a dairy. He was immediately hired to be the service manager for MGs. Lossman Motors also sold Volkswagens from Midvo, the VW distributor in Columbus owned by Don Marsh, John and Bob Fergus; it also sold MGs. As VW began to grow, it suddenly decided it didn't want its dealers handling any other brand, so the MG operation had to move. When it did, Bob Shea went with it, and Cadwallader became the manager. Art Brow stayed at the VW store as a mechanic and his wife Dutch was employed in the office on warranty work and other details. Incidentally, Art says, both Bob Shea and Ralph Cadwallader were combat infantry veterans of the Battle of the Bulge in World War II.

The Ralph Cadwallader MG TC, #22, gets ready for the rolling start at the Put-in-Bay races in 1957 (courtesy Joe Brown).

Artwork by Chuck Pervo of MG-TCs racing at Put-in-Bay in the early fifties (Ralph Cadwallader collection).

Meanwhile, in about 1950, Ralph bought an MG TC. He put a carpet in the garage and disassembled the entire car on it. He drove it on weekends and then, when the Put-in-Bay races came up, entered them. "I ran my TC every year but the first one," Ralph said. "I missed 1952, and I never won at the 'Bay. I didn't have very good luck — one year I broke an axle, another year the brakes went out. The closest I came was in 1953. I was ahead of Chuck Dietrich for eight laps. But my exhaust pipe came loose. Every time we came by the marshal, Chuck would point to the pipe hanging from my car. Finally I was black-flagged and had to come in. I ripped the exhaust off my car and I got back in the race. I had lost the lead but I still finished the race."

As Art Brow recalls, Ralph sold the TC about five years after the last 'Bay race in 1959. Much later he bought a Morgan and then an MGC GT. Ralph never forgot the wonderful races at Put-in-Bay, and on their 40th anniversary he staged a meeting of former drivers at the Cleveland Sport Car Club banquet in 1992. Everyone savored the unique character of the event and in closing Ralph paraphrased King Henry V before the Battle of Agincourt, saying, "We few, we happy few, we loyal band of brothers; He who races with me this day shall always be my brother."

∞ Jim and Sally Carroll ∞

The Carrolls have been fixtures in the MG and Midwest sports car scene from its beginning to the present, in spite of Jim's death a few years ago. It began when Jim was a young man working as a Diesel mechanic at the Collinwood Yard of the New York Central Railroad in Cleveland. He knew cars pretty well and decided to get a second job in the sales department of Jaguar Cleveland, on Kinsman near Lee on the east side.

Jim Carroll leans jauntily against his new 1951 MG-TD. In 1952 he bought an MG-TC and started racing (courtesy Sally Carroll).

This was 1950, and he was dating Sally Vaughan at the time. In the spring of 1951, Jim bought a 1951 MG TD and they started on a life in the sports car scene.

About this time, as the sports car movement was underway, Jim and Sally were involved in the formation of two notable car clubs, the Cleveland Sport Car Club and the MG Car Club. The CSSC would be the organizer of the Put-in-Bay and Akron Airport road races, before SCCA got underway in Cleveland. Then, the Lake Erie Centre of the MG Car Club was formed by Jim and Sally, as a branch of the Chicago MG club. Originally, the meeting place of the CSSC was Sports Cars Limited at 45th and Euclid. The MG club originally met at a tavern on Lee Road just south of Mayfield in Cleveland Heights. Later, it would have a longtime gig at Linsay's Tavern in Shaker Heights.

A year later, Jim traded the TD even for a TC. They ran it at the Akron Airport sports car races and the famous island race at Put-in-Bay. Later Jim began working full time for Sports Cars Limited, which was initially at 45th and Euclid and later went to 69th. They always had a number of very interesting cars, including the Siata Gran Sport that Dick Irish had driven to 3rd overall at Sebring in 1952. They also had a beautiful Cisitalia 202 coupe and a Ferrari 212 with right-hand drive and a 5-speed gearbox featuring an amber shift knob with Roman numerals indicating gear positions.

While working for Sports Cars Limited, Jim had an opportunity to drive a Siata Spyder of theirs, once again at one of the Put-in-Bay races. This, the smallest of the Siatas, was powered by a 750cc Crosley engine and ran in the H-Modified class. The Spyder weighed about 1000 pounds and was noted for its perfect handling qualities.

Top: The staff of Sports Cars Limited, on Euclid Avenue in Cleveland, lines up behind a new Cisitalia coupe, just like the one that the Museum of Modern Art has. Jim Carroll is third from the right and Sally Carroll is in the car. *Bottom:* Six people in a Siata: Jim Carroll is in the passenger seat. Jim helped to organize two car clubs in the Cleveland area: Cleveland Sport Car Club (which sanctioned the Put-in-Bay races) and the MG Car Club (which put on most of the rallies in northeastern Ohio) (courtesy Sally Carroll).

Jim and Sally drove a few hillclimbs, including the Giants Despair out east near Brynfan Tyddyn, which Sally contested in a Riley.

Subsequent car dealerships were Jaguar Cleveland and Stoddard's in Willoughby. Jim was originally the parts manager at Stoddard's and the service manager. It was the dealership of Chuck Stoddard, who drove a Siata Spyder before switching over to Alfa Romeo, which brought him three national SCCA racing titles.

After that, Jim went back to working on heavy equipment, in the form of the massive Terex and Fiat/Allis machines, and the sports cars were put in the background. After the passage of years, his younger son sent him a poster picture of an MG with the note, "I hope this influences you to do something foolish." This was all Jim and Sally needed to get an MG TC, which was found in an ad in the *Cleveland Plain Dealer*. MGs can be a little like Alfas, of which the letters of the word are said to mean Always Looking For Another. So the next thing they did was get an MGA. It was a 1960 model with the 1600 engine, bought from a customer of Stoddard's. After that there was the MG TF that was found in New Mexico. The beautiful YB sedan, resplendent in glossy maroon, was a little harder to find—it came from northern England and a lucky tip while on vacation. Then came the MGB GT. Those are still owned, together with a Morris 1000 pickup truck, and that's all for now.

These days, besides presiding over the collection of MGs, Sally is busy as president of the club that Jim founded, the Cleveland Sport Car Club.

∽ Sam Collier, Miles Collier ∽

As the prewar MG importer in the U.S., in a business named Motor Sport, Sam and his brother Miles raced the Octagon in the late thirties before hostilities broke out again in Europe. In 1934, they founded ARCA, the Automobile Racing Club of America, along with George Weaver, George Rand, George Huntoon and race official Roy Cramer, who were also figures in the sport postwar. The Colliers published *The ARCA News*, and organized the road races at Alexandria Bay, New York, between 1936 and 1939. One of their notable MGs was the beautiful Leonidis MG, a re-bodied special that Miles Collier raced at Le Mans

Left: Winner of the 1949 Watkins Glen Grand Prix is Miles Collier in the #39 Riley-Mercury. Here Miles beams as the trophy is held out to him (courtesy Don Snelbaker).

The #39 Riley-Mercury of the Collier brothers poses in front of the Ford-Mercury dealer in Watkins Glen, 1949. Sam Collier is at the wheel (courtesy Don Snelbaker).

Miles Collier in the #8 MG Special tries to pass the #38 MG-TC of Frank O'Hare at the June 10, 1950, Bridgehampton race. The car driven by Collier was owned by Donald Millager (courtesy Don Snelbaker).

Top: The beautiful Leonidis MG of the Collier brothers is seen in the town of Watkins Glen before the 1951 race there — rear view. *Bottom:* As seen in profile, the Collier brothers' Leonidis MG is seen in the town of Watkins Glen before the 1951 race there (courtesy Joe Brown).

in 1939. According to George Jasberg, the car was a PA/PB model, displacing about 850cc with a crankshaft-driven supercharger. In an account of the first race at Bridgehampton by Bruce Stevenson, he noted, "Sam Collier took the lead immediately in a blown MG and was never headed." The following year, the Leonidis MG won with Miles Collier at the wheel.

The Collier brothers were good drivers and later joined with Briggs Cunningham to co-drive a stock two-door Cadillac at Le Mans in 1950. It finished 10th. Sam was driving a Ferrari 166 Corsa Spyder at Watkins Glen in 1950 when he got into some gravel, the car rolled, the seat belt broke, and he suffered fatal injuries. After that, Miles was forced to use a pseudonym, a common ruse in racing, in order to compete without his parents' knowledge. Many people believe that the nom de plume was Brete H. Hannaway, a Britisher living in Connecticut. But Hannaway was a partner of John Fitch's at Sports & Utility Motors and even helped to build the V8-powered Fitch Model B. John says that Collier's mother was going to disinherit him if he continued racing and so he, Fitch, arranged with Louis Chiron for Collier to race here and abroad under a variety of aliases including "John Marshall." Miles raced several cars under several names, including a Bandini at Sebring in 1954. He died of polio about a week after the '54 Sebring. In memory of Sam Collier and his brother Miles, the Collier Brothers Memorial Trophy Race was instituted at Watkins Glen in 1954. It saw its 50th anniversary in 2004.

↝ Harry Constant ↜

Harry Constant, prominent racing official in SCCA's Detroit Region, started racing in an MG, then an Alfa Romeo and a Siata at Put-in-Bay, then a Maserati 150S. After racing he became an SCCA official, staging everything from drivers' schools at Waterford Hills to the Detroit Formula One Grand Prix. We'll let Harry tell the story in his own words:

"About two years out of college, in 1953, I was having lunch at a friend's house and he had a TD in the back yard. I asked him what he was going to do with it and he said, 'Race it.' At that time you had to own a sports car and be sponsored to join the SCCA, so I bought a used TD and my friend sponsored me.

"My first race was Lockbourne AFB in 1954. It was a blast. They even assigned a GI to each car. I raced a stock MG for three years. Put-in-Bay was fun. You could practice and race on Saturday and then party all night. We also raced Harewood and Greenacres in Canada. Even on two dirt tracks in Maumee, Ohio, and Mt. Clemens, Michigan. They put hay bales on the course to make you shift gears. That's how I learned about four-wheel drifts—not intentionally.

"I decided to go to Elkhart Lake, September 10 and 11, 1955. I went to my local MG guru Bill Sands to get his advice on car prep. He pulls out a ruler and says each inch will cost you $100 and you need all twelve inches to be competitive. Well I gave him $100 and he put in competition brake linings. I came in tenth and you would have thought I won the race.

Top: Start of the 1954 race at Lockbourne Air Force Base in Columbus, Ohio. The hands are up, the engines are revving and they're waiting for the green flag. Seen are cars #162, #158 and #65. *Bottom:* Harry Constant corners briskly at Elkhart Lake, September 11, 1955. Harry says, "Note the one-handed driving technique — I was just hanging on" (Harry Constant collection).

Top: Harry Constant waits on the grid at the Tri-Cities Michigan race, in his #1 Alfa Giulietta. The #2 car is a bit unusual, a G-Production Porsche with a 1300cc engine. Tom Payne brought a few of these 1300s in to race with the Alfas. *Bottom:* Looking behind him after a driver change at the 1956 Elkhart Lake 4-Hour enduro is Harry Constant in the #81 Morgan Plus Four. A driver change was required every hour (Harry Constant collection).

At speed in the #81 Morgan during the 4-Hour Enduro at Elkhart Lake in 1956. Harry Constant is at the wheel — he co-drove with Dick Kennedy (Harry Constant collection).

"I bought an Alfa from Tom Payne in 1956 and raced that with some success. Then the Veloce model came out and they were tough to beat. I got into a Siata and raced H-Mod. for a few years. I was able to come in second to Martin Tanner in a couple of races but everyone in the class was going to fiberglass and two-cycle engines.

"I co-drove a Morgan at the Elkhart Lake 4-hour race and was asked to drive at Sebring the next year in the factory entry but a mammoth snowstorm hit Detroit so I could not get out of the driveway and the airport was closed.

"Had a ride in a Maser 150S. It was a thrill just to be in the seat let alone race it. I only had five laps in the car. It was right-hand drive with a five-speed on the left. In addition, the accelerator pedal was between the brake and the clutch. Fortunately I was young and had a fast learning curve. I do remember Tom Payne in his 550, waving to me as he passed.

"After that I really got involved in the stewards program and the Detroit Region. After 53 years, I am still involved in road racing."

∽ DENVER CORNETT ∽

Denver is a legend at Watkins Glen, for his many years of racing and his colorful entrée into the sport, at the wheel of his favorite MG TC. As a novice driver, he entered the first races at Watkins Glen, in 1948, driving the #7 black 'TC. It was in the Junior

In a picture taken right after Denver Cornett rolled his #7 MG-TC at Stone Bridge during the 1948 race at Watkins Glen, the driver (wearing gloves) is thankful to be OK. The car landed upside down. A spectator asked, "I wonder if he's dead." From underneath the car, Denver replied, "Why don't you roll the car over and find out?" (Don Snelbaker collection).

GP that he rolled his car at Stone Bridge, down a hill into a dry stream bed. An odd car number meant he would land upside down and when it stopped rolling a crowd began to gather. "I wonder if he's dead," one of them finally exclaimed. "Why don't you roll the car over and find out?" was Denver's reply. Noting that the rugged little car was not badly damaged, Cornett framed his plans to race in the regular Grand Prix event. He had two bent wheels but only one spare. Always generous, Briggs Cunningham offered a wheel and tire so Denver could race. He placed 2nd in class and 7th overall.

The next year he drove the 'TC at Bridgehampton. We don't know where he finished but he went to the beach and lost his car key. Another MG racer said, "Try this" and his spare key fit. Then that fall, in the Seneca Cup at Watkins Glen, he DNF'd. In 1950, the first year for racing at Elkhart Lake, Denver entered his 'TC there. Then, at Watkins Glen he set aside the MG and drove the "Speedcraft Special," a DuPont that had run at Indianapolis, and had a Ford V-8 built by Otto Linton. Unfortunately, he had a short event as he went off course on the first lap. A photographer for *Speed Age* magazine, Don O'Reilly, the magazine's publisher, saw a Jaguar driven by M.E. Abendroth run him off the road. The following year he ran the DuPont special in the Seneca Cup and the engine blew, but he was credited with 18th place based on laps completed.

Then, in '52, he went back to the MG and started on the pole in the Queen Catharine race at the 'Glen, placing 14th in class F. The year after the Watkins Glen accident, he did not race there, but drove a Porsche Super to 4th in the First Race at Chanute AFB, Rantoul, Illinois; the #72 Porsche to a 3rd in F-Production at Lockbourne AFB, Columbus, August 9th, 1953; and the #121 Porsche to a 3rd overall at Turner AFB in Albany, Georgia, October 25, 1953. Denver bought the ex–Kimberly 166 Ferrari and won the hillclimb at French Lick, Indiana, on November 22, 1953. He drove a 2-liter Arnolt Bristol in the 1954 season. He drove the #180 Arnolt at Lockbourne AFB in Columbus, Ohio, August 8, 1954, to a 5th in class E. Back at Watkins Glen, on the interim course, he took a 2nd in class and 18th overall in the Seneca Cup, and the following year, 1955, a 3rd in class and 12th overall. After that, as Jim Sitz notes, he raced a 300SL in 1956, in 1957 he raced an MGA, and in 1960 he raced an Austin-Healey Sprite.

After 1962, he took a break from racing and bought a nice Maserati 3500 Spyder in silver with blue leather, for the road. Then he came back to racing in vintage events beginning 1994. No need to get a new racing car for that — he had kept his old #7 MG-TC. He raced it every year in SVRA events, from '94 to 2001, skipping the year 2000. In 1996, he won the Collier Cup at Watkins Glen — an award voted him by his fellow drivers.

∽ Tom Countryman ∽

Before getting his first MG, Minneapolis resident Tom Countryman's first interest in, well, very interesting cars was a captured German "Swim Vagen," which he had the opportunity to drive while in North Africa during World War II. But after that, he spotted his first childhood desire: a 1937 Cord 812 Phaeton which he bought while attending photographic school in Los Angeles in the post–World War II era. He was shortly recalled back into the army during the Korean War, and that was after 4½ years during World War II with the 34th Infantry Division. The 34th saw more combat than any other division — it was in the invasions of North Africa and Italy and then went all the way to the Swiss border.

He had returned to college on the GI bill, attending the University of Oklahoma, where he received an ROTC commission. As a new Army lieutenant he was recalled for the Korean War and ordered to Camp Pickett, Virginia, where he spotted his first MG. He had stored the Cord in Nebraska so he just had to have another interesting car and the TC was perfect.

"I had a very big German shepherd," says Tom, "who loved to go for a ride in that little TC. I would drop the front windshield and he would sit up in the breeze on that left side passenger seat while I would slouch way down behind the wheel. Oncoming cars would nearly run off the road when the saw this funny little foreign car coming at them with a dog driving. I sure wish I had a picture of that.

"Our division, the 43rd Infantry Division, was sent to Germany, instead of Korea.

Tom's #10 white Speedster with a 16mm sound camera mounted behind the headrest, at Sioux Falls, South Dakota, in 1962 (courtesy Tom Countryman).

What a break! As an officer, I was able to take my own car along. I had my wife sell the MG and I took a new 1951 Chevy convertible to Germany. I was notified that it was at the dock at Bremerhaven. I went to pick it up, and returning to my base it was a thrill to drive this flashy new convertible down the Autobahn. Even this long after the war there were still relatively few cars in Germany, and the Autobahns were mostly free of traffic.

"They were in good shape except for the occasional bombed-out bridge. Although the Allies had a 50 mph speed limit, it was meant for army trucks rather than civilian cars. Returning from Bremerhaven, it was a rainy miserable day and I was going maybe sixty when a silver car went by like a bullet. I had no idea what it was; I'd never seen anything like it before, and he was out of sight in a second.

"Driving though Augsburg another time, I noticed this little car in my rear-view mirror, and after he passed by I sped up, passed him and then pulled in front of him — I mean literally cut him off. Jumping out of my car I ran over and said in my silly German, 'Vas is das!?' Surprised, he replied 'Das ist ein Porsche.'" We talked a while and he told me where I could find out about one. I went to Munich the following day, to a car lot where they had two Porsches, one of them used. It belonged to the owner of the Four Seasons Hotel in Munich, who was buying a new Porsche (the 1500 engine had just come out). At that time, a used car dealer only acted as a broker for the owner of the automobile so I ended up buying this 1300 coupe from the hotel man. It was a 1951 coupe with a 1.3 liter engine, Volkswagen brakes and a crash box transmission. Because

Top: It is September 11, 1955, and Tom Countryman's 1951 1.3-liter Porsche Coupe, #110, is on the grid for the 1st race at the Road America at Elkhart Lake, Wisconsin — F, G and H-Production. Tom is in G-P along with the 1300cc Alfa coupe beside him. *Bottom:* Tom Countryman, Lake Phalen, Minnesota, in 1954, driving his 1951 1300N Porsche. "Note the camera mounted inside the car. I was wearing a World War II tanker helmet." Tom not only won his class but won overall in the event, which was covered by the NBC network (courtesy Tom Countryman).

Driving a Porsche-powered Autodynamics Formula V car that he built (courtesy Tom Countryman).

I needed money to buy the Porsche I called a friend of mine in Scotts Bluff, Nebraska, and sold him the Cord over the phone for 1300 dollars.

"At that time if you needed any service, you took your Porsche to the factory in Stuttgart. There Huschke von Hanstein allowed me to wander all over the factory taking photos. While there I was invited to Le Mans and was given a pit pass to the 1952 24-hour race. Porsche had entered three aluminum cars, and it was there that I got to meet Briggs Cunningham and his team.

"I brought my Porsche back to the U.S. and of course, having watched them race at Le Mans, I just had to try it so I entered the 1954 St. Paul Winter Carnival ice race on Lake Phalen. Because I won 2nd in my class I was invited to enter the feature race which included an Allard, Healeys, an XK120 Jag, a Corvette, a couple of hot rods and several MGs. I won overall in this feature event, which was covered by John Cameron Swayze for the NBC network. Needless to say, the hook was set deep. Thus started a 20-year career of sports car racing. My 1.3 liter Porsche was on the grid in 1955 for the very first green flag ever to fall at Road America. After that I bought a '55 Porsche Speedster, and then a '56 Speedster which I raced for over 15 years. I ran Brainerd, Blackhawk, Greenwood Raceway, Lyndale Farms and Meadowdale, just to name a few.

"In the year 1958 I decided to make a film on Road America. So at the next race I mounted a 16mm sound camera on my roll bar and headed out for practice. As I left the pits I saw Bud Seaverns, the chief steward, nearly fall over looking at me. I knew darn well he was going to black flag me, and sure enough I was pulled in. 'Who told you

Tom Countryman in the #10 Porsche Speedster leads a group of production car racers, silver Porsche #4, black Triumph #47 and a Lotus 7 (courtesy Tom Countryman).

that you could do this?' 'Nobody,' I said, so he shook the camera trying to make it come loose but I had it well mounted. 'Ok, but just for practice, not in the race.' Subsequently all of the racing footage in *Road America* was shot during the first practice session. Later when I showed the finished film at the Chicago region Bud came over and said, 'Why in the hell didn't you tell me what you were doing?'

"As the years went by we would do all the things to the Speedster that would keep it competitive. I converted it to a Carrera in 1960. I bought a wrecked Carrera coupe and switched everything over including the oil tank. When I sold the speedster, I put the 1600 pushrod engine back in because the 4-cam went into a 550 Spyder I found without an engine."

In addition to running his own car, Tom drove for the NODAK racing team, Bert Horton's North Dakota racing team. "I ran his 904 Porsche at Elkhart and the RS-61 in the USRRC and the IMSA series," Tom recalls.

"Around 1970 I built an Auto Dynamics Formula Vee car with a Porsche engine which ran as a Formula B. I didn't do too good driving it so when Porsche came out with the 914–6 I had to give it a try. Now here was a car. A mid-engined six-cylinder 2-liter car that really handled. In '72 I ended up finishing 2nd in the central division in C production.

"We had a film production company in Minneapolis, Countryman-Klang Film Productions. We did industrial films, TV commercials, traffic safety films. We worked with most of the advertising agencies in Minneapolis and produced industrial films for Cargill and the 3M Company. We traveled around the world filming the manufacture and use of reflective license plates and reflective highway signs."

At 87, Tom doesn't race any more but he still has a Porsche, a 1980 911 cabriolet, and he still goes to the local 356 Porsche get-togethers to talk of old times.

Some of the racing films he produced are:

The Ice Race 1954
Road America 1958
The MeisterBrausers 1959
Dynamite 1975
Road Atlanta 1976
The 24 Hours of Daytona 1979
Trans Am 1982

∽ Briggs Cunningham ∽

Briggs Cunningham is probably the second most important figure in American sports car racing, second to Cameron Argetsinger who staged the first postwar event here, in 1948 at Watkins Glen.

Cunningham was not only a fine driver and excellent team manager, he was a great all-around athlete, excelling in everything he attempted: football, bobsledding, yacht racing, golf and aviation.

By way of example, he not only won the 1958 America's Cup in sailing but he was virtually unbeatable in the Star class, Atlantics and Six Meters. He won the Cup so decisively with *Columbia* going against the British boat *Sceptre* that he felt sorry for it. He told Denise McCluggage, "I wish we could trade boats and sail the series over again."

His interest in motorsports began in the immediate prewar era. Initially, he did not drive himself, but he was a car-owner and a car-builder. In 1934, Cunningham had an MG J.2 that he, himself, raced in ARCA events. Later, in 1936, he owned a supercharged MG K.3 Magnette. This car was borrowed and raced by both Sam Collier and George Rand, on the European continent and in Ireland. Later, he watched on the sidelines as Miles Collier took his MG Special to Le Mans in 1939. It was the beautiful Leonidis MG, a re-bodied former 1935 team car.

The first car Cunningham built was a Bu-Merc, the combination of a Buick Century chassis and the body from a wrecked Mercedes-Benz SSK. Built and modified with the help of Charles Chayne, who was Buick's chief engineer, it first ran at the New York World's Fair, October 6, 1940, with Miles Collier at the wheel.

During the war, Cunningham was too old to serve in the regular military, so he volunteered to fly submarine patrol on the east coast. This was not a simple job, as thousands of tons of cargo were being lost in Atlantic waters just off American shores, due to German submarines coming in close. If they could be spotted and their positions

Briggs Cunningham drives the #46 OSCA down a street in Bridgehampton just before the big race between his driver Phil Walters and the Ferrari of Bill Spear (courtesy Alix Lafontant).

radioed to naval destroyers or light bombers, they would be sunk. That was Cunningham's job. Cunningham at first bought a Fairchild plane and later a Sikorski S39B amphibious plane.

After the war, the Automobile Racing Club of America did not re-start. It was superseded by the Sports Car Club of America, founded in 1944. A tremendous boom in recreational activities occurred at the end of the war. People were sick of the killing and destruction. They wanted to forget it all. They bought boats. They went camping. They built little cottages out in the woods. And they began to think about racing sports cars.

They had time trials at airports. They ran rallies. They planned hill climbs. It was difficult to just close off public roads and race on them, but that's just what Cameron Argetsinger did. He was able to get this one little town behind the idea and put on a race. It was scheduled for October 2, 1948. Briggs Cunningham was there with two cars, the Bu-Merc and a supercharged MG-TC. He decided to drive the special himself, and asked Haig Ksayian to drive the MG. The Bu-Merc was 2nd overall and 1st in class in both of its races— an 8C Alfa Romeo won the Grand Prix. The MG was 3rd overall and 1st in class in both of its races. That race was Cunningham's only one in 1948, although he did buy another racing car that year. It was made by a man who had directed racing for Alfa Romeo and it was called a Ferrari. It was sold to him by Luigi Chinetti. It had a V-12 engine of 150 hp, in a light chassis designated the Type 166 Spyder Corsa, and it was the first Ferrari sold in America and the fourth one built (there was the Auto Avio and then two Type 125s).

Cunningham driver Phil Walters waves to the camera after winning the race at Thompson Raceway in 1953, with a Chrysler-powered Cunningham C-4R (courtesy Alix Lafontant).

The second road race in America was like the second chug of an engine — it gave momentum and a sense of continuity. Bruce Stevenson organized the race at Bridgehampton. He was the son of the man who financed Walter Chrysler, and had just come back from Europe, where he was a fighter pilot, first in P-40s above North Africa and then in P-47s stationed in Italy and France. Bruce was the national president of the MG Car Club and owned a TC. He attended the 1948 Watkins Glen race just to see how it was organized. Then he incorporated many of Argetsinger's ideas into his own event out at the end of Long Island.

Cunningham first raced the Ferrari 166 here. It was 1949. His friend George Rand drove it for him. The car showed its potential but unfortunately an oil line parted and the car did not finish. Sam Collier drove the supercharged TC to a 1st place in Race 2 and a 3rd in Race 3. Briggs also drove the MG but blew a head gasket in his turn at the wheel.

In the fall of '49 they were back at Watkins Glen, with three cars: the Ferrari, the MG TC and the Bu-Merc. This year, Briggs was driving, at the wheel of the Type 166. In the Seneca Cup, Cunningham took a 1st in class and 2nd overall, after the Grand Prix Maserati of George Weaver; in the Grand Prix, he again took a second overall, to

Out in force, the Cunningham team fields two D-Type Jaguars (#60 and #61) for the feature race of the 1957 Watkins Glen Grand Prix (courtesy Alix Lafontant).

the Mercury V-8 engined Riley driven by Miles Collier. The MG did not fare as well in the hands of Sam Collier as it had when driven by Haig Ksayian the year before, with only a 3rd and a 15th overall.

As noted in the Larry Berman chronology of the Cunningham team, Briggs bought the race preparation business Frick-Tappett Motors and moved it from Long Island to West Palm Beach to form B.S. Cunningham Co. The first real task of this fine, creative race shop and its staff of people from the aircraft industry was to get a couple of Cadillacs ready to run at LeMans. That's right, Cadillac sedans. He got a pair of them, with the manual transmission option, from Ed Cole at General Motors. Cunningham wanted to enter an American car at Le Mans and that's the only thing the organizers would let him bring. It had the advantage of having one of the most advanced engines anywhere, a very fine overhead-valve V-8. One of the two cars was re-bodied by an aircraft engineer in hopes of achieving higher speeds. It did, but the added weight affected acceleration and brake wear in a negative way. The special car finished after the standard Cadillac, 11th and 10th overall, respectively.

In only nine sports car races, Cunningham was already running high-level events, and three cars were entered at the first Sebring endurance race, in 1950: a Cadillac-engined Healey Silverstone, an Aston Martin DB2 that Cunningham himself drove, and a new Ferrari, a 195S, piloted by Luigi Chinetti and mechanic Alfred Momo—they took 7th overall.

As part of a team of Americans invited to compete in the Argentine GP at Buenos

Alfred Momo and the Cunningham crew stand at attention as the National Anthem is played just before the Formula Junior race at Watkins Glen in 1959. The team is represented on the track by Walt Hansgen in the #64 Stanguellini (courtesy Alix Lafontant).

Aires, Cunningham sent the Type 166 Ferrari for George Rand to drive. Cunningham himself did not go. The race was won by a new driver from America, an ex-fighter pilot named John Fitch, who drove a Cadillac-Allard. After the race, Cunningham gave him a call and invited him to drive with them at the next Le Mans. Cunningham was going to race a team of his own cars at the French 24-Hour event in 1951. Fitch would be teamed with a former circle-track driver by the name of Phil Walters. Two of the model C-2R racers went out, but Fitch and Walters managed to nurse their car to the finish in spite of damage caused by bad French gas.

While the C-2R was being raced, the great C-4R was being developed. It weighed

Seen at the 1961 Watkins Glen Grand Prix are left to right: Briggs Cunningham, crew chief Alfred Momo and driver Walt Hansgen, in a Cooper F1 car (courtesy Alix Lafontant).

1000 pounds less than the C2, it was simpler, more reliable and more powerful. It debuted at the 1952 Bridgehampton race where, driven by Phil Walters, it led briefly before being flagged in for a dragging exhaust pipe. At Le Mans again there were two team retirements and one car finishing, the car of Cunningham and his Connecticut neighbor Bill Spear — they finished 4th overall and 1st in class.

While the C-4R was being raced, the C-5R was being developed, with its streamlined body, beam front axle and 17-inch brakes. This was entered in the 1953 Le Mans and Fitch and Walters took it to a 3rd overall and 1st in class at Le Mans, setting a 104.04 mph average speed and fastest top speed of 154.8 mph. The last good finish at Le Mans was in 1954, when new team driver Sherwood Johnston and Bill Spear finished 3rd overall and 1st in class in the old C-4R. Despite his determination to win Le Mans, Cunningham never heard the Star Spangled Banner played at the end of that race. In 7 years of racing at Le Mans, his best finishes were the two 3rd places, in 1953 and 1954. He did, however, win the Sebring 12-Hour race three times, in an OSCA, a Cunningham and a Jaguar.

Besides concentrating on important endurance races, he ran a full schedule of SCCA National events, for 18 years. He ran the SAC base races in '53 and '54. He ran the races on closed-off public roads. And he ran on the growing number of purpose-built road racing courses, from coast-to-coast.

As an heir to the Procter & Gamble fortune, he could get any racing car he wished to buy. Sir William Lyons of Jaguar told him if he would stop building his own cars, Lyons would give him a team of D-Type Jaguars. Noting that it cost far more to campaign the machines, Cunningham said, "That was the most expensive decision I ever made." A list of his racing cars traces the technology of the sport, from his own Cunninghams to the D-Types, then the Lister Jags, Corvette, Porsche Spyders, Maserati 300S, OSCA 1500, OSCA 750, Stanguellini F. Jr., Maserati Birdcage, Fiat Abarth Record Monza, Cooper F. Jr., Lotus F. Jr., Jaguar 3.8 Sedan, Cooper Monaco, Brabham F. Jr., Jaguar E-Type and Porsche 904. According to the list compiled by Cunningham historian Larry Berman, there were 99 of them.

Briggs Cunningham had an uncanny knack for identifying great drivers and getting them into his cars. These include Phil Walters, John Fitch, Sherwood Johnston, Ed Crawford, Bill Spear, Walt Hansgen, Marsh Lewis, Frank Bott, Denise McCluggage, Dick Thompson, Dan Gurney, Bruce McLaren, Paul Richards, Lake Underwood, Roger Penske and many more.

To describe each of the races he and his team ran would take a book, because there were over 800 of them. Cunningham inspired and influenced scores of racing drivers and enthusiasts. By entering races, he built the attendance at race courses which, in turn, built the courses themselves. He and his friends were involved in an official capacity in the SCCA. From the beginnings of the sport in postwar America in 1948 to when he stopped racing in 1966, Cunningham *was* sports car racing in America.

David E. Davis Jr.

"I grew up in Burnside, Kentucky," notes Davis, "in the south central part of the state. My father moved up to Detroit during the Depression, as soon as my mother was able to travel. There was a sort of circuit taken by the people who were looking for work, from Kentucky to Detroit to New Jersey and back to Kentucky.

"A Russian immigrant named Roman Krauchuk was a friend of my father's. He taught my father how to build cabinets and my father taught him English. He was a friend of our family and we called him Uncle Ohman. They would go to new Sears stores that were opening, to install new furniture and repair furniture owned by the store and its customers. Then they would move on to another store and do the same. My family was fairly comfortable through the Depression. We got through the Depression that way. I was just out of grade school and World War II was approaching.

"In 1936, we settled in Royal Oak, Michigan. My father worked for furniture stores in Detroit. Later he was a restorer and seller of antique furniture. He was an avid hunter. And the hunting was good in southeast Michigan. At the time the limit was two pheasants a day. He would rush home after work, pick up our dog, an English Setter named Pick, and go out hunting. As soon as he would kill two birds, he would come back home and leave them for my mother to prepare for dinner, then go back out and kill two more before dark.

"As a first awareness of cars, my chew toy on those long drives from Kentucky was the shift knob from a Model A Ford. When we traded in that car, I cried and so did my mother when I had to give up that shift knob. People recall that I could identify all of the different cars on the road when I was four or five years old, from the sound of the engines. In Detroit we were lucky to see many interesting cars including Graham Hollywoods, which you wouldn't find just anywhere.

"At the time we had lots of dirt roads around Royal Oak. When I was a teen-ager we would take a Nehi soft drink sign, curve the front to make a toboggan out of it and tow it behind a Model A Ford in the winter. One time we were going along in a section of Royal Oak called Vincetta, and I was standing on the running board, going fast around a curve. The car was starting to get out of control and I thought it would be best to jump. I did, and then I tumbled around a little and found myself on the side of the road. Just as I was feeling sorry for myself at having gravel rash on the palms of my hands, the car went over. Junior Delew had rolled it into the ditch and I would have been under it if I hadn't jumped.

"Frank Winchell was a friend of mine. He was the head of R&D at Chevy, then he was VP of Engineering at GM. We worked together at the GM Allison plant in Speedway City, Indiana, trying to get more horsepower out of the Allison engine for the fighter planes. Around the time of the Indy 500 many of the GM workers went out to the track to work with the teams. Frank told me about a GM photographer who went there in 1940 and pulled up to his favorite place at turn one, with his family. He was just getting out of the car when he heard the characteristic sound of a race car losing it. Just then Maury Rose came over the fence, about 35 feet in the air. Most of the drivers would head for the basement but Maury was hanging over the side of the car and looking for a place to land. I wonder where that picture is today.

"I started going to midget races at Motor City Speedway right after World War II. I went with a friend of mine. To me, the most beautiful thing I'd ever seen was a Frank Kurtis midget. At the Race of Two Worlds, between the Kurtis cars and the European formula cars at Monza, the Europeans were astonished at the workmanship, and the performance, of those cars. So between 1947 and 1951, the midget was it.

David E. Davis with his MG TD at the Cumberland road races (courtesy David E. Davis).

"My moment of inspiration was seeing a Jaguar XK120 on Woodward Avenue. It was black with a tan interior. I followed it to Long Lake Road. The owner parked it at a bar and went in. I walked around that car looking at every detail. It was so sleek and so small. It was the turning point of my interest in cars. Shortly after that I bought a 1935 Mercedes roadster. It had a custom body with twin side-mount spares. It was pale gray with red wheels, with a 2½-liter 6-cylinder engine and a 4-speed overdrive transmission. The overdrive was a kind of clockwork mechanism — you had to move the lever right and forward, almost touching the dash. It was too nice a car to race, and besides it was down on power for its weight. I sold it to a Buick dealer who lost it in a garage fire.

"Then I bought an MG TD from Sports Cars of Ypsilanti. Doug Mahoney ran it for investors who included Max Goldman, Bernie Koerner and someone named Dave. It was not a happy investment for them, but Max was a very good journeyman racing driver. Through his business contacts, he got a lot of good rides. He gave me my competition license.

Buckling his helmet in the Mercedes Benz W196 GP car is magazine editor and publisher David E. Davis (courtesy Mercedes Benz).

"With the MG I did all the usual MG Car Club and SCCA events — rallies, races, quarter-mile ovals, airport courses. I drove in national races at Cumberland, Lockbourne and Chanute Field. The airport races were fun but they were tough on tires. You could use up a set of tires in a week. Then I got a job with Sports Cars of Ypsilanti. That was good until Tom Payne bought it and wanted a VW agency. We thought of ourselves as a sports car dealership. I quit and went to Larry Falvey in the spring of 1955 and bought the TF then. Detroit racing driver Harry Constant and I had coffee at Falvey's in about April '55 and I told him I'd like to go to work for *Road & Track*. He thought it wasn't too likely and I went out to California and worked for North American Aviation. I married my first wife in June — she had been a classmate of mine at Royal Oak High School. As we approached California, I decided to cross the desert at night, so the MG would not overheat. At dawn we came over the mountains and had our first look at California. I'll never forget the palm trees and the open bay garages, the emphasis on cars and evidence of speed equipment as we drove into San Francisco and south to Los Angeles.

David E. Davis tries out the fabled Mercedes W196 Grand Prix car — in the wet, no less (courtesy Mercedes Benz).

"I became an expediter for North American — I had experience working in four automotive factories in Detroit, trying to pay for the college degree I never got. My first assignment was testing two jet starter motors, and to do that we took them over to Meyer Drake, where Gus Salley, Sam Hanks's mechanic, did the test. While this was going on, virtually everyone in racing stopped in at the shop. I had stumbled onto the car culture out there. I decided to enter three SCCA races and the first of these was October 30, 1955, in Sacramento. I prepared the car and towed it up there with Chet Advent, a friend of mine.

"I was relatively fast in practice. Ken Miles introduced himself to me. He commented, 'You looked pretty good out there,' and offered some advice on a problem I had with the right rear tire lifting in the corners. He said to let the car settle down and the problem would take care of itself. At the start of the race I was leading the F-Production MGs, Porsches, with an HRG and a Singer, too. At the end of 3 laps my mirror was shaking, so I looked over my shoulder to see if anyone was trying to pass. In a moment of lost concentration, I brushed one of the hay bales lining the course. The cops had watered them down to keep the kids from lighting them on fire and it was like hitting a house with the front end of the car. It went over, and this was before the roll bars came in, so my head was caught between the back of the seat and the pavement. There were 130 compound fractures in my head. It took me 18 months to recover and the bill was $24,600. The track had $5000 and North American had $5000 and I

Windshield folded down, cap turned back, David E. Davis truly experiences the kind of wind-in-your-face drive that only an MG TC can provide (courtesy *Automobile Magazine*).

paid the rest myself. My friends told me to keep paying and pay any amount. I sent in checks for $15 and $20 and it never was turned in to a collection agency. When I later got an advertising job for $16,000 in 1960, I sent in the rest of the payments.

"Before all this happened I had been elected to the board of SCCA out there and their meetings were in Manhattan Beach so John Bond would pick me up to go to board meetings. He was one of the partners at *Road & Track*; the others were Oliver Billingsly and Bill Brohoe. They were enthusiasts but they had run up a big printing bill. The owner of the printing company called Bond and told him, 'Take over the outstanding debt and you own the magazine.' Their offices were in Playa del Rey and when they paid off the debt, they had a party that I was invited to. I wanted to stay with cars. I had written newsletters and I wanted to be an editor. I wrote to all the magazines and had bites from *Motor Trend* and *Road & Track*. They hired me, but it was as a space salesman. It was a big disappointment that I was not hired as an editor. Pete Molson was the editor and I was sure I could do a better job than he was doing.

"I was calling on Campbell-Ewald as a salesman. They were Chevy's ad agency. I knew Barney Clark through the sports car club and he had them recruit me, he put them up to it. Then he went on to Kenyon & Eckhardt to work on some Ford business. I turned them down but then Bob Brown, the advertising director at Peterson Publishing, caught wind of it and told *Road & Track* at the New York Auto Show. Bob would ingratiate himself to people like Lee Iacocca by buying Cuban cigars for them in Toronto. So *Road & Track* fired me even though I had not initiated the contact and I turned down the offer. I was so mad I cried when I pulled into the driveway at Costa Mesa. Then I told my wife and kids. Barney had left Campbell-Ewald and was over at K&E. But he called his old agency and told me, 'Put your house on the market and get out of there.' Well, that was the end of my marriage. We had moved about ten times and that was one too many.

A portrait of David E. Davis (courtesy David E. Davis).

"The job at Campbell-Ewald was waiting for me when I got to Detroit in 1960. The copy supervisor I worked with was Elmore Leonard, the novelist. He was great to work with and made a huge contribution to my writing ability. I had gotten into the agency business at the perfect time. In the postwar era, agencies were full of well-rounded, well-educated guys whose influence put the final polish on me. Even now, when it comes to captions, cut-lines, headlines, et cetera, I've got the edge with my advertising background. I was at Campbell-Ewald for three years.

"I had been writing an occasional article for *Sports Cars Illustrated* and they came up with an idea for an assignment. They said, 'Why don't you get a motor home and do a piece on the Watkins Glen Grand Prix?' So I got a Travil Motorhome and drove to Watkins Glen. I got myself all set up in the paddock and some people from *Car and Driver* came over; they said they were supposed to get a motor home to entertain their clients but it never came through. They asked if they could use my motorhome. Bill Ziff was there and so was Brad Briggs, vice chairman at Ziff-Davis. *Sports Cars Illustrated* was up for sale for $2 million but they got them down to $25,000! Karl Ludvigsen, a popular editor, had quit and a man named Bill Pain was in his place. The magazine was dead in the water. They offered me the job as editor of *Car and Driver*.

"This was wonderful for me, because all the people at the corporation were standing back so they wouldn't get anything on them in case something went wrong. I could do pretty much what I wanted. I got a great second-in-command, John Jerome, who had been writing *Sports Car Digest* in Texas. It was very funny and that gave our magazine that little extra snap. He was only there about a year and then he went to Campbell-Ewald to write ads with Bruce McCall. He was later the editor of *Skiing* magazine.

"One of our better-known features was the GTO comparison: Pontiac versus Ferrari. Jim Wangers at the D'Arcy agency called with a GTO for us to test. We didn't know it had a 421 engine but the test numbers were incredible. Jim tried to supply a Ferrari GTO but couldn't. So we had to skip the car-to-car comparison and use separate figures. One time in '64 or '65, Wangers and Brock Yates and Steve Smith were talking and Jim said, 'Street racing is the next big trend; street racing is what's happening.' Smith disagreed with Wangers and replied, 'What's happening has already happened.'

"I went back to Campbell-Ewald for awhile, as executive vice president and creative director, then I returned to *Car and Driver*. I left in April of 1986 and started *Automobile* magazine."

It seems that David E. never got far from *Car and Driver* because he was back there as a columnist at the time of his death in March 2011. After all those years of driving interesting cars to interesting places and writing about them in his own colorful way, he never got tired of it.

∽ Bob Dickens ∽

Bob Dickens, his dad and mom all became interested in sports cars when they lived in Chicago. "In 1949 my father Sid bought a 1948 MG TC as a birthday gift for my mom, Ruth. It was black but he had it painted her favorite color, a chartreuse green. Dad and I were amongst the six founding members of the original Elkhart Lake road course along with Jim Kimberly, Clif Tufte, Bayard Sheldon and Everett Namitz. Our whole family raced the 'TC there. My dad drove it off a corner, which now sports a National Historic Registry sign titled 'Dickens Ditch.'

"We raced it for two years in the country, on the short course, which was a trapezoid shape. Then the next year it went into town and around Elkhart Lake itself. In 1952 an MG driver went through a barricade, hitting a spectator. When Wisconsin officials stopped our racing on roads, it was decided to build Road America.

"After mom retired from racing, dad had the 'TC painted the 'Dickens Red,' a golden-brown color, and had the crank magnafluxed, polished and balanced. We campaigned at Road America, the Iowa City and Lawrenceville, Illinois, airports, plus Chanute Air Force Base in Rantoul. When I was an engineer in the Army

The face of Bob Dickens, Chicago Region driver, is captured on the 1957 Road America racing program (courtesy Bob Dickens).

I went to Chanute on a long weekend pass and at 2 A.M. I got stopped by a sheriff in eastern Kentucky who thought I was a moonshine runner. He took the car all apart. Before leaving Ft. Jackson, my 1st sergeant asked me who my contact would be and I told him 'General Gates,' who paraded with my folks in dad's 1934 Duesenberg dual cowl phaeton. I was just a private but on my return my company commander saluted me and they looked at me differently after that.

"At Elkhart Lake, we kept our car in the same garage as Briggs Cunningham's three C-2R entries. We, of course, were much in awe of them. As we were all getting ready to leave the garage, Phil Walters turned to Briggs and said, 'I'd better fill up the gas tank. Do you know how much is in it?' Cunningham replied, 'No. The gas gauge doesn't work.' That told me they were just like the rest of us human beings, and we felt more comfortable with those hero drivers after that.

"True gentlemen!

"We also raced at Wilmot, Wisconsin's nice little one-mile track. When we went there, we would flat-tow the MG. If you watched in the mirror, the wood frame would twist front to rear. But it held up very well, even when rear-ended by a Sprite!

"My dad, mom and I raced the TC for several more years. Mother was only 4' 8" tall so we extended the pedals with blocks that were 9 inches long. I still have them! They later lived in Venice, Florida, and when the brakes went out on her Mini-Moke, she drove it home — about 9 miles — slowing by downshifting and using the emergency brake. When she died, on September 11, 2001, I got a call from the *Chicago Tribune* and I told them about her. They printed a full-column remembrance of the 'famous woman racing driver.'

"After the MG, we raced a Siata Spyder, a Bandini and an XK-120MC. Then I built a couple of specials. The first, a '29 Ford roadster with a flathead V-8 engine, came in 5th behind Ernie Erickson's D-Jag, a C-Jag and a couple of Ferraris at Milwaukee's race track. The other, with a sectioned Victress S4 body on a 1926 Dodge frame, had a 1939 Ford V-8 with a Mercedes 540K compressor. Naming it the 'Mooselette,' I did a 44-second lap at Wilmot and that, I believe, equaled the time of the great Hal Ullrich in an Excalibur. My car had a distinctive sound, a 'whistle.' (There must have been an air leak in the intake manifold.) I liked the sound and I told my mechanic Rosie, 'Don't ever take the whistle out of the car!'

"In 1957, at Road America, I ran the B-Modified 'Mooselette' in the main event, finishing 2nd behind Augie Pabst, who drove a Bocar. My top speed was 154.

"In the '70s and '80s, as a member of Midwest Council's Drivers Club, I raced two Mini-

Bob Dickens in a 1957 photograph at Road America (courtesy Bob Dickens).

Sid Dickens's massive 1934 Duesenberg phaeton — the gang all goes for a ride with the top down at Chanute Air Force Base, Rantoul, Illinois, in 1954 (courtesy Bob Dickens).

Coopers, rolling one four times, end-over-end at Blackhawk — my last race. Ahhh ... but I was in 1st place at the time!

"The five fastest cars I ever drove were our Lamborghini Espada at 156, the Miura at 165 and my Countach at 187 (the latter clocked by the Arizona State Police). My ex–Richard Burton Ferrari 400i ran 145. My '82 Aston Martin could do that all day, according to the manual. It did!"

Now Bob is a fine artist, full time, painting under the name "Little Blue Hand" and living on a ranch west of Livingston, Montana, with two dogs, Jazz and Reba. They're blue heelers and they appear in some of his paintings. The closest he gets to the old sports car scene any more is reading *Vintage Racecar* magazine and driving his short wheelbase full-race Mini-Moke now and then.

✑ CHUCK DIETRICH ✑

Dietrich, of Sandusky, Ohio, is a former Volkswagen dealer who won his first race in 1951, in a stock TC at the old Detroit Fairgrounds, then drove a supercharged MG-TC in the E-Modified class. His next car was a Lester MG purchased from Don Marsh and raced in F-Modified. He raced everywhere from Put-in-Bay to Watkins Glen to Harewood Acres, a former RCAF base in Canada. Then he began a long relationship

Top: Chuck Dietrich's #24 supercharged MG-TC sets up for a pass on Bob Kuhn's Siata 208S, at Put-in-Bay in 1956. *Bottom:* The Dietrich MG TC, with Chuck and Suzy in it at Lockbourne AFB, 1954 (Betty Henn collection).

Cutting the corner closely puts a little sand on the course and it looks like Chuck Dietrich isn't the only one doing it, in the #34 rear-engined Elva Formula Junior. With all that sand, it has to be Bridgehampton, in about 1961 (Chuck and Jane Dietrich collection).

with Elva cars. In fact, he raced every model of Elva ever made except the Mark 8, from the nimble Mark 1 to the powerful Mark 7 Elva-BMW.

As Jeff Allison has noted, he's the man who put Elva on the map, right up there with Cooper, Lotus and Lola, the English Big Four. In 1960, he was in England, driving a factory Elva Formula Junior against Jim Clark and John Surtees. In '61, he had ten consecutive wins in a Series 2 rear-engine Elva FJ. In 1962 he set an FJ record at the new Mid-Ohio track, the first of many. He won the G-Modified SCCA National Championship in 1963, driving a Bobsy-Ford. He was in the big leagues, on the starting line at Mosport in 1965 with Jim Hall's Chapparal, and had an 8-race FJ winning streak in 1967. Also in 1967, he continued driving the Elva-BMW and won the SCCA National Championship in Formula B driving a McLaren M4B sponsored by Ron and Peggy Amey; in 1968, he finished 2nd nationally in FB in the beautiful M4. In 1969, he placed 3rd in the Formula 5000 National Championship at Daytona. Chuck drove at Sebring four times, with a best finish of 2nd in G-Modified in the Elva Mark 4. Along the way, he attracted a cadre of friends and fans, people who would sit on the turn seven hill at Mid-Ohio and scream, "Come on Chuck!"

He was a man who could win even if his car wasn't the fastest. A favorite Chuck Dietrich story concerns his old Elva Mark 7. The time came to sell it and the new owner

In the USRRC race at Laguna Seca, May 3, 1964, Chuck Dietrich gets a little crossed up in the #176 Elva-Porsche ... but he still managed a 2nd in class and 9th overall (courtesy Jeff Allison, Chuck and Jane Dietrich collection).

was not content with a car that had won dozens of races. He wanted to win even more. In taking it apart, he found much of the suspension out of alignment, the corner weights were all vastly different, and the car was in general disrepair, at least according to this restoration expert. In putting it back together, he made sure that everything lined up perfectly and the car specifications were flawless. After that, the car never won another race. Could it have been Dietrich all along?

He concluded 51 years in racing on 63 different racing circuits, as the holder of the oldest SCCA active competition license in the country, dating from 1951. For dedication to the sport, SCCA retired License #1 in honor of holder Chuck Dietrich. At the age of 77, he drove a Martini Formula Atlantic at Mid-Ohio to a 6th place among 14 newer, faster cars. While most of his racing was as an amateur, he competed in many professional races, particularly in the 1968 season. He is a longtime member of the Road Racing Drivers Club.

∽ Suzy Dietrich ∽

Suzy was Chuck's wife during the '50s and '60s and went to all the races with him. "Chuck came home from the service and I had saved my $100 a month that they gave

Top: Out at a club event in their green MG TC, Chuck and Suzy Dietrich look back at the camera, with Suzy at the wheel (Suzy Dietrich collection). *Bottom:* After winning the ladies' race in an Elva Mark I, Suzy Dietrich takes the victory lap without a helmet at the Akron Airport sports car races in 1957 (courtesy Joe Brown © Carl Goodwin).

At a Midwestern airport course Suzy Dietrich sits in the #30 Porsche Spyder before her race. She raced both the Spyder and Speedster Porsches and they were among her favorite cars (Suzy Dietrich collection).

all the service wives. I never drove a car until I was 19. We looked at two TCs. I wanted the red one but it was sold. We got the green one. I didn't really like it. The radiator hose broke and I just about cried. But pretty soon we started racing it."

She joined SCCA in 1951 and first raced an MG-TC at Chanute Air Force Base in Rantoul, Illinois. When Chuck got the Elva, Suzy took over the supercharged TC. She raced it at Akron Airport, Bryfan Tyddyn and other venues. Then she began driving the Elva and faster cars including a Porsche 550 Spyder. She won the first ladies' race at Watkins Glen in an Elva Mark II. In 1964 she finished the 24-Hour endurance race at Daytona Beach, co-driving with Donna Mae Mims.

A perennial competitor was Peggy Wyllie, wife of Doc Wyllie, both good drivers. "They had Lotuses," Suzy says, "a little better car than an Elva. I used to think 'Oh, if I only had a Lotus!' One time we were going to race and then Bob Fergus gave Peggy his Porsche Spyder. I was supposed to get that, but instead I drove our Elva. Then we got to see who's the best. We went into the first corner and both went off. I got back on the course and set the 2nd Fastest Time of the Day. I came back into the pits and they said, 'Who were you mad at?'"

In the heyday of Formula Junior she had a BMC-engined Cooper and also drove an Elva and a Lotus 20 FJ. In 1967 she was driving a Porsche Speedster. Other cars she

Top: Through years of driving other cars, Suzy Dietrich would say, "Oh, if I only had a Lotus." Finally she got one: this Lotus 20 Formula Junior. Here she is in the #7 Lotus at Road America.
Bottom: On the false grid at Road America, Suzy Dietrich gets a little last-minute advice from Chuck before going out in her Lotus 20 Formula Junior (Suzy Dietrich collection).

has driven include Lester MG, Elva Mark I, II, IV and V sports racing cars and a Porsche RSK. Other courses she has driven include Brands Hatch (England), Nassau Bahamas, Caguas (Puerto Rico), Sebring, Road America, Nelson Ledges and Mid-Ohio. For several years she served as an official of the Neohio Region, Sports Car Club of America, including a term as regional executive.

❧ FRANK DOMINIANNI ❧

Frank is best known for his antics in distance races on the East Coast, and as a Corvette driver who won an SCCA National Championship. But he started in an MG. "Actually my interest in racing started when I was 10 years old," says Frank, who grew up in Brooklyn. "The people downstairs had a midget racer with a homebuilt frame and a Henderson 4-cylinder motorcycle engine—I worked on that." In World War II, Frank was an Army infantry soldier in General Patton's unit, the 103rd Division of the Third Army. As a rifleman in the European Theater, he earned the Bronze Star, the Purple Heart and a Presidential Citation. On returning to the States, he started a shop called Hi-Speed Power Equipment in Valley Stream, Long Island, and bought a 1946

By 1954, Frank had moved on to a Nardi that was race-prepared by Bernard Taraschi and thought to be a Giaur. Photographer Dolin noted, "748cc Crosley-engined Giaur—Frank Dominianni—a good driver cursed with bad luck all season." Here's Frank in his Giaur at Thompson, September 4, 1955 (courtesy Irv Dolin, Frank Dominianni collection).

Top: The #169 Elva FJ of Frank Dominianni chases the #62 Lister Jaguar entered by the Cunningham team. It was unusual to mix open-wheel cars with sports racers but here it is done. It looks like Bridgehampton (courtesy R. Pelatowski, Frank Dominianni collection). *Bottom:* Frank Dominiani wins the B-Production race in his Corvette at Bridgehampton in 1964 (courtesy Stanley Rosenthal, George Jasberg collection).

Top: Frank Dominianni tries to keep his 1962 Corvette roadster ahead of the #59 Corvette coupe in back of him (courtesy Kenneth J. Fagan, Frank Dominianni collection). *Bottom:* Frank Dominianni in the #69 Corvette holds off the #17 Cobra to win 1st overall at the September 1968 Bridgehampton National (courtesy Spectrum Photos, Frank Dominianni collection).

MG TC from David Ash at J.S. Inskip. He first raced it at Westhampton in 1950, then Linden Airport and Watkins Glen.

He and his engine man, Art Drury, built a flathead Ford for road racing, called the D & D Special. It had a body built by Joe Gertler at Raceway Garage in the Bronx. It also raced at Watkins Glen in 1950. He later supercharged it. "I bought 300 superchargers from Tony Pompeo. I supercharged everything! Tony Pompeo was a bon vivant and a lovely person!" At the end of the season he got a rapid small-displacement Italian car, also from Pompeo. It was a Nardi transformed into a "Giaur" (pron. "Jower"). "It had Fiat disc wheels and at the Glen I lost a wheel. I said to Tony, 'Get me some brakes and Borrani wheels.'" Then, in 1957 he moved up to a Corvette. "I knew Charlie Bast, a Chevrolet dealer on Long Island. I said, 'We could run a Corvette.' So he got a 3-speed fuel-injected car. We did well until Cumberland, where Carroll Shelby, Dick Thompson and Bark Henry were racing in factory cars with 4-speeds and big brakes. Then we got a 'real' factory car and started winning."

Frank ran at most of the eastern tracks: Thompson, Bridgehampton, Lime Rock and the 'Glen. The '57 Corvette was followed by a '58 Corvette, '59, '60, '61 and '62, then a '68 and '69, which ran at Daytona and Sebring. Backing up to 1960, he acquired a Huffaker BMC Formula Junior from Briggs Cunningham then, and a rear-engined Elva FJ from the Mavino Brothers' Puerto Rican racing team. For awhile, he raced both the Corvette and an FJ, towing one with a station wagon and the other with his Cadillac. He stopped racing in 1995 at Bridgehampton. Frank's favorite course was Bridgehampton, where he could take the blind downhill turn one flat out, and beat the Cobras there in 1963.

∽ Bob Donner ∽

Bob Donner raced sports cars from 1953 to 1983. Holy smokes, that's 30 years! He has a map in the garage of all the races he's traveled to, from Riverside to Bridgehampton. "All told, it's 150,000 miles in a transporter," Bob quipped. Growing up in Colorado Springs, he was one of that group of Rocky Mountain drivers who should be better known, for their abilities and their enthusiasm. Two other top competitors were Danny Collins and Charlie Lyons.

Like many drivers of his era, he started in an MG. His first race was driven on the streets of Estes Park, Colorado. Misreading the schedule, he was eating lunch when the race began, but he jumped in his car, chased after the field, and still finished 7th. In the hillclimb at Lookout Mountain, he took a 1st in class with the MG. "My TD of 1953 was black with green," said Bob. "It was very reliable and I even drove it to El Paso, Texas, with my sister, to attend a wedding."

Bob drove the MG in the street race at Salida, Colorado, finishing 1st in class but 3rd overall with the Glockler Porsche taking 1st. At this point he gave the MG to his sister. "My father attended the Mexican Road Race in 1953 and 1954," Donner noted, "and brought back stories about how well the Porsches had run, and how impressive

On the starting grid at the street race in Salida, Colorado, 1953, is Bob Donner's #77 MG-TD with his sister ready to start the ladies' race. Next to her on the grid is Doreen Phipps, who had raced in the UK, and her well-modified MG (Bob Donner collection).

the Ferraris were." In December 1955, Bob got a Porsche 1500-S coupe from Competition Motors in Los Angeles, which he raced at Palm Springs, California, in a Cal Club event. He was a Marine training at Camp Pendleton, and the commanding officer of his unit was his pit crew. He also raced the Porsche coupe at Torrey Pines and Santa Barbara before getting a 550 Spyder in 1956. He bought it from John von Neuman's, where Ken Miles and Richie Ginther were mechanics. Donner got some coaching from Miles, who called Bob "The Lieutenant." "Miles helped me a lot," Donner said. "He would tell me how to drive a course and then say, 'Now Lieutenant, I don't want you to go too fast, but I don't want you to go too slow!'"

Bob's son David notes, "Dad did all of his own mechanical work during the Porsche days." Undaunted by the complexity of the Spyder engine, he did that too. "An aircraft mechanic who worked for his father guided him through the air-cooled Porsche 4-cam gear-driven valves, which revved to 8000 rpm on the Porsche 550, RS, RSK and RS-61," David adds.

After mechanical problems at Bakersfield, Bob finished 5th at Pomona, June 1956, following Ken Miles, Richie Ginther and John Porter. Then Bob had a string of seven 1st place finishes, at La Junta airport; Casper, Wyoming; the Kremling, Colorado, hill-climb; Socorro, New Mexico; Coffeyville, Kansas; La Junta again; and the Ft. Worth Nationals. At Casper, Donner beat two of the Ferraris entered by Temple Buell of

Bob Donner and wife Joan are all smiles after a run in the #17 Porsche RSK at Pikes Peak in 1960. It rained that year and Bob went up the hill "with wipers on high and lights ablaze." Competitors were amazed at how quick a small-displacement car could be (courtesy Stewarts Photo, Bob Donner collection).

Denver. In the following race, June 1957 at Elkhart Lake, he placed 3rd after Lake Underwood and Don Sesslar.

In May 1958, Bob acquired a 550RS Spyder, but DNF'd at La Junta using an experimental Carrera engine. Then at the Road America June Sprints, he finished 2nd to Don Sesslar in spite of a clutch cylinder failure. In May 1959, Donner got an RSK Spyder. He ran 23 events in this car, of which 12 were firsts in class. These included the Elkhart Lake national race in which he beat Don Sesslar and George Constantine, the race at Continental Divide Raceway, and the National at El Paso, Texas. In the first year with the RSK, he entered the Pikes Peak Hillclimb, only a few minutes from his home. But a driving mistake in 1959 meant he would have to wait until 1960 for a win at the hill, which he did in spite of a hailstorm. This was the first time a rear-engined car had run up the hill. Porsche racing manager Huschke von Hanstein was delighted that Bob had made the run and done so well. In March of 1961, Bob teamed with Don Sesslar to race the RSK at Sebring. They finished 2nd in class after Bob Holbert and Roger Penske, and 7th overall.

In January of 1962, Bob bought a new Porsche RS-61. It was run 14 races. That included one Sebring, a Daytona race, Mosport in Canada and a long tow out to the great Bridgehampton course on Long Island, which netted a 1st in class. At Sebring with co-driver Don Sesslar, the new car unfortunately went out with transmission

Top: The starter waves the green and Bob Donner gets off to a fast start in his #19 Porsche RSK at the 1961 Pikes Peak race. He took 1st in the Sports Car Division with a 14:36.5. *Bottom:* Drifting at the edge of the world, Bob Donner hangs out the tail of his Porsche RS-61 as he gets the checkered flag for a record time of 14:23.3 going up Pikes Peak in 1962. The car took another 1st place in the Sports Car division, which made the Porsche factory very happy (courtesy Artemis Images, Bob Donner collection).

failure but Bob was first in the 3-Hour event at Daytona. The RS-61 ran once at Pikes Peak, taking a 1st place in the Sports Car division in 1962 and setting a record, with a time of 14:23.3. He beat all the sports cars, all the stock cars, and his time would have given him a 12th place in the Open Wheel class. David Donner notes that a 2nd place in the Elkhart Lake 500, after the Chaparral, led to a call from Jim Hall to drive a second Chaparral at the 1963 Sebring enduro. Hall led the race but retired after 3 hours; at the 4th hour Donner was still running, in 3rd place. Shortly afterward, the rear axle failed just in time for Donner to pull the Chaparral into the Porsche pits. There von Hanstein chided, "Donner — I told you not to drive that car — it would never finish!"

Bob dropped out of racing for 13 years and then bought a Ferrari in 1976. A high point was competing at the Le Mans 24-Hour race in 1981 with his 512 BB/LM. The invitation came from the factory — the car was prepared at Goodyear in Switzerland and sponsored by a Belgian company, with Belgian co-drivers. Donner's son Bobby was in the pits handling refueling. Donner's Ferrari finished 7th overall after 24 hours in France. In 1983, Bob wrapped up a 30-year racing career at La Junta, the nice little airport course out in southeastern Colorado. In 2006, Bob Donner was inducted into the Colorado Automobile Hall of Fame.

☙ Ralph Durbin ❧

Ralph Durbin was known around the Detroit Region SCCA as the World's Fastest Bus Driver. Besides driving a Greyhound, he drove a variety of cars and all of them well. He was 3rd nationally in F-Production in 1954, with his MG in the Porsche class. He was 5th nationally in G-Production in 1955, with his MG TF. He was 3rd nationally in 1956, still with an MG, in the Alfa class. Then he got an Alfa and slipped to 22nd in points in 1957. He only raced a couple of races with the Alfa. He sold it to Ken Askew that year. The rest of the season was with an Austin-Healey 23rd in D-Production. Then he went back to 3rd nationally in 1958, again with an Austin-Healey. He got an 8th in E-Production in an Arnolt Bristol in 1959. In 1960 he was 3rd in an Arnolt Bristol in D-Production. Then, in 1961 he was 4th in C-Production in an Arnolt Bristol, and he seemed to get out of racing after that.

According to Bill Green at the International Motor Racing Research Center, Durbin competed in about fifty races. Many of the early ones were airport races, including both of the Lockbourne AFB events, Turner AFB in Georgia and Atterbury AFB. He began taking firsts at Andrews AFB in Washington, D.C., and soon became the MG driver to beat. He raced often at Road America and Cumberland, did a hillclimb at Giants Despair in 1955, and even got out to Bridgehampton in 1960 — that's a 21-hour drive from Detroit.

Two of his friends in the Detroit Region remember him: longtime driver and race official Harry Constant, and racer Ken Askew. Ken notes, "I first saw Ralph in 1951, when he arrived at the Janesville, Wisconsin, Airport for the races. I was much

Ralph Durbin's car, MG-TF #211, sits forlornly in the paddock at Watkins Glen, 1955, with a split gas tank. When new asphalt on the course began to disintegrate, they applied dry cement. This created dust clouds, and while passing through one, Ralph's TF was hit by another car (courtesy Ken Askew).

impressed, being a Detroit native, to see the cream-colored MG being towed by a cream-colored Oldsmobile."

As Harry Constant remembers, "Ralph raced a TF at first. He had already been racing for about a year when I went to my first race, at Lockbourne Air Force Base in 1954. I was a little uncertain of the course and I mentioned this to Ralph. He said, 'Just follow me around and you'll learn it.' He took off and I lost him on the 3rd corner.

"The next year, we were racing together at Put-in-Bay. Going down the straight, Ralph passed me, but I kept on his tail. A TC passed me, then got behind Ralph and gave him a nudge as we approached the gas station. He spun Ralph and Ralph drove backwards down the sidewalk, hit the front straight, went forward and continued. A very interesting bit of driving. I'll never forget Ralph looking over his shoulder, driving backwards in the race.

"After he had the MG, he got an Alfa. Then he drove an Austin-Healey. He drove a modified T-Bird for a short time and then drove for Wacky Arnolt on the Arnolt Bristol team. He was a very good driver, very versatile and he was always in the national points."

Ken Askew notes, "Ralph and I became friends when I moved back to the Detroit area in 1954. I worked on his pit crew in 1955 and enjoyed his company. A fierce competitor on the track, he was a gentle and humorous friend. When I got a chance to drive

The Austin-Healey of Ralph Durbin leads a Jaguar and two other Healeys at Ithaca, Michigan, in 1956 (courtesy Ken Askew).

an Alfa Romeo owned by Jack Downey, I knew Ralph had to change cars to win in the under 1300 class. The night before the Put-in-Bay race of 1956, I took Ralph for a ride around the course in the Alfa. The Alfa was entered in the G-Production class, until after the morning practice, then it was moved to G-Modified. I finished second to Chuck Dietrich, who drove a Lester MG ahead of the class F MGAs. Ralph won the 1300 MG race that day but was convinced about the Alfa's future.

"Then Ralph arranged with Falvey Motors to be an Alfa dealer and he got four Alfas, one for himself. The weekend after it arrived, we went to Elkhart Lake, the second year of the new course, 1956. We went to a 4-Hour enduro and won our class there.

"Soon, other Detroit drivers got Alfas. Harry Constant got one and took it to the airport course at Harewood Acres, Ontario. I wasn't quite sure whether the Alfa would roll if it lost adhesion and I was glad to see Harry spin one time because that told me it wasn't going to go over. In 1957, we went to Elkhart and took both the Alfa and the Austin-Healey. A driver named Scotty rolled his tan Porsche so we brought it back on the trailer and I drove the Healey back without a windshield and when we got home I bought the Alfa. Ralph didn't like the Alfa. He liked British cars where you're close to the steering wheel. He bought a new six-cylinder Healey and won 23 out of 24 races with it. Another place Ralph raced in Canada was Kincardin, near Grand Bend on Lake Huron. It had been an RCAF base in World War II, just like Harewood.

"When Tom Payne went with the Arnolt Bristols to Sebring in '57, Ralph was one of the drivers." Actually, he was in the only Arnolt Bristol (#71) that finished the race.

Ralph Durbin's #164 MG TF passes the #114 MG TC of Harley Watts of Columbus, Ohio, at the 1954 Akron Airport sports car races (courtesy Ken Askew).

Co-driving with J. Cook and L. Karber, he finished 30th overall and 6th in class G3. The car was entered by J. Cook of Detroit. "John Cook was a very consistent driver," says Ken, "and careful. His tachometer had a small dollar sign ($) at the 5500 mark." Three other Arnolt Bristols entered by Wacky Arnolt of Chicago were DNFs in the race. In fact, they withdrew, due to the death of driver Bob Goldich. In the 1958 Sebring race, Ralph was in the #40 Arnolt Bristol, one entered by S.H. Arnolt. Co-drivers were Wacky Arnolt himself, and competition driving instructor Max Goldman, along with Ralph. They finished 35th overall and 4th in class that year. Trying once again in 1959, the team of Wacky Arnolt, Max Goldman and Ralph Durbin finished 25th overall and 4th in class once again, in the #26 car. But wait, that's not all! In 1960, the team of Max Goldman and Ralph Durbin came in 14th overall and first in class, in the #31 Arnolt Bristol entered by S.H. Arnolt!

Well, after all that racing in an Arnolt Bristol, it was time for a change, and Ralph drove what amounted to a T-Bird Funny Car. This is the one that people said was a modified Thunderbird. Well, it sure was modified, but it wasn't a T-Bird. According to Ken Askew, it was a Kurtis Kraft chassis with an aluminum body made to look like a 1957 Thunderbird. It had a Lincoln engine, a Jaguar transmission and a Halibrand quick-change rear end. "The Fords were nicknamed 'Battle-birds' and were built by Ford to beat Corvettes. The factories were supposed to be out of racing, but Corvettes were entered by Doane Chevrolet of Dundee, Illinois, and the 'Battle-birds' were entered by Dearborn Steel Tubing's owner Andy Hotten."

The Halibrand caused Ralph a problem one time. He went out for practice and the car felt fine. Then Hotten's crew thought they would make the car even better. So

The #68 Alfa Romeo Giulietta of Ralph Durbin rounds the corner into town and the front straight at the 1957 Put-in-Bay race (courtesy Ken Askew).

they put a lower axle ratio in overnight. The next day, Ralph ran out of RPM out on the race course.

"Durbin was a very good driver," says Ken. "He always said the object was to win at the slowest speed. He said, 'Don't use a lower gear if you can use a higher gear.' After being a bus driver for so long, he later got into the contracting business. One of the most satisfying times of my adventures with sports cars was when, as the starter of a race at Michigan State Fairground, I watched my friend Ralph leave the entire field behind as he cruised around the dirt track. He built up such a lead that the NASCAR promoter working with us suggested that I black flag Ralph to make the race closer!"

Harry Constant picks up the thread here: "Then he retired to Florida. When we had the 50th anniversary of the Detroit Region SCCA, he came up for that. His son wrote a biography of him. And then shortly after that, he died."

∽ Fred Egloff ∽

Fred Egloff credits his grandfather Gottfried "Fred" Egloff for his lifelong interest in auto racing. A Swiss immigrant, he often recalled witnessing the first American auto race in 1895. He worked and lived a few blocks from the race course in Evanston at the estate of Francis Peabody, founder of the Peabody Coal Co.

Fred Egloff sits on the grid ready to start the Rio Grande Prix road races at El Paso, Texas, in 1957. This car, with wire wheels, is the first of two MGAs that Fred raced (courtesy Fred Egloff).

Fred became a well-known figure in the Chicago Region SCCA as editor of the National Award winning *Piston Patter*, the region's newsletter. He also served as Midwest correspondent for *Sports Car Graphic* and *Sports Car*. He knew all the pioneers: Wacker, Kimberly, Ullrich, Bott, MacArthur, Haas, Uihlein, etc., etc. That was primarily because Fred got an early start on it, working in the pits and on corners when he was a 17-year-old high school student. "You had to be 21 to race but they would let you work in the pit area and course work stations—sometimes that's just as dangerous." In fact, he was active so young that years later, when Karl Brocken mentioned Fred's name to the Rose brothers—you know, the ones who owned the garage in *Ferris Bueller's Day Off* where the Ferrari exits through the rear window—they said, "Fred Egloff? Oh, we know his son!" When told of this later on, Fred corrected, "No, that was me."

The first club he joined was the Midwestern Centre of the MG Car Club, which covered several midwestern states. Bud Seaverns and Larry Whiting were the officers and the membership included Karl Ludvigsen. For his first speed events Fred borrowed a TC MG from a neighbor. Another of his neighbors, Ernie Erickson, inspired his visit to Elkhart Lake to witness the through-town races. He was hooked and had an official pass at the 1952 event. He served as a gofer for a group of MG racers during the SAC racing days, Bob Larson with a blown TC, Bob Krasberg, Bob Gary with TDs. When he finally turned 21 he purchased the first MGA in the Chicago area with help from Wacky Arnolt. He soon had a license and in the ensuing years raced primarily in the

Fred Egloff drives his red MGA in the Carrera San Ignacio in Chihuahua, Mexico. Blurred in the foreground is a competing Triumph TR-3. This was an open road race with very little crowd control (courtesy Fred Egloff).

Midwest at State Fair Park in Milwaukee, Wilmot, Lyndale, Blackhawk, Meadowdale, and Road America. Elkhart is the best but, due to its length, not ideal for an MG. The shorter courses such as Wilmot and Lyndale, a small Road America, were better suited and more fun.

"When I was in the army stationed in El Paso, I drove in the Rio Grande Prix on the Enchantment Park Course. Also, they held a two-mile hillclimb up in the Sacramento Mountains of New Mexico near Cloudcroft that featured a hairpin turn with a sheer drop-off on both sides. Most memorable while I was stationed there, they held a Carrera San Ignacio town-to-town race. It was held in Mexico just southeast of Juarez with virtually no crowd control. It was about 50 miles between towns so you raced to one, turned around and raced back at your first leg interval. Stutz Plaisted, then stationed in San Angelo, was also driving an MGA. He had a problem in the race; though he usually beat me he was having engine trouble and finished after me on leg one. Despite the desert dust he had removed his air cleaners. He opened his hood during the layover and discovered someone's undershorts had blown up from the road and into his carburetors. After it was removed he beat me on the next leg. On one leg there was a multi-car accident directly in front of me. An RS Porsche had thrown gravel onto a high-speed turn before a pack of six cars arrived. A Triumph TR3 spun, taking out two other cars, causing a dust storm obscuring the view of the road ahead. I looked to

Top: Fred on the starting grid at the Algonquin Hillclimb in 2005, in his #8 BMW 328. *Bottom:* At Road America in 2006, the 70th anniversary of BMW was celebrated with a vintage race. Fred Egloff won the prewar class in his #8 BMW 328 (courtesy Fred Egloff).

A close-up of Fred in the white BMW 328 (courtesy Fred Egloff).

my right and intentionally spun into a vacant village square accompanied by the sounds of the unseen accident. Realizing someone else might follow in my direction I quickly headed through the village, regaining the road beyond the accident. The SCCA learned that some of us had participated in this banned event and had our licenses lifted. Later on I had to go through driver's school all over again to get a national SCCA license."

In the meantime Fred specialized in serious competitive rallying, winning the Chicago Region individual championship as well as team championship with his MGA. He became the only three-time winner of the National Lake Michigan Miglia, an over 1000-mile national event with 100 competitors. Two of the three wins were in MGs, a standard MGA and a twin cam.

In 1955 Fred was an officer in the Army reserve in summer camp at Sheboygan, which was 15 miles from Elkhart Lake. One of the privates in his outfit, Frank Isaacson, had a new Corvette and the thought crossed their minds to exercise the car at the new Road America course. Fred said, "I'll call Clif Tufte." Clif said, "There is a problem, Fred. I'm going to be in Milwaukee all weekend at a business meeting, but why don't you stop by the house? I'll leave the keys to the track with my wife." Fred and Frank had Road America to themselves for two days and the Corvette got a good workout. "We trusted one another in those days," said Fred.

The following year Fred beat a newcomer, Augie Pabst, who was driving in his very first race, with both driving Triumphs. Augie was a very fast learner and seldom lost any race thereafter. In the early sixties Fred took driving lessons from Stirling Moss at the Meadowdale Course, and then assisted Moss in a presentation to the region at the Edgewater Beach Hotel. This experience served in convincing Fred to abandon the increasingly professional scope of racing and pursue vintage sports car activities. He was asked to join the VSC (Vintage Sportscar Club), an exclusive club made up of road racing pioneers in the Midwest states.

After driving many years in "real" racing, mostly in an MGA, Fred bought a 1937 BMW 328 that qualified for vintage races. While the 328 was being worked on, Bill Victor lent Fred a Railton, and a LeMans Replica Frazer Nash. With the Frazer Nash he won the 1970 Competition Trophy of the VSC. According to *The Automobile* magazine of England the 328 BMW was "one of the most significant sports cars of all time."

The VSC Competition Trophy presented to Fred Egloff in 1997 for driving his BMW 328 nicknamed "Smoke" (courtesy Fred Egloff).

Further research has uncovered the legend behind his very car. It had been sent to Holland to their auto and motorcycle champion, who drove it to first overall in the 1939 sports car Grand Prix of Holland at Zandvoort. Its escape from the Nazis in World War II was described in a Dutch racing book. Fred once again won the VSC Competition Trophy in 1997, this time with his 328. In 2008 the historic car was on display in the International Motor Racing Research Center at Watkins Glen, New York. After 41 years of owning the car he sold it to a man he believes will keep it as original as an old race car can be kept.

After a decade of research, Fred's book *Origin of the Checker Flag* was published in 2006, answering one of racing history's most puzzling questions. In her review of the book Denise McCluggage said it consisted of "impeccable research," while it also received high praise from auto historian Beverly Rae Kimes in her very last review. Fred is also a noted western historian having received several lifetime achievement awards in that field. Recently his 1981 book *El Paso Lawman: G.W. Campbell* was voted one of the one hundred outstanding nonfiction western books published during the 20th century. Is it any wonder he has retired to the Texas Hill Country, where his home overlooks the old cattle trail to Dodge City? He still keeps in touch with friends from the heyday of sports car racing in Chicago.

∽ Gus Ehrman ∽

Gus immigrated to the United States after World War II, during which he was a Spitfire pilot in the Royal Air Force. He had his flight training in Canada at Goderich,

Gus Ehrman drives the #60 MG-TC, white with green seats, to 12th overall in a field of 43 cars at the 1949 Watkins Glen Grand Prix (Gus Ehrman collection).

Ontario, in Tiger Moths. After training at three other bases in single-engined planes, he was sent to a Liberator squadron flying sub patrol in Ireland. He told the base commander, "I can't even count those engines." The reply: "We have you, and we're going to keep you." But the captain who taught him to fly the bombers said, "Gus, I'm going to help you get out of the squadron." Shortly afterward, he was sent to Elmden near Birmingham, England, to fly Spitfires. After coming to the States, he had an MG dealership in Greenwich, Connecticut, from 1948 to 1951. "I played with motorcycles while I was a pilot," Gus says, "and then I decided to race something with four wheels."

He began racing at the inaugural Bridgehampton event, June 11, 1949, in a TC, followed by Watkins Glen, September 17, 1949 (car #60). "I also took the TC to Palm Beach Shores," he notes. May 7, 1950, was another early race, this time at Westhampton AFB, in a supercharged Crosley Hot Shot. He then was president of the Rootes distributorship in Boston before joining the J.S. Inskip dealership in Providence, selling MGs. "When the TDs came out, of course, I raced one of them, in the usual places—Bridgehampton, Watkins Glen, Thompson, Mt. Equinox and the Somers hillclimb in Connecticut." An early racing adventure occurred at the 1952 Sebring, where he was

Top: Driving the #27 MG-TD, Gus Ehrman takes a first-place finish at the 1954 Watkins Glen race. That year they raced on the beautiful 4.6-mile course up on the hill in Dix Township.
Bottom: Here Gus Ehrmann tracks out from the apex of a corner at the Palm Beach Shores race in January of 1950, driving his #11 MG TC (Gus Ehrman collection).

expecting a promised ride in a Singer roadster. When he learned the car would not arrive, he approached Steve Wilder, driver of a Morgan, who had traveled all the way from California in it. Gus persuaded him to enter the race — they finished 9th overall and 1st in class. In 1954, Gus co-drove the Motto-bodied MG TD of Fred Allen and they finished 11th. He was reunited with the car at the 2005 Amelia Island Concours.

In 1955 he was recruited by Hambro Automotive Corporation at Nuffield as sales manager, and in 1961 he was sent to California to take over the MG and Austin lines from the Gough distributorship. Then, in 1963, he became the president of Hambro. Due to manipulations by U.S. Customs, which wanted to charge double the duty on some cars, Gough Industries was renamed Hambro Distributors. Then BMC came to Hambro and said, "Thank you for your service, now we're going to take this over," and Hambro Automotive was morphed into Hambro Distributors, with Gus Ehrman as its president. As Gus explains it, "They shot the father but not the son." In 1964, Hambro was sold to Kjell Kvale in northern California. In the East, BMC was not happy with J.S. Inskip and there was a need for new management. BMC said, "We have just the man for you," and Gus was installed there as president. Finally, in 1969, British Leyland bought out Inskip and Ehrman was made a Leyland vice president. "Different company, same chair," Gus notes.

Getting back to the racing, he had been on the winning MGA team at Sebring in 1957, and later raced Austin-Healeys. In 1959, Ehrman went to the Bonneville Salt Flats to co-drive the EX-219 Austin-Healey streamliner with Tommy Wisdom and Ed Leavens. Twelve

Top: In victory lane at Watkins Glen in 1954, Gus Ehrman wears the laurel wreath for his win in the MG race. With the #27 MG-TD, he beat national champion Ralph Durbin by two car lengths. *Bottom:* Gus Ehrman sits in the cockpit of the EX-219 Austin-Healey streamliner with the canopy open, at Bonneville in 1959 (Gus Ehrman collection).

The #7 flat-radiator Morgan Plus Four of Gus Ehrman leads the Deutsch-Bonnet of Steve Landing at the 1952 Sebring race. At the finish, the Morgan was 9th OA and the D-B was 7th OA and 1st on Index of Performance (courtesy Bill Foster).

records were set by the team. Gus posted a record speed of 146.64 mph for the 200-kilometer distance. Ehrman and Tommy Wisdom averaged 138.39 mph for 1000 Ks and Ehrman, Wisdom and Leavens drove at 138.75 for 12 hours ... all in a Class G car of under 1100cc.

∽ Charlie Ellmers ∽

Ellmers is the man who gave Roger Penske his first competition license. As a long-time race official in the Neohio Region of the Sports Car Club of America, Charlie was the head of the Contest Board at the time Roger wanted to go racing with his new Jaguar XK-120M. Another Contest Board story involved license applicant Bob Parsons driving at Akron Airport, with Charlie observing. Bob recalls, "I went roaring down this hairpin turn to the right, onto the dirt, sliding around in my TR-3. All of a sudden I'm upside down. I hit one of the ruts and rolled my car. I scrambled out through one of the cut-down doors. Then I went back to see Charlie. I thought that was it for my competition license. He said 'Ahh, don't worry about it, Bob. We're not going to let a little thing like that keep you from racing.'"

Charlie Ellmers of the Funny Face Auto Racing Team wins the MG race at Put-in-Bay in 1952 and stops to pick up the checkered flag for the victory lap. His #3 MG-TD has a masking tape number and competition windscreen (Ruth and Charlie Ellmers collection).

Ellmers was a Navy combat veteran of both World War II and the Korean War before he got into sports cars. "I was discharged from the Navy after my stint aboard the *Essex*," Charlie said. "I had some money saved up and thought I would buy a new car and drive it home. I was considering a Studebaker but thought I would check out the new MG TD. The TD was $2020, about the same as the Studebaker. The guy at the MG dealer's wouldn't let me drive one of the MGs in the showroom, but he did take me for a ride in his TC. That cinched it."

Ellmers joined the Cleveland Sport Car Club in 1951. He was an excellent driver and won the first race, the first year at Put-in-Bay in 1952 in his black MG TD. He also drove the TD at Put-in-Bay in '53 and '54, and drove at Elkhart Lake and Lockbourne Air Force Base. "He raced it at Watkins Glen," notes Ruth Ellmers, "and blew up the engine. He was so disgusted he sold it on the spot. Besides, he didn't have a tow bar."

After the TD, he bought a Jaguar XK-120. "It was red and he painted it black," Ruth recalls. "He drove it in rallies for a couple of years before we were married and won several of them, including the Ohio 24. That was about 1956 or '57. We did some rallying afterwards, too." To continue racing at Put-in-Bay, since the Jag could not race there, Charlie borrowed an MG-TC from Ben Hitchcock, which he drove in 1955, '56 and '57. As Ruth recalls, that was the year that he missed the corner into town, went

Charlie Ellmers, left, shows off the grille of the Funny Face Auto Racing Team MG-TC, at Put-in-Bay, where the team entered two cars (courtesy Joe Brown).

straight down the escape road, backed up, and still won the race. "I was impressed when he won that race," she adds.

After the TD and the TC, in about 1957, he and four other drivers bought Chuck Dietrich's Lester MG and ran up in the modified class with the Porsche Spyders, OSCAs and occasional Kieft MG. The group racing the Lester was called the Funny Face Auto Racing Team, or FFART, for short. It included Meach and Ben Hitchcock, Frank Floyd, Ted Jayne and Charlie. Ted and Charlie drove the car at venues including Watkins Glen, Akron Airport, Cumberland and Dunkirk. Charlie also drove the Giants Despair hillclimb near Brynfan Tyddyn. "We were married on the Ides of March," says Ruth, "and we went to the 1958 Sebring race for our honeymoon. At the end of the race I was almost run over by Stirling Moss." Ruth adds, "We were true MG aficionados. Over the years we had three T series MGs and three B series MGs."

One of Charlie's many friends, Triumph driver Bob Morrison, shares this story: "Of course the Lester was rapidly outclassed by the Porsche Spyders and then the Elvas and Lolas as they came along, but Charlie had an interesting philosophy. He told me this at Cumberland: 'When I race, I consider that I'm racing only two people, the guy in front of me and the guy behind me. If I pass the guy in front of me, then I have a

Charlie Ellmers in the #10 Lester MG takes the corner at the Roundhouse Bar in the 1956 Put-in-Bay road race, a fabulous event on an island in Lake Erie (courtesy Joe Brown).

new race, but it still only involves two cars. The same is true if the guy behind passes me.'"

Charlie and Ruth later drove Cleveland Sport Car Club rallies in their VW Microbus. It was after he stopped racing that he got into officiating. "Putting on a race was a major project," he noted, "and only a region with a lot of members was able to do it in the early days." Charlie was the chief tech inspector and chief steward, the Steward of the Meet at Mid-Ohio, etc., as well as head of the Contest Board, and Ruth worked at the races, too. In addition to sports cars, he was a racing sailor at Mentor Harbor Yacht Club, a great club east of Cleveland. Charlie and Ruth's Ensign class sloop was well-known on the south shore of Lake Erie. Charlie named the boat *Lieutenant*, because, he noted, "It's been an Ensign too long."

❧ BOB FERGUS ❧

Bob is no longer with us so we'll let his friend and business partner Don Marsh tell his story. "Bob started racing a little earlier than I did," says Don. "He was extremely good at it. I was working in his sports car business with him. Harley Watts prepped the TC and Bob ran everything from stock to cycle-fender-modified. He won the Collier Trophy. He was RE of our SCCA Region. His dealership was named Columbus Sports Car Co. That was before the Volkswagen. Bob had a distributorship called Midwest

Bob Fergus shows off the new Austin-Healey 100 at his Ohio dealership, Columbus Sports Cars. The store was the center of plenty of activity as the sport grew and new racing courses sprang up every year (courtesy Tom Householder).

Volkswagen Co., then we decided to modernize it, so we called it "Midvo," our cable address.

"After racing the MG TC, he gained some fame as co-driver of the Dick Irish Siata Gran Sport: 1st in class, 2nd on index and 3rd overall at the 1952 Sebring, ahead of 4 Ferraris and 3 Jaguars. Then Bob bought a C-Type Jaguar to race along with the TC, at the 1953 Lockbourne Air Force Base event. In the MG race, Bob finished first and his pit crew, Don Marsh, was 2nd, also in a TC. In his early drum-brake C-Type, Bob took a 5th.

"In about 1953, Bob had polio, so he backed off a little on the racing," Don says. "Afterward, we never drove the big cars because he didn't have the strength in his arms." When Bob sold the 120-C, he bought a Healey 100S. It was a beautiful car with an aluminum body and disc brakes. "He put a patch on the fender every time it beat a Ferrari," notes Marsh. Then he stopped racing in the late fifties. Like Don Marsh, he got into vintage in the late seventies. Bob took up vintage racing in a big way. "He had a Lotus 15, a 200S Maserati and a Lola T210, with an 1830cc FVC engine," Marsh continues. "As well as Chuck Deitrich's old Elva Mark 7 BMW, a 250S Formula One car, a lot of nice cars ... Lotus Elite, 500TR Ferrari, and a Frazer Nash Le Mans Replica. He had a J2X Allard — Chevy powered, but never liked it — it was too heavy. Then there was his flying. He was a fighter pilot in World War II, but not in combat — at the close of the war. He had a Pitts — a little bi-plane, a Youngmeister stunt plane and he loved gliders. He bought one from Elmira, New York. He could fly a Lear but never did, though he was qualified for it."

~ JOHN FITCH ~

Fitch was a World War II airman in the U.S. Army Air Force, with two tours of duty in combat. He flew an A-20 light bomber in North Africa and a P-51 fighter plane over Germany. Captain Fitch was one of the first to shoot down a German jet and was shot down himself three months before the end of the war. After Patton liberated Fitch's prison camp, he was a highly decorated airman. When he came back, he ran a seaplane shuttle service for awhile and then opened a car dealership in White Plains, New York. Named "Sports and Utility Motors," it sold MGs and Jeeps. He drove his first race on his honeymoon. As OSCA driver Otto Linton recalls, John and Elizabeth arrived at the 1949 Linden, New Jersey, airport race in a TC loaded to the gills. John took all their luggage off the rack, unpacked the rest of the car, drove and won his race and went on his way.

A triumphant Elizabeth Fitch celebrates John's big race win at McDill AFB, Tampa, Florida, in the Cunningham C-4R (John Fitch collection).

Top: John Fitch (center) takes a break from activity at the 1953 Le Mans race. In the foreground is the Cunningham C-4RK; second from the right is Fitch's co-driver, Phil Walters (John Fitch collection). *Bottom:* Briggs Cunningham and John Fitch converse before the start of the Road America race in 1956, in front of #58 D-Type Jaguar (courtesy Alix Lafontant).

Top: John Fitch beams after a magnificent triumph in the 1955 Mille Miglia: first in GT class and fifth overall in a 300SL Mercedes coupe. With him is passenger Kurt Gesell, appearing to be glad that the race is over (John Fitch collection). *Bottom:* Fitch's last race was at Bonneville in this borrowed 300SL. He was 88 years old at the time. The adventure was made into a film by Chris Swedo, titled *A Gullwing at Twilight* (courtesy Larry Berman).

In this amusing fashion, Fitch began a racing career that included a Sebring win, 3rd at Le Mans, the Cunningham Team, the Mercedes-Benz team, and a final race at age 88 in a gullwing Mercedes at Bonneville. His most important race was at Buenos Aires, Argentina, in 1951, when he repaired a crashed Allard and won the race against Tommy Cole, Fred Wacker and Jim Kimberly. This put him on the Cunningham and Mercedes teams. Of his Mexican Road Race drive in the prototype 300SL roadster, he said, "In 1945 I was shooting at the Germans and seven years later I was driving their race cars." For driving the Cunningham cars, his partner in the long-distance events was the great Phil Walters. "We would go out and practice in the same car and take turns scaring each other," Walters once quipped. They beat the Aston Martin factory team at Sebring in 1953, to the astonishment of team manager John Wyer. Fitch also won a number of the SAC-base races.

In 1955 he drove in Europe for the unbeatable Mercedes team. His best race was the '55 Mille Miglia, driving a thousand miles in 11½ hours in a production 300SL coupe and finishing ahead of many sports racing cars as the only American in the race. Fitch was Stirling Moss's co-driver at the '55 Dundrod Tourist Trophy—they won the race on Stirling's 26th birthday, September 17. In 1957 he was involved in the design of the Lime Rock racing circuit, and became its general manager. In 1961, he invented an energy-absorbing device for highway safety—the Fitch Barrier, those yellow barrels you see on the highways. He is an advocate of racing safety and is promoting the practice of paving gravel traps and the use of energy-absorbing barriers.

THE FUNNY FACE AUTO RACING TEAM

In European road racing, the teams were usually named for a car constructor: Scuderia Ferrari, Daimler-Benz, Jaguar, etc. Sometimes it was the sponsor or his company: Ecurie Ecosse, David Brown (Aston Martin), etc.

Americans took a far broader and more creative point of view, such as George Schrafft's "Ecurie Shoestring," intended to describe the budget used to race his Siata 208S at Sebring and elsewhere, and the closely related "Scuderia Shoestring" of Boris Said and his OSCA, "alone and broke in the fabulous city of Paris."

A well-known team in the Midwest was the "Funny Face Auto Racing Team," otherwise known as FFART. The group campaigned a Lester MG, an MG TC and 1½ MG TDs. The "½ TD" was that of Ruth Ellmers, Charlie's wife, and it was never raced. "I think Charlie married me because I had a 'TD," Ruth explains. The team members initially were Charlie Ellmers, Ted Jayne, Meach Hitchcock, his brother Ben Hitchcock, and Frank Floyd. They all owned the Lester. If it had been a yacht, the group would have been termed a syndicate. As it was, they were just some people who all liked the same car.

The car was the cycle-fendered, 1250 XPAG-engine, aluminum-bodied creation of Englishman Harry Lester, built on a prewar MG TA frame. Thought to be one of the original Monkey Stable cars, it was originally owned in America by Don Marsh; then it was raced extensively by Chuck Dietrich and later sold to the FFART.

The Cleveland, Ohio, group, in turn, expanded as its friends got into racing. When John Tame put his MG TF on the track, Charlie Ellmers said, "Let's put a funny face on your car too." As John recalls, you had to win a race or come close to it to get a funny face on your car. At the Put-in-Bay race it was customary for competitors to drive their racing cars around town after the races. The drivers liked it and the spectators liked it. One of the perks of being on the team was getting the Lester to drive around, which John Tame did in '58.

"Charlie was the cheerleader of the team," Tame says. "He was the one who came up with all the ideas. He and Ted drove the Lester. The TC was Ben's— sometimes he raced it and sometimes Charlie did. Meach raced later, he drove a bugeye Sprite. Meach's wife was Robin, and they lived in Bratenahl. The nickname of Ben's wife was 'Spook'— I'd like to know what her real name was. She was from the Augustus family in Waite Hill, where Art Modell of the Browns lived. The Funny Face team raced at Put-in-Bay, Akron Airport, Watkins Glen and Lockbourne Air Force Base, a General Le May race. It was a nice safe course, with no cliffs to fall over. At Cumberland, Maryland, there was a cliff at the end if you didn't make the first turn. Race officials advised you to spin your car to avoid going over the cliff. We also raced at the Dunkirk, New York airport in '57, '58 and '59 ... maybe 1960.

"At the races, we always started out with a happy face. Then, if something happened, we could change it. When Charlie blew the engine up, we just turned down the corner of the mouth on the face. I blew my car up too. Not in a race, but on the way to Watkins Glen. I left it at a gas station in Erie, Pennsylvania. I was operating on a pretty low budget. The head came off a valve and it holed a piston. If you used the heavy springs, it put a strain on the valves. After that I put in new valves every year. I got them from Chuck Stoddard. He sold the BAP line of British parts when he was working out of the garage at his house."

The time came when the Lester was rapidly outclassed by the Porsche Spyders and then the Elvas and Lolas as they came along. The Lester was already uncompetitive in the late fifties. So it was retired in the early sixties and the team became involved in running the races.

As John Tame notes, "Charlie was the Chief Steward at the first Mid-Ohio race. He made Ted and I 'official observers.' We were supposed to watch for cars with problems. But we were used to driving decrepit cars that were falling apart. It didn't bother us to see a car that was spilling a little gasoline. It would soon evaporate."

Ellmers is the man who gave Roger Penske his first competition license. As a long-time race official in the Neohio Region of the Sports Car Club of America, Charlie was the head of the Contest Board at the time Roger wanted to go racing with his new Jaguar XK-120M. "We just wanted to have a look at whoever's applying, see if they can drive and maintain a car in safe condition," Charlie said. "Well, here was Roger Penske and he's got a shiny gold Jaguar with wire wheels. I asked him to drive me around the block and then I said 'I think we can sign off on this, Roger.'"

All of the FFART drivers were also sailors, and when the sports car racing slowed down, the Marine Auxiliary Division was formed. "Someone had given us a boat," says Tame. "It was a free one, a 25-foot wood boat. It had fallen off its trailer and had some damage. The hull was cracked and the mast was broken. We patched up the hull. Fred Steger built a new mast for it. It had an outboard motor well and I provided the outboard. It was not the best-looking boat, and the people at Mentor Yacht Club looked down their noses at it. Later we all got different boats. I sailed a Thistle and crewed on Pat Black's 41-footer. Fred Steger was also in FFART and raced an MG TD at Dunkirk and Put-in-Bay. He later got the 1½" carbs and had more power than my car. Fred worked for Carpenter Printing. He was a salesman for them."

Another one on the team, though not a racer, was Charlie Ellmers's friend Johnny Reinhart. When Charlie mustered out of the Navy after combat tours on the *Essex* in World War II and Korea, he bought a black MG TD with red seats in San Francisco and drove it cross country to park it at the Monticello Bar, a favorite watering hole in Cleveland Heights, next to an identical TD, which Reinhart had just bought. Ben Hitchcock worked with Jim Rand of Rand Development, an engineering firm. He didn't really have to work. He could just as easily have spent his wife's money. But he wanted to get out of the house. Ellmers and Jayne worked for him too, on engineering projects. They did the development on a molybdenum disulphide lubricating system for pretreating engine parts and making them last longer. Meach Hitchcock worked for Industrial Leasing Corporation, which provided funding for manufacturing equipment. They funded electron beam microscopes for Clevite, for instance.

As the years went on, the team got away from sports car racing and got out of the SCCA. They did more sailing. Charlie Ellmers got an Ensign class keel boat. Fred Steger got a 32-foot wood-hulled Alden design named *Banshee*. Gerry Steger recalls what led up to it: "Fred and I went to Put-in-Bay in 1953 with Ruth and Charlie Ellmers. Charlie had a TD and he decided to watch the race from the last-place car. He entered it and won. Later on, Charlie and Ted Jayne raced the Lester MG — it was modified, to say the least. Fred got a '53 TD and did not race at Put-in-Bay, but he did race at Dunkirk, Watkins Glen and a few other places. He raced for awhile, then had it redone, from white to maroon, and sold it — for $1250, the same as the engine size. They were kind of going out of fashion at that time.

"When Fred got out of sports car racing and into sailing," Gerry continues, "it made my mother very happy. She was always worried about the racing. I told her, 'Mom, they're all going the same direction.'" Besides, Fred had done a few more dangerous things than sports car racing. He was a Marine combat rifleman in the Pacific during World War II. Assigned as a scout to his platoon, he participated in three invasions in the Philippines. "And by the way," Gerry continues, "I didn't go to all the races — I was taking care of three kids. I didn't go to Cumberland but I enjoyed going to Dunkirk, and Mid-Ohio was very nice."

John Tame did a few more races on the Pat Black boat. But their hearts were never very far from sports cars — Tame continued his membership in the Cleveland Sport Car Club. Ted Jayne found an old Berkeley sports car just like the one he bought from Stoddard, and he started restoring it. Ellmers put in appearances at the Put-in-Bay

∽ RICHIE GINTHER ∽

According to Jim Sitz, Ginther began racing in an MG, but it was one with a V8-60 engine. At the first Pebble Beach in November 1950, he was on Hill's pit crew when Phil won in his black Jag. Ritchie's first race was the next year's Pebble Beach, driving the ultra-fast MG "2 Jr." to a 3rd place behind winner Phil Hill in a 2.9 Alfa and Sterling Edwards Special. In 1953, he rode with Phil Hill as co-driver in the Panamerican Road Race in a 4.1 Ferrari. George Jasberg adds that Ginther was also Phil Hill's riding mechanic in the 4.5-engined 4.1 Ferrari that took 2nd overall in the 1954 Carrera Panamericana. Then he went to Korea as a helicopter mechanic and returned to racing in 1955 at Pebble Beach in an Austin-Healey from a dealership he worked for. His real entrée into serious racing came, as the story goes, when he was helping Phil Hill prepare

Richie Ginther slams the bank in 2 Jr., the V8-60 powered MG Special, on his first attempt at the Sandberg Hillclimb in 1951. Later he made the 5th fastest climb of the day, at 36.64 seconds (courtesy Bob Canaan).

Richie Ginther enters a corner at Santa Barbara in 1956, in the #211 white Porsche Spyder (courtesy Jim Sitz, Int'l Motor Racing Research Center).

Ferraris for John von Neumann late at night. Von Neumann said, "Well, the least we can do is give you a Porsche Spyder to race." Richie was amazed to learn von Neumann had an extra 550 on hand!

Photographer Sitz was a good friend of Ginther's. "Richie did a lot of free-lancing in the late fifties," Jim says. "He drove for von Neumann, John Edgar and Paravanno. At the end of 1956, he took over Josie von Neumann's car in a race and went from 10th to 5th. In March '57, von Neumann started the Ferrari dealership and they had the 4-cylinder Testarossas—a 2-liter and a 2-and-a-half liter. Then in '58 they got the 250 TRs, the V-12s. Richie became manager of the Ferrari shop. He was very proud of that. The factory invited Ginther to test drive. They offered him a ride but in sports cars only, not Grand Prix. I had lunch with him when he came back from Nassau. He was in a quandary. He had a good job and he wanted to settle down and get married. He decided to discuss it with Eleanor von Neumann, who owned the dealership then.

"She said, 'This is a great opportunity—don't miss this chance.' She encouraged him to go. The people in Europe had never heard of him. They knew Phil Hill, but not Richie. After a number of good sports car drives, he did some GP testing. He drove the rear-engined car at Monaco. Monaco '61 was when Moss beat all the Ferraris. Richie was having a good day and so Phil waved him by to go after Moss. Richie and Moss set the lap record with identical times and they credited Richie. After Ferrari, he drove for Tony Rudd at BRM."

According to Tim Considine's Grand Prix book, his best years were in '63, 3rd in World Championship points, and 4th in 1964. He made the podium 7 times over those two seasons, both in BRMs. When he had an accident, Rudd invited him to his house to be around people rather than sit alone in his hotel. While he was there, he fixed the TV, fixed the radio and everything else in the house. He also drove the kids to school. But Richie got tired of finishing second to Graham Hill and left the team. In '65 he was driving for Honda and gave them their only victory in the 1.5-liter formula, at Mexico City. Richie made them a winner.

When they brought Surtees on the team the next year he felt slighted and left to go to Dan Gurney's team. Then he couldn't qualify for the Indy 500 and he said, "I don't enjoy

Richie Ginther (center) is seen at the 1963 Watkins Glen Formula One race, talking with racing great Jim Clark of the Lotus team as Pedro Rodriguez listens in. Richie, in a BRM, was 2nd to Graham Hill (also BRM) and Clark was 3rd; Rodriguez DNF'd (courtesy Alix Lafontant).

it any more." Gurney's Eagles were getting ready for the Dutch GP and he sent a telegram that he wasn't coming. But they kept the car for him right up to the start. By 1967, says Jasberg, he had amassed 110 career F1 Championship points between '60 and '67 — two more than Gurney.

Richie got his motor home in mid–1967. He was a person of wide-ranging interests, including American Indians and American history. He drove out to the Indian lands, from Four Corners down to Cow Springs and Tuba City through the Navajo Reservation on the road to Flagstaff, and went down into Mexico.

∽ CAL GLEASON ∽

Detroit MG driver Cal Gleason recalls a race at Grand Island, New York, near Buffalo, in August of 1952. "I almost put Bill Spear into the bushes on that course in practice. I was going flat out at about 70 miles an hour in my TC. The steering was

Cal Gleason's third car was his third TC, this red one. Here he is competing in the Haven Hillclimb west of Pontiac, Michigan. Cal notes, "By the next year we had to wear helmets!" (courtesy Cal Gleason).

loose and it wandered into the middle of the road just as Spear was coming up in his Ferrari at 120. He sped by me with two wheels on the road and two in the dirt. Later that day I tore up a rod bearing and Chuck and Suzy Dietrich gave me a set of used bearings so I could drive back to Detroit. I had graduated from high school the year before and I lied about my age so I could race.

"Grand Island was my first race," Gleason explains. "A guy I knew about a block up the street, Frank Smith, had a TC with 16" wire wheels. That got me cranked up about cars. My dad would not let me get a '40 Ford but, to his thinking, an MG was little, and I couldn't get hurt in it. I got my MG from — you'll never believe this name — Jim Crowe, in Detroit. [Crowe was a newspaperman and a founder of the Detroit Press Club.] It was a black car, titled a '48, but was probably a '46. I never raced that but, a year later, I got a second TC, this one a cream-colored car with 16-inch wire wheels. They put a lot more rubber on the road. It was a 5.50 or 6.50 × 16 versus a Model A tire. We used Sears tires before the Dunlops were available.

"Later on I bought an Arnolt MG coupe out of Wisconsin, through *Road & Track*. I bought it from the business manager of William Wuesthoff. Hal Ullrich had changed the engine from the MG to a 90 hp Willys F-head. I flew to Milwaukee to pick it up and drove it home. It was dark green, or more like an emerald green, with a light green top. At that time I also had a Mark VII Jag sedan that I bought from a bank for $450 — the car was damaged. I had those when I was going to college, at the Detroit Institute

An interim car for Cal was this MG TD, which he raced in a couple of SAC base events. The #70 TD is seen here in an aircraft hangar, probably at Atterbury AFB in Indiana, in 1953 (courtesy Cal Gleason).

of Technology. I parked both of the cars in a garage near the YMCA where some of the classes were held.

"After the TC, in about '53 or '54, I bought a '52 Porsche. It was a 1500 roller bearing car. These were supposed to be indestructible but the Hirth crankshaft went bad on mine. It left a bad taste in my mouth for Porsches. After that I got a '54 MG TF."

Cal was driving the red #44 MG TF at the 1954 Watkins Glen race. He was there with a good friend from Detroit, MG driver Ralph Durbin. By then, many competitors were beginning to trailer their cars, but not Gleason. "I drove there and drove back," he recalls. "I started on the grid in 10th place and I finished in 10th place, but I passed a few cars and was passed by a few to get there." Durbin took 2nd place in his TF, after the TD of Gus Ehrman.

Gleason also drove at Chanute AFB; Lockbourne AFB; Cumberland, Maryland; and Put-in-Bay. "That place was a pain to get to," says Cal of the 'Bay, "but it was my favorite race."

In about 1958, Gleason got a Jaguar XK-120 with a Motto body. It had belonged to Knute Skillman, of Detroit. The original body was damaged and he had it replaced with an Allard-like body with cycle fenders. Unlike most Motto bodies (e.g., the beautiful Motto MG), this car was ugly. Someone gave it the nickname of "The Hookie

In the #44 MG TF is Cal Gleason, at the 1954 Watkins Glen race. He finished 12th out of 25 cars in the Collier Brothers Memorial Trophy race (courtesy Cal Gleason).

Boo." It had one redeeming aspect and that is it weighed about 800 pounds less than a stock 120. "I took it to Harewood Acres in Jarvis, Ontario," says Gleason, "and got a first in class B." They had a Formula Libre race for anything you would like to drive there. Someone brought a Pontiac Catalina with the aluminum front end used in drag racing. That was about 1962. The Pontiac was fast, faster than anything else there, but it had no brakes.

"About that time, I stopped racing. But my wife Andrea wanted to race and I got her two MGAs, but she rolled both of them at Waterford. She didn't hurt herself and then she got a Corvair. It was from a Cadillac Development engineer. It had a turbo and some special equipment. Once she took it into a shop for clutch replacement and other service. She told the mechanic to be sure he put a heavy duty clutch in and proper oil in the transaxle, for the Positraction. The mechanic insisted that the heavy duty clutch was not available and the non-slip axle was never made for these cars. She said, 'Why don't we jack the car up on one side and you put your head in front of the front tire? If there's no Positraction, you won't be hurt.'" Mrs. Gleason also had an Abarth 750, in '63 or '64. "She never wrecked it or blew it up," Cal remarks.

Gleason had a number of interesting road cars, including a Vignale-bodied 4.1 Ferrari Mexico, one of three coupes; the one roadster had been raced by Bill Spear. The coupes were raced in the Panamerican road race by Chinetti, Viloresi and Ascari. Cal's car was s/n 0224, the Chinetti car. No. 0226 was recently restored by the Marriott family, and no. 0228 is in California with a Chevy engine, last he heard. Cal had two other Ferraris, a 1961 250GT with a Farina body (not a short-wheelbase) and a 1965 275 GTB coupe.

As if all this were not enough, Gleason has had a lifelong affinity for Corvette, having bought his first one in 1953. He's had 17 of them in all, including a blue 1965 coupe that he used to surprise the owner of a short-wheelbase Ferrari. "What have you got in that car?" asked the Ferrari driver. He couldn't believe that the car was stock. But it had a fuel injection engine and a 4:01 rear axle ratio—the last year for FI, the first year for disc brakes.

As late as the year 2000, the oneupmanship that began in Detroit on Woodward Avenue was still apparent as the Chevy engineers cooked up something special to embarrass the Viper developers, in the form of a new C5 Corvette with two superchargers, 800 horsepower and a stick shift—so they said! We did not get a look at the engine but there was no a/c or heater. It sure seemed fast!

Today, Cal drives a year-2003 50th Anniversary model Corvette and goes to the Saturday morning breakfast club to get the latest car news. It meets every Saturday at 7 A.M. and it's always interesting to see what people are driving there.

∽ Isabelle Haskell ∽

Isabelle Haskell's first sports car was an MG. Then she raced a Siata, Bandini, OSCA, and Maserati. She raced at McDill AFB, Watkins Glen, Bridgehampton, Thompson Raceway, Lockbourne AFB, Cumberland and Sebring, racing mainly in the men's events and very rarely in the Ladies' Race. She also raced in South America and Europe: Argentina, Venezuela, Cuba, Italy, Germany, Belgium. Isabelle won Class G-Modified at the 1954 SAC-base race at Lockbourne in her Siata and took a class win at the 1958 Sebring in a factory-entered OSCA 750. She was from a well-to-do family in Red Bank, New Jersey. Her brother drove a Mercedes 300SL roadster. For awhile she dated Alberto Maglioli, the Formula One driver. She married automaker Alejandro De Tomaso, lived with him in Italy and, after his death, moved back to the States to live in Palm Beach.

On May 23, 1951, Otto Linton sold her an MG TD from his Speedcraft Enterprises dealership in Exton, Pennsylvania. It was blue with a tan interior, ser. no. 6220EXLU. "I don't think she actually raced the MG," Otto says. "Shortly after that she got a Siata from Tony Pompeo. It was one that I was supposed to receive. I could only pick it up at Tony's from his 'allocation'—if you knew Tony you would know what that meant. I was supposed to get three Siata Spyders. The third one suddenly disappeared and Isabelle got it. She got this car from Tony, but without an engine. I believe she bought the engine that was in the prototype I drove in 1951 at the 'Glen. It was built by friends of Tony's, Don Sauvignon and his brother. Isabelle got this engine after more modifications for her car—it was a Crosley and over 800ccs."

Here Jim Sitz adds some details on Isabelle's racing the Siata: her first race was in January or February of 1953, at McDill Field near Tampa, Florida—that's where John

Isabelle Haskell corners her Siata Spider at the Bridgehampton road course in 1953. Note the huge crowd behind the snow fencing (courtesy Alix Lafontant).

Fitch learned to fly bombers in World War II. Then she raced at Bridgehampton in 1953 and Thompson, Connecticut, on September 6, 1953.

Dick Irish drove with her at Sebring in 1955 in a Siata Spyder and remembers: "Tony Pompeo sold the same Bandini to both my brother and Isabelle. Tony would do things like that. Tony quickly realized that she had a lot more money than we did, so the car went to her. I would co-drive with her at Sebring.

"The Bandini was a great car. It had a Fiat 1100 engine and it didn't weigh anything. We had faster acceleration than the Healey 100S that the factory brought for Stirling Moss and Lance Macklin. We would hit the brakes and they were great. But we couldn't keep it cool. We'd go 1½ laps and it would boil. We opened up the grille, we soldered copper tubing onto the radiator, and nothing would work. When we dropped the oil pan, there was a rag inside, all chewed up. We decided to swap the engine from Isabelle's Siata into the Bandini. But it was a Crosley engine and wouldn't fit. There was an interference between the steering column and the exhaust manifold and we didn't have the time to fabricate a new exhaust manifold. So we decided to run her Crosley-powered Siata. The Crosley from her Siata was a sprint engine and not set up for endurance racing, so we knew going in that longevity was a crap shoot. It actually was over nine hours into the race that we lost a cylinder.

"About nine hours into the race, we dropped a valve. Then we made a mistake. We should have pulled the plug out and grounded the wire. I was driving along and heard a loud noise. The car stopped running. There had been an explosion in the engine and it blew out both sides of the block. You could reach in from each side and shake

Top: Taking the checker for a win is Isabelle Haskell from Redbank, New Jersey. She drove her Siata Spider to a first at Lockbourne Air Force Base, Columbus, Ohio, August 8, 1954. *Bottom:* The #63 Siata Spider of Isabelle Haskell, at speed on the vast runways of Lockbourne AFB, Columbus, Ohio in late summer, 1954 (courtesy Alix Lafontant).

Isabelle Haskell waits for her race to come up, at Lockbourne AFB, Columbus, Ohio, 1954 (courtesy Alix Lafontant).

hands with yourself. I believe that the fuel-air mixture inside the crankcase had ignited. That was too bad because Isabelle was actually a good driver."

According to the records of American photographer Jim Sitz, on July 22, 1956, Isabelle drove a Maserati 2-liter at the street race on the Adriatic, in Barri, Italy. Isabelle raced a 1500 Maserati in Argentina in 1956. She raced this car at Sebring in March of 1956 and in the summer of 1956 she drove a 2-liter Maserati in Italy. In November of 1956, she went to Cuba to race, in a Maserati 1500. Later that year, she went to Caracas, Venezuela. The crowd cheered her driving there.

On April 11, 1957, Sitz watched Isabelle race her OSCA in Sweden. Jim Sitz recalls seeing a British magazine feature Isabelle's new 1500 Maserati, painted American racing colors and shown at a Modena test track. For the 1957 season, she switched over to an OSCA and an Alfa. She took a 6th overall in the 1957 Argentine Grand Prix and drove an Alfa 1300 Giulietta at the Nurburgring in '57. She took a 3rd at Spa, also in the OSCA.

On March 9, 1957, Isabelle married Alejandro de Tomaso. People called them 'the odd couple' because he was short and she was tall. In 1967 and '68, de Tomaso went on a spending spree and bought Ghia and Vignale, took over Maserati, and made other acquisitions, most of them reportedly with money from Isabelle's family. Jim Sitz is uncertain whether that money came from GM or DuPont, or a little of both.

Still racing as of June 8, 1958, she drove a 750 OSCA that summer. According to Sitz, her last race was in 1959 driving an OSCA 1500 at the Nurburgring 1000K race.

"The last time I saw her," says Dick Irish, "was when Barbara and I were in Modena after I'd picked up the 275 GTB/4 in 1967.

"In 1968 I was in Italy with Toly Arutunoff. I must have spoken with her because I remember her telling me that she was going back to the States to vote. She left word at the plant that we would be visiting. Seems to me our conversation was to tell me the test driver hadn't returned due to fog. She greased the skids for Toly and I to drive the Mangusta. He told me the redline was 6700, but the tach was redlined at 6200. Toly was not impressed with its handling. 'What a pig. I almost hit the gate,' he told me. The test driver spoke little English. Then he looked at me and said, 'You don't remember me? Last year I worked at Scaglietti. I put the roll bar in your Ferrari 275.' I asked him what the redline was. He replied '6200' and we drove off. A little ways down the road we were approaching a tunnel entrance and a couple of Fiats suddenly pulled out around a truck, without looking in their rear view mirrors. I found that the brakes were great and managed to stop 3 feet from the Fiat. But the handling was poor."

Isabelle Haskell De Tomaso disappeared, her husband died, and then she reappeared in Palm Beach. Tony Pompeo, on the other hand, disappeared and was never seen again. "Isabelle told me," says Dick, "that Tony was working at the American Embassy in Rome." But nobody, including a U.S. Senator, has been able to confirm this.

∽ CHUCK HASSAN ∽

During World War II, Chuck Hassan was an aide to Admiral Stump, the naval commander of the Pacific Fleet. As a transport pilot, he also ferried planes from their builders in the United States across the Atlantic to bases in England. At the end of the war, he came back to Cincinnati and worked for Charles V. Maescher & Company, a family-owned construction company, managing one of the divisions.

"Then one day in 1947," says son John Hassan, "my mother read an ad in the *New York Times* for a little car called an MG. It must have been a TC. They flew to New York and drove it back to Cincinnati. There were so many people who asked them 'Where did you get that?' my mother thought, 'We should be selling these.' They contacted the distributor and arranged to become an MG dealer. They formed a dealership that they called 'Raymond Motors,' in the Indian Hill section of Cincinnati — Raymond was my father's middle name. My mother ran it during the day and my father worked there nights and weekends, as he kept working at the construction company.

"They soon added other British cars," John says, "Austin-Healey, Jaguar, Triumph, Austin and Morris Minor. So, basically, my mother Jane started the first MG store in Cincinnati. Then my father left his job and managed the dealership. In the late 1960s, the British cars went out and it became a Toyota store. Basically, it became difficult to sell and service such a wide variety of cars. Toyota became a high-volume opportunity.

It's the Hassan family in the Hassan family MG-TC: Chuck Hassan, son John Hassan, and Jane Hassan (courtesy John Hassan).

In about 1950, dad also got a Volkswagen dealership. That really took off. It was separate from the MG business and was called Hassan Motors. In the early '80s, my parents opened up a Porsche/Audi dealership in Palm Beach."

Chuck's first racing car was a Bandini. It was a lightweight, small-displacement racing car from Italy. He first raced it at Vero Beach, Florida, in 1952, then at Sebring in the first 12-Hour race there, and he later raced the car at Elkhart Lake and Watkins Glen. He moved on to a Jaguar XK-120 and XK-140. In 1953, he co-drove the C-Type Jaguar of Harry Gray to a 3rd overall in the feature race at Floyd Bennett Field. Then, according to racing mechanic Walter Rye, he began to drive Ebby Lunken's 2-liter Ferrari. In 1956, Chuck drove a Corvette with Chicago driver Ernie Erickson at Sebring.

As one of the celebrated "Cincinnati Gang" of Ferrari drivers, Chuck Hassan was 3rd in SCCA national points, driving a 2.9 Ferrari. The other members of this team were Ebby Lunken, John Quackenbush, Howard Hively, Jim Johnston and Roger Bear. They frequently gathered at road races in the Midwest, lining their cars up in the paddock to form a wonderful "Ferrari Row."

A highlight of the team's adventures was the 1956 racing season. At the beginning of the season, everyone bought new cars. In May, Chuck bought a Ferrari 500 Mondial from international playboy Porfirio Rubirosa. Lunken, Johnston and Quackenbush all bought Ferrari 500TRs, and Howard Hively bought Jim Kimberly's 4.9 Ferrari.

After the MG, the Hassans owned this silver Jaguar XK-120, seen with Jane Hassan at the wheel and son John Hassan on the passenger side (courtesy John Hassan).

At the 1956 Road America June Sprints, or at least what were to become the June Sprints, Hassan (car #132), Johnston (#15), Quackenbush (#75) and Lunken (#6) were all gridded in Race Three, for Class E and F Modified cars. Unfortunately for the boys from Cincinnati, this was the year that Porsche upgraded the 550 Spyder into the 550RS, with its suspension improvements and horsepower boost. Worse yet, two of the best Porsche pilots were driving them that day: Jack McAfee from the West Coast and Chicagoan Ed Crawford. They finished first and second, relegating the cars from Modena to positions down in the pack. Nevertheless, it was a safe race and a good time was had by all.

At the 1956 Akron Airport sports car races, the chief steward was Richard Lamport, who had also been a steward at the original Elkhart Lake races, and Roy Cramer was the chief starter. Besides serving as the steward of the meet, Dick Lamport also brought some young people from Christ Episcopal Church in nearby Shaker Heights. One of them, Roger Penske, would continue his new-found interest in motorsports. The race observers were Dick Gent and Dick Irish. John Tame was an observer at a later race and he explains what they did: "An official observer goes out and watches the cars," John says. "Then one of the corner workers calls him on the headset and says, 'It looks like car No. 18 is falling apart.' Then we watch the car and call back to say, 'Ah, he looks OK to me.'"

The Ferraris drove in Race 7, the one-hour-long Lake Erie Grand Prix at Akron,

Top: Cornering the #51 Bandini on the Sebring runway close to the swamp grass is Chuck Hassan. This is 1952, the first Sebring 12-Hour race. Chuck drove with New York car dealer Beau Clark. Their Crosley-engined Italian racing car retired after 55 laps (courtesy Jess Woods, John Hassan collection). *Bottom:* Chuck Hassan powers the #75 Ferrari though a corner on an airport course. On the inside of the turn are hay bales to mark the course and protect the corner workers (courtesy Leo Cummings, John Hassan collection).

Happily taking the checkered flag for a win in the #71 4.9 Ferrari of Howard Hively is driver Chuck Hassan. Car owner Hively is in the passenger seat (John Hassan collection).

in '56. Chuck Hassan was in first at the start but then John Quackenbush took over the lead on the seventh lap and was hounded by teammate Hassan, driving his older Mondial against the leader's Testa Rossa. Don Sesslar of Lancaster, Ohio, was third in Cyrus Fulton's Porsche 550. Ebby Lunken came in fourth after the two-driver team of Doc Wyllie and Bob Fergus in the latter's Porsche 550RS. Ohio Valley Ferrari driver Roger Bear was seventh overall and second in Class D. At the end of the race, Quackenbush finished with a lead of 18 seconds over Hassan, averaging 70.6 mph during the race with a top speed of 145 mph timed on the straightaway.

On October 6 and 7, Hassan entered the race at Smartt Field, near St. Charles, Missouri. Al Baeyen was the assistant starter in the SCCA's St. Louis Region, which sanctioned this airport race. Al says, "Smartt was an auxiliary field for the Naval Reserve during World War II, auxiliary to Lambert Field in St. Louis. There were four or five like it in the area. The Navy pilots would practice their landings and take-offs here so they wouldn't tie up the main field. There were up to 100 training planes here at one time. When the war was over, the city of St. Charles got the field, and we rented it from them. The course was nearly two miles long. And U-shaped. We used sand bags to mark the course and had six races that weekend."

Chuck Hassan took thirds in each of the two races for his class. In Race 2, Lunken had led in his Class D Ferrari, but then the drain plug came out of his oil sump. This allowed Loyal Katskee to take the win in his Ferrari 750 Monza. Quackenbush was second in the new Testa Rossa and Hassan was third overall in the Ferrari Mondial, and second in Class E. Then, in Race 6, Lunken took off in his Testa Rossa with the new 2.5-liter Grand Prix engine. Katskee was second but blew a tire and then Quackenbush moved up, followed by Chuck Hassan in the Mondial, in a field of 26 cars.

The last race of the season, December 5–10, was the gala extravaganza Nassau Speed Week, intended by the Chamber of Commerce to get an early start on the tourist season and fill empty hotel rooms with spectators. The drivers—by invitation—got free shipping for their cars and themselves, as well as free hotel rooms, and the spectators paid their own way. The Cincinnati Gang had three cars at Nassau—Chuck Hassan had the 500 Mondial Series II, Howard Hively had the 500 TR and Ebby Lunken had the 500 TR, with a 625 engine of 2.5 liters displacement. In all, there were 18 Ferraris entered at the 1956 Nassau.

In the Ferrari race, Masten Gregory beat Fon de Portago, while Ebby Lunken finished sixth and Chuck Hassan was eighth. Not bad finishes, considering the top-flight international drivers on the entry list.

Most of the Cincinnati Gang, including Hassan, left racing in 1959. Chuck Hassan died in 1995, a few years after the others. He and his friends were front runners at many of the major races and they'll be remembered as part of the golden age of sports cars in the fifties.

⁓ CHUCK HENRY ⁓

Chuck Henry was a student at Wittenberg University in Springfield, Ohio, when he became interested in sports cars. He met his wife Gerrie at Wittenberg. In 1954 he purchased a 1948 MG TC at Inskip's in New York. Suzy Dietrich remembers the car. "He was driving a black TC," she says. "His father was Colonel Henry, who owned the Northern Ohio Telephone Company. We had gotten the bug. We went to Watkins Glen the year the kid was hurt [1952]. There is a photograph of us standing at the bottom of the hill. Later, when we saw Chuck Henry, he was tooling along and we thought, 'We want to get one.' Then we saw an ad in the paper. Leach Cracraft in Wheeling, West Virginia, had two cars.

"One was a red one. I really wanted that, but it was sold. But he had the green one. It had a Marshall-Nordec supercharger on it. He said, 'Take the car out and drive it.' We went out in the car and I didn't really want it. It was right-hand drive and you had to shift with your left hand. So we went back to Ohio. But Chuck [Dietrich] really wanted the car. We had the money. It was about $1500. So we got the TC and started driving it. Soon we encountered Mr. Henry again. We got to know him and, when we started racing, he did too. He built a double-deck trailer, for the two TCs—his wife didn't want him driving anything faster. We were like a team. Everywhere we went, he went."

Chuck Henry in 1958 at Put-in-Bay. His TC featured the shorter, fatter 16" tires that many of the serious racers favored (Paul Henry collection).

Chuck Henry began racing the car in 1955, a year after his son Paul was born. Actually, his first race never occurred. He entered the '55 Akron Airport sports car races and it was canceled because event sponsorship fell through. But he did enter the Bellfontaine hillclimb that year.

Then, in '56, the Bellvue, Ohio, resident ran the Put-in-Bay road race. In the #6 MG TC, he competed against well-known area drivers including national champion Ralph Durbin, Detroiter Harry Constant, Cal Gleason, Bill Staufer, Charlie Ellmers and Art Brow. Hampered by a poor grid position (drawn out of a hat, as was the custom), he was unable to move up to the front before the end of the 10-lap race.

In the 1957 season, he entered both the Put-in-Bay race (placing 4th in Race #1, as car #5) and the Akron Airport sports car races, as car #85. In 1958, he again ran at Put-in-Bay, as car #17. By this season, he had switched to 16" wheel rims, as some of the other TC drivers did, for better acceleration and higher cornering forces. He strung these together himself using the TC centers and 5½" wide Ferrari rims. 1958 was the beginning of the Milan Hillclimb, which Henry used to compete in. That year he set the Fastest Time of Day with the rapid TC.

According to Chuck's son Paul, he did not race in 1959 or 1960. By the time he

Here in a grassy paddock, Chuck Henry checks the tire pressures on his #85 MG TC at Road America in about 1956 (Paul Henry collection).

reactivated, in the 1961 season, racing at Put-in-Bay was over. The Milan Hillclimb was still going, but Mid-Ohio and Nelsons Ledges had yet to be built.

This is a partial list of Chuck Henry's racing achievements:

Giants Despair Hillclimb, Wilkes-Barre, PA—1956—1st MG G Production
Kentucky Derby Festival Road Races—1956—1st
Kentucky Derby Regional Road Races— May 1957—1st in Class MG-G
Lake Erie Invitational, W.NY Region, Dunkirk, NY—June 2, 1957—1st
Cumberland Nationals— May 1958— Second
Kentucky Derby Regional Road Races— May 1958—1st in Class MG-G
Cherry Festival Race—1958— First
Lake Erie Invitational, W. NY Region, Dunkirk, NY—1958—1st
Glen Classic 1958, Watkins Glen—1st in Class
Lake Erie Invitational, W. NY Region, Dunkirk, NY—1961—1st
Road America June Sprints—1961— 2nd H Production

Here again, fate presents a new situation. "We opened up a VW dealership," says Suzy Dietrich, "and they gave us a trip to Europe. I fell in love with Porsche. A dealer was there who told me, 'I got a car for you.' It was a cream-colored Speedster. I wanted

The MG TC #17 of Chuck Henry tracks out to the exit of Town Turn at Put-in-Bay ever so nicely. His astute cornering technique is captured on 8mm film by the cameraman in the background. This is about a 45 mph corner for an MG and look how little body roll there is. The year is 1958 (Paul Henry collection).

my own car for the Ladies' Races because sometimes Chuck would bring the car over after his race and say, 'Well the clutch is gone.' So then I got a Porsche.

"Chuck Henry liked the Porsche, too, even though Gerrie didn't want him to drive anything faster then the MG. One time we were coming up from Columbus. The two MGs were in the trailer, the two Chucks were driving the tow car and I was driving the Porsche. I was a little tired so I pulled off to take a nap. Henry said, 'You get in with Chuck and come back tomorrow and get the car.' I didn't like anyone to drive my car but I was tired. I had to work at the dealership on Monday — I was the accountant — and I didn't know how I was going to get my car back. But then Chuck comes over with the Speedster.

"Then we go up to Elkhart and I go out in practice and Henry is out with the MG. I didn't pass him but I was close. And there was a driver that Chuck saw as a competitor of his. We both came in off the track and Chuck said, 'I wonder if you are really getting the most out of the car. Somebody ought to take it out and check it.' So he got in the car and took it out. Somebody who was following saw the other guy he was dueling with. In the back of the course there's a fast sweeper. The tail came out there, he tried to save it and climbed up the side of the bank, then he flipped and the roll bar broke. The corner workers came out with his helmet and there was blood in it. They took him to a hospital about 15 or 20 miles away. It might have been Plymouth. Gerrie and I drove over. We went inside and a doctor came over and gave Gerrie his personal effects."

～ PHIL HILL ～

America's first Formula One Champion started racing in an MG-TC at a California airfield, the Goleta Marine Air Force Base at Santa Barbara. It was a time trials, racing against the clock.

He sold his 1946 Ford to buy an MG TC in 1948, and soon ordered a Shorrock supercharger for it. With race courses limited in the early days, Hill drove at a nearby oval track several times and bought another new TC to race. This was in July of 1949, Jim Sitz notes. Hill raced at Carrell Speedway in Gardena, California, where he had a number of wins. Then he went to England in November of 1949 to do a 6-month

Here Phil Hill drives the #3 MG-TC in a time trials at Goleta Marine Airbase. Of all the MG drivers, this one would be the World Champion. Wonder if photographer Jack Campbell sensed that as Phil raced by with confidence (Jack Campbell, courtesy Malcolm Campbell).

Like many West Coast drivers, Phil Hill drove the famous "2 Junior" modified MG-TC. In this photograph, the car is driven by Bill Stroppe (courtesy Bob Canaan).

apprenticeship at Jaguar. He bought a Jaguar and left in May, came back to the States and drove an Allard up Pikes Peak. He acquired an 8C Alfa and then went back to Carrell Speedway in 1951 to drive Bill Cramer's MG, which was powered by a Ford V-8 60 (the "2 Jr." car).

He appeared on the SCCA national scene in 1952, driving XK-Cs for Jaguar distributor Charles Hornburg Jr. His first Ferrari? A 1952 Type 212 Export, 2.6-liter Touring Barchetta, acquired in time for the April 1952 Pebble Beach race. Five years later, in August 1957, he was at Bonneville at the wheel of the record-setting MG EX.179 streamliner, sharing the billing with Stirling Moss. He came back again in 1959 for the ultimate Class E record run, in the MG EX 181. "I was the fastest guy in an MG," Phil reminds us. "I set a record on the Salt Flats at 254.9. I loved Bonneville. That was 1959, a lot of years ago. It hasn't been broken yet, though I'm sure it will be." The next year he was at the wheel of a Formula One Ferrari, driving high on the wall at Monza. Two years later he became the first, and only, American-born driver to earn the World Championship.

As George Jasberg notes, between 1956 and 1962, he won a major endurance event at least once a year, and also in '64 and '66: Le Mans—'58, '61, '62; Sebring—'58, '59, '61; Swedish GP—'56, with Maurice Trintignant; GP of Venezuela—'57, with Peter

Top: An early win for Phil Hill was this one at the main event at Pebble Beach in 1950. It was Hill's black Jag 120 and he won without brakes and without a clutch (Jack Campbell, courtesy Malcolm Campbell). *Bottom:* Phil Hill charges up Pikes Peak in the #14 Cadillac-Allard, in 1950 (courtesy Stewarts Photography, Bob Donner collection).

On the front row at the 1955 Beverly, Massachusetts, airport race is Phil Hill in the #3 Ferrari Monza, flanked by Jim Kimberly in his #5 Ferrari 4.5 and Bill Spear in the #1 Maserati 300S (courtesy Alix Lafontant).

Collins; Buenos Aires—'58, '60; Nurburgring—'62, '66; and Daytona—'64. At Daytona in 1964, he won the 2000 Kilometer race in a NART GTO, with co-driver Pedro Rodriguez. All of these except Nurburgring '66 (Chaparral 2D) were won in Ferraris. George Jasberg reminds us that Hill and co-driver Mike Spence won the 1000-km race at Brands Hatch on July 30, 1967, in a Chaparral 2F, the winged coupe. At a party for Carroll Shelby—actually, it was a roast—Jim Sitz said to Phil Hill, "There are hundreds of guys racing MGs. They race for a year and then you never hear from them. How were you different?" and Phil said, "I never had the ambition to go to Europe. I just went there."

After his racing career, Hill operated the Hill & Vaughn restoration shop. He and his wife Alma lived in his parents' house in Santa Monica, California, and enjoyed a large collection of player piano music, including Bach, Vivaldi and other composers of the Baroque era. Their son Derek is also a professional racing driver.

∽ BOB HOLBERT ∽

He was born in November of 1922 and served as a mechanic on PT boats in World War II. The Bob Holbert you know best was a longtime Porsche driver who later raced

Above: At the 1954 Brynfan Tyddyn race, Holbert takes the checkered flag in 3rd place, in the #60 MG-TD. *Below:* Bob Holbert smiles from the cockpit of his Porsche Spyder at Watkins Glen in 1957. This was a classic race against the larger 300SL roadster of Paul O'Shea. Bob won one race and Paul won the other (courtesy Alix Lafontant).

Cobras for Carroll Shelby. But the Warrington, Pennsylvania, Porsche dealer got his start in racing with an MG TD in October of 1952 at Thompson Raceway. Then he got a TF, followed by a TC. Another early race was at Brynfan Tyddyn, Pennsylvania, a dangerous 3.5-mile course on public roads, July 25, 1953. Run between 1952 and 1956, it served as a place to race until permanent circuits could be built at Bridgehampton, Lime Rock and Watkins Glen. Holbert also ran there in the last year. In the modified race, he saw Jack McAfee drive his Porsche Spyder to an impressive second place behind Carroll Shelby's Ferrari Testarossa. McAfee had previously finished behind the D-Type Jaguar of Walt Hansgen, at Cumberland. This influenced him to get a Spyder, the first of many.

Elinor Holbert smiles as Cam Argetsinger pours some of that good Gold Seal champagne into the trophy bowl for Bob Holbert. Bob just had a big win at the 1963 USRRC at Watkins Glen (courtesy Alix Lafontant).

Bob drove all the Spyders: the 550, 550RS, RSK, RS60 and RS61. Highlights would include a long-remembered race against Paul O'Shea in the Mercedes 300SL roadster at Watkins Glen, July 5, 1957, actually two races: "He won one race and I won the other," Bob comments. "That was a great race, with lots of lead changes," driver Art Brow recalls. "The SL was faster on the straight but the RS was faster in the corners." Jim Sitz believes that Watkins Glen July '57 was the first time Holbert raced a 550 Porsche. Holbert was 2nd to Charlie Wallace in the F-M class national points in 1957. He won the championship in 1958. And he was 2nd to Don Sesslar in 1959, in the RSK. When he moved up in class to E-Modified with the 1.7-liter RSK, and Roger Penske won F-M, in addition to taking 2nd in E-M. Holbert again won the national championship in E-Modifed in 1961, this time with a Porsche RS61; he won again in 1962. Of all the Spyders he drove, he liked the RS61 best. "I bent the original car and they sent me a special chassis," Holbert explains. "It had a longer wheelbase that had originally been designed for the flat-8 engine."

He raced and won against the factory many times. He drove at Le Mans in 1961, to a 1st in the under-2-liter class and 5th overall. His co-driver was Masten Gregory.

Top: The crowd gathers for the victory celebration as Bob and Elinor Holbert pull into the winner's circle with their Porsche Spyder. Cameron Argetsinger, with the French Legionnaire's hat, is getting ready to pour the champagne (courtesy Alix Lafontant). *Bottom:* Bob Holbert in the #14 Porsche RS-61 drives to a win at the first Watkins Glen USRRC race, held June 30, 1963. Second was Clevelander Herb Swan, also in a Porsche RS, and third was Ken Miles in a Shelby Cobra (courtesy Alix Lafontant).

"He was quite a character and a very good driver," Holbert notes. At Sebring in 1961, he drove the top-placing Porsche, a Brumos entry, with co-driver Roger Penske (1st CL, 6th OA). By 1963, he was in professional racing, in the USRRC, with a Porsche RS61 and a 289 Cobra, as a member of Shelby's team, with Ken Miles and Dave McDonald. He recalls McDonald: "He was a good driver, but overanxious. At Indy, he knew he had a bad car but he wouldn't give up." Holbert and Ken Miles had a great mutual respect for each other and teamed up for a race at Pensacola in May of 1963, which they won.

Holbert drove production Cobras for two years, '63 and '64, and the King Cobras, which were Cooper Monacos with a Ford 289 and influenced creation of the Can-Am series. "The King Cobras were great cars but they had growing pains," Holbert remarks. "We led a number of times but didn't win anything because of overheating." In 1964, he had an accident at Kent, Washington, May 10, and quit racing. His best year was 1963, when he drove both Porsche and Cobra and won the USRRC Manufacturer's Championship. After driving at least fifty road courses in twelve years of racing, his favorites were Laguna Seca and Mosport in Canada.

ED HUGUS

Like most World War II veterans, Ed Hugus was born in the 1920s, 1923 to be exact, according to an email sent to historian Pete Vack. Ed was descended from a family who came to Philadelphia from Alsace-Lorraine in 1767 and his mother's ancestors came from England at about the same time. His childhood was spent on farms in Pennsylvania and Ohio, mostly Ohio, in the New Philadelphia area. He could drive a tractor by the time he was 10 years old. In 1941, his family moved to Pittsburgh and his father and brother both went to work in the steel mills.

When war came, Ed joined the army. Art Evans was a friend of Ed's and he notes, "After basic training, he was posted to Ft. Benning, where he became a paratrooper with the 11th Airborne Division. Of his service in the Pacific, Ed told me, 'I was one of the few who survived. Not many of us did.' After the war, he served with the occupation in Japan."

Continuing the email to Pete Vack, Hugus noted that his first sports car was an MG-TC that he bought new from J.S. Inskip in New York. In 1950 he became involved in racing through a friend of his, Leach Cracraft of Wheeling, West Virginia, who campaigned Offenhauser cars driven by Spider Webb and the great one-legged driver Bill Schindler. In 1950, Ed bought an Allard K2 roadster from Tony Pompeo. Ed's first sports car race was at the wheel of an 1100cc Siata Spider entered by Tony in the 1952 Grand Island, New York, road race. He was leading his class but spun on the last lap and finished second to an MG TC.

"The first time I saw Ed Hugus," says longtime Steel Cities racer Don Baker, "was at an SAE meeting in 1953. He had three car dealerships in Pittsburgh: European Cars, Continental Motors and a VW dealership. I think European had Porsche, Continental

The Ed Hugus Porsche Spyder that he co-drove with Carel de Beaufort at the 1957 Le Mans 24-Hour race. They finished the race 2nd in class and 8th overall. The car is s/n 550-0132 (courtesy Gerry Weyer, 356 Registry).

had Alfa, Lancia and Citroen. I remember as early as 1955, the first issue of *Steel Cities Drift* had a report about him racing at Le Mans."

According to the email from Hugus, "We became the sole dealer in Pittsburgh for Porsche, Mercedes-Benz, Volkswagen, MG, Jaguar, Morris and other British cars and later the area dealer for Fiat, Alfa Romeo, etc. I worked with Alesandro de Tomaso in developing his first Formula Jr. race car and was the U.S. importer—distributor." He also sold a number of Siata Gran Sports imported by Tony Pompeo. Ed was able to set up these dealerships with the help of his friends and mentors Lucille and Pete Davis, who were wealthy Pittsburgh sports car enthusiasts. They funded the businesses and were rewarded by Ed's success. The name "Lucybelle II" was painted on the side of many Hugus racing cars—that was Lucille's nickname.

Ed drove a Mercedes 300SL in the 1955 race at Watkins Glen. "I was running first," Ed said after the race, "with a 10- or 20-second lead and Paul O'Shea behind me, when I was black-flagged because my hood was open. Well, it opened at the back and I could have been going 100 or even 200 and it wouldn't have opened any more. But they brought me in and I lost my position. It kind of ticked me off to get a second place."

In 1956, as Pete Vack notes, Hugus drove at Le Mans with writer John Bentley and finished an incredible 8th overall in a little 1100cc Cooper Bobtail. He finished 8th overall again, in 1957, driving a Porsche Spyder with Carel de Beaufort. This began the practice of driving two endurance events a year, Sebring (March) and Le Mans (June), since Hugus and Bentley had driven the Bobtail at the Florida 12 hours and DNF'd. The Spyder raced in '57 was later used to start Porsche champion Don Sesslar's sports car career.

In the mid-fifties, Hugus drove at the Put-in-Bay road races for three years: 1955 and 1956 in a Porsche Speedster with his lucky number 13, and 1957 in an Alfa Giulietta Spider. In the 1956 race at Akron Airport, he drove a Porsche Spyder to a second place after Bob Fergus and ahead of Doc Wyllie in the Lotus. He also raced at Cumberland, Maryland, and became involved in the beginnings of the Steel Cities Region of the Sports Car Club of America. In the inaugural race at Bridgehampton he was leading in his red Veloce when he lost a wheel, and he remarked, "It was on the second turn at the bottom of the hill. The center pulled out of the wheel. It must have been fatigue. That Alfa brake drum was big enough to roll on and I finally came to a stop."

A close-up of Ed Hugus, who drove an Alfa Giulietta at the 1957 Watkins Glen race (courtesy Alix Lafontant).

Meanwhile, in 1956, Hugus became what is thought to be the second Ferrari dealer in the country. He was a good friend of Luigi Chinetti, but the first competition Ferrari he raced came from Denver racing patron Temple Buell, via Chester Flynn, a General Motors executive with an interest in racing. The Ferrari was a 500TR, s/n 0652MDTR.

In 1957, Ed's friend Chet Flynn bought a new Ferrari 250TR (s/n 0732TR) and entered it in the 1958 Sebring race with Hugus as co-driver, but the car retired with a broken valve spring. Flynn suffered an accident and never raced again. Before Le Mans, Hugus became the owner of the car, painted it white with a blue stripe and drove it with Ernie Erickson to a 7th overall, later racing the car again at Watkins Glen in the fall.

In 1960, Hugus teamed with Augie Pabst to drive a short wheelbase Ferrari at Sebring, where they placed 4th overall and 2nd in class. Then they raced a similar car — the competition version with alloy body and six Weber carbs— at Le Mans. Having the advantage of disc brakes, they finished 7th, ahead of the 8th-place Corvette entered by Briggs Cunningham and driven by John Fitch and Bob Grossman. Dick Thompson said if the Corvettes had disc brakes, they could have won the World GT title three years in a row before the SWB came out.

For a little change of pace, Hugus drove an OSCA at Le Mans in 1961. It was s/n 1001, Type S. It did not last the race. Then, in the September '61 Road American 500, he took a 2nd overall driving a Ferrari 250TR 59/60 with George Reed.

One time early in his driving career, Hugus fell into conversation with Briggs Cunningham in the paddock at a race. As he was walking away, Ed turned and said, "I hope I can drive for you some day." Cunningham replied, "Oh, I'm sure you will." Hugus later drove for BSC in 1960 and 1962. According to Larry Berman's records, he drove a Lister Jaguar at Watkins Glen in 1960, taking a 1st in class, then he drove a Fiat Abarth 1000 at Bridgehampton in 1962, taking a GT Class win.

In the early sixties there was another business expansion as Hugus said in his note to Pete Vack: "In 1962 I became the Cobra distributor for Shelby for east of the Mississippi. The first 3 Cobras in the U.S.A. were assembled and sold at my shops in Pittsburgh."

Over the years, he drove other Ferraris in competition: a 250GT SWB Speciale, a GTO, the rear-engined 250 P, and a 250 LM in addition to Porsche RSK and 906 models, recalling, "I enjoyed every single minute of it."

Looking back on his racing career, Hugus told Pete Vack, "It was all just part of the business. I had no hobbies, and I guess you could say that race driving was my hobby, even though it was tied to business. I just had no time — or desire — to do anything else."

∽ Dick Irish ∾

Dick is the driver who demonstrated that a Siata Gran Sport handles better than a Ferrari by beating four of the machines from Maranello at Sebring in 1952 with co-driver Bob Fergus. His almost-first race was at Bridgehampton on June 9, 1951, in a borrowed TC. He was in 3rd place when his flywheel broke on the last lap. Next he got a Jaguar 120 (an early one with the aluminum body — according to Jim Sitz it was s/n 670116), but he didn't race that.

He soon traded the Jag for a Kieft-Norton FIII and a Ford pickup truck to haul it to races. He ran it at the May 1951 Giants Despair hillclimb, taking 6th in class. He became notorious as a record-setter at venues such as the Janesville, Wisconsin, airport and 1952 Brynfan Tyddyn race, where an innovative shortcut, involving a near miss with a tree, soon became known as "Irish Corner." The Norton twin-cam engine was tuned by a Canadian wizard. Its megaphone exhaust created an ear-splitting shriek and fumes from the alcohol fuel made your eyes water.

When he was at Watkins Glen racing the Kieft in 1951, he met ace mechanic Charlie Kirschoffer, who was with Hector Sheffer's Siata Gran Sport, the first race for this car in the U.S. They would work together later.

In the early fifties, Irish knew a number of characters in the sport, including Tony Pompeo, celebrated importer of Italian cars such as Siata, Bandini, Cisitalia, Giaur, Stanguellini and others. Pompeo had locations in and around New York City, he was active in the racing scene although not a very good driver, and he was known as a ladies'

Top: Car #60F at Bridgehampton gets crossed up a little near the hay bales. It's a little like sailing: "If you don't capsize once in awhile, you're not sailing fast enough." The car is one that Dick borrowed from Frank White and its license plate — AB6436, 1951 Ohio — is plain to see. Dick advises, "Oversteer out of the last corner onto front straight." This is the race for Novice Drivers in the Mecox Trophy, 1951 (courtesy Tom Weber, Dick Irish collection). *Bottom:* Ace mechanic Charlie Kirschaffer talks with Dick Irish in the #210 Ferrari at Watkins Glen in 1954. Dick beat Walt Hansgen in the C-Type Jaguar in this car, racing in the rain (Dick Irish collection).

Top: Whoops! Dick Irish gets a little sideways at Chanute in '54. The front anti–roll bar of the #152 Ferrari was disconnected, which produced a squirrely quality to the handling. Mechanic Art Bly figured it out and re-connected it. *Bottom:* The #152 Christiansen Ferrari in the paddock at Chanute AFB, Illinois, 1954. Christiansen had a company called Motoresearch, in Racine, Wisconsin. It built electric induction motors for the Air Force. The car was later given to the University of Wisconsin, which later sold it to a party in Germany (Dick Irish collection).

man. He also kept company with John Perona, who owned the El Morocco night club. Dick Irish facilitated construction of an interesting car, the Siata-Ford. He worked for Mulgrew Ford, a dealer in Euclid, Ohio. In 1951, owner Jim Mulgrew wanted to put an Italian body on a Ford chassis, but didn't know how to do it. Irish picked up the phone and called Pompeo, suggesting that Siata could convert a Ford chassis into an Italian-bodied American car. Mulgrew tried to get a bare chassis from the factory but was unable to. Once he concluded that Ford was not going to send a chassis, he reached behind him and picked a set of keys off a board. They were for a 1951 Ford he had on the lot — he told Irish to have Pompeo ship it to Italy. When it came back it was a beautiful car, smaller and shorter, with a Siata badge on the nose and a Ford V-8 under the hood.

In 1952, Irish was working for a dealer named Blauschild Chevrolet in Shaker Heights, Ohio. They wanted to get into the sports car market and Dick suggested selling Siatas. To promote them, Dick took one of the cars to Vero Beach and Sebring in 1952. He enlisted Bob Fergus in Columbus as a co-driver because Bob could put together a crew from his dealership. In the Vero Beach 12-hour race, the Ohio boys struggled to keep the Siata on the track. The head gasket blew four times and they used up all their spares. At one point, the engine was filling the cylinder with water so fast, they had to start it without the spark plug and then Dick's brother Bud put the spark plug in while the engine was running. Don't try this at home, kids!

For the Sebring race, Tony Pompeo came down from New York with a spare head gasket in his briefcase and, most importantly, the shop manual which advised re-torquing the head after installation. The factory head gasket blew out in practice and the crew had to make a replacement out of soft aluminum. This held during the whole race. With the engine reliable, there was nothing to stop the little Siata. These cars handled better than the Ferraris of the era, and the brakes were very good, too. Noting the practice speed of the Irish/Fergus Siata, the Porsche factory team withdrew. But the Siata not only beat their rival MG team, they beat four Ferraris and three Jaguars, car-for-car. Dick Irish and Bob Fergus finished 1st in class, 2nd on Index and 3rd overall.

After the Kieft and the Siata, Dick began to drive the Marty Christiansen 4.5 Ferrari coupe, in which he beat Walt Hansgen in the rain at Watkins Glen in 1954. Other venues included March AFB and Chanute Field in Rantoul, Illinois, both in the 1954 season. He was scheduled to drive the 4.5 coupe at the '54 Panamerican Road Race. According to an agreement between owner Christiansen and Luigi Chinetti, the car would be entered there to be driven by Chinetti and Dick Irish. But later, Christiansen reneged on the agreement and the car did not go to Mexico.

"The racing mechanic who took care of the Christiansen Ferrari, as well as Bill Cooper's Ferrari 500 TRC," says Dick, "was Charlie Kirschoffer. Charlie was an institution in the Chicago area. He was a S.P.A.D. mechanic in the French air force in World War I. He was from Alsace. He was a Bugatti mechanic for Nuvolari. He came to this country and worked with Lou Welch, Leo Goosen, et al. on the Novis at Indianapolis, and was there with Luigi Chinetti and the Ferrari. He had his own shop in Winthrop Harbor, Illinois, just south of the Wisconsin border. He took care of Chapin's cars — the honcho at American Motors — and was the person who got me the ride in Marty Chritiansen's 4.5 Ferrari coupe.

Dick Irish and actress Claudia Hall with the 4.5 Ferrari on a windy day, November 7, 1954, at March AFB, Riverside, California. The car had previously been driven to a 4th-place finish by Italian driver Guido Mancini in the 1953 Mexican Road Race. It was supposed to have been driven in the 1954 Panamerican by Dick Irish and Luigi Chinetti, but Christiansen reneged on the deal, putting him on Chinetti's Less Favored People list (Dick Irish collection).

"Charlie took me on a conducted tour though Travers and Coons' TRACO Engineering," Irish continues, "and the Meyer Drake facilities when we were out to run March Field AFB in '54, and they treated him like visiting royalty. Charlie was the one who got Snap-On into the foreign car business. If you bought a foreign car in the early fifties, all you had to do is contact Snap-On and they would tell you what tools you needed — after they checked with Charlie."

In 1955, Irish co-drove a Ferrari 500 TRC with owner Bill Cooper. Before the endurance race at Road America, Charlie Kirschoffer recommended replacing the brake drums but the owner had them turned instead. "The liners came out in chunks," Irish recalls, "wiping out the brake shoes, so we had to finish the Elkhart 500 with no brakes!"

In 1956, a might-have-been drive evaporated for Irish at Sebring. He went down there with Chuck Hassan and was a reserve driver on John Fitch's Corvette team, with two possibilities to drive. Either he would be a third driver of the Fitch/Hansgen car or he would replace Ray Crawford in case he was not able to drive. Unfortunately for Dick, Crawford got to Sebring and a third driver was not needed on the Fitch/Hansgen car.

His last race was in 1958 at a race in Colorado driving the Christiansen 4.5 Ferrari. In following years, Dick kept in contact with the sport and bought a new Ferrari 275 at Maranello. As Jim Sitz notes, he was there every day, watching them build it.

~ ROWLAND KEITH ~

Keith owned a 1948 TC and first raced at Watkins Glen on September 17, 1949. He DNF'd that year but won the Queen Catherine Cup in 1950. For two years the engine was stock but then he supercharged it and took the advice of a Canadian mechanic, Jim Ferguson. "Jim said to sleeve the engine down to 1100cc to stay in Class F. The small loss in engine size was more than made up by the blower." Then he got a Formula III Cooper-J.A.P. It was probably a Mark IV. At one race, they didn't want him on the track — his engine was dripping oil. "Of course," he said. "All these JAP engines leak — that's the kind of oiling system they have." They finally let him race.

A couple of years later, Jim Ferguson was going to England on business and he picked up a new Cooper for Rowland, with a d.o. Norton engine. Keith was the Formula III national champion for 1956 and was 2nd in SCCA points in both '54 and '57. One

In his first race, Rowland Keith's black MG-TC leaps over the railroad tracks on the old Watkins Glen road course in 1949. His main recollection of the race? "Coming down the hill into town, the front end started jacking when I put on the brakes. It got so bad I had to take my foot off the brakes. But I made the corner anyway" (Rowland Keith collection).

Above: Here Rowland Keith hustles the #71 Allard Le Mans through a corner. "It was a race in eastern Massachusetts, I think they only held it one year. I don't think I did very well in that race." The event was Westover AFB in Chicopee, Massachusetts, in 1954 and Keith took a 3rd in C-Modified. *Opposite, top:* The Mark IX Cooper Norton of Rowland Keith charges up Mt. Washington to set the Fastest Time of Day, at 10 mins. 42.2 sec., ahead of Carroll Shelby in a 4.4 Ferrari GP car. Keith's 1955 record, he recalls, lasted a little over ten minutes, or until Shelby made another run and set a time of 10:21.8. Both drivers broke the previous record, a 10:44.8 posted in 1954 by Sherwood Johnston, in a Jaguar. *Opposite, bottom:* The J1 prototype Allard of Bob Wilder takes in the sun at Vero Beach, Florida. It was powered by a Ford V-8 with Ardun heads. Wilder and his friend Rowland Keith co-drove it in the 12-hour event the week before Sebring in 1952, placing 1st in Class III, and 6th overall, just behind Briggs Cunningham's 2-liter Ferrari (Rowland Keith collection).

of the highlights was a hillclimb. "At Mt. Washington, I held the record for about ten minutes in my Cooper. Then Carroll Shelby took it away with an Indianapolis Ferrari." In August of 1956, he raced an Allard-Olds up Mt. Washington. At the same time he was driving an Allard in road racing. It was the one Bob Wilder had been killed in at Bridgehampton in 1953. "We were all friends. When Bob died, we fixed up his car and ran it the next year. It was a Le Mans Allard, entered by Len Walker who had the Chevy agency in Palmer, Massachusetts. The mechanic was Bebe Zelinski, a very good mechanic."

Rowland's favorite car, though, was an Austin-Healey 100S that he ran at Sebring and at Harwood Acres in Canada — he won the Indian Summer race there in 1956.

Rowland Keith takes the checkered flag to start on a victory lap after an overall win in the Indian Summer Trophy Race, September 1956, at Harewood Acres, a popular airport course in Canada. In the car with him is Jack Barr, who came over with the car, from Scotland. "Jack said he could get me an invitation to drive for Ecurie Ecosse, but I didn't want the pressure of driving for someone else," Rowland says. The Austin-Healey 100S was his favorite car. "It handled so nicely," he remarks. In the race he beat a Corvette: "He had tremendous acceleration and almost caught me," he comments. On the back of the picture, car owner Alice Ferguson wrote, "You lapped the other Healey 100S" (Rowland Keith collection).

There was one other 100S in the race, which he lapped. He raced until 1958 and then sold his Cooper and used the proceeds to pave his driveway.

LeRoy Kramer Jr.

Roy Kramer was a racer, a racing team manager, and an SCCA official in the prewar and postwar eras. He was a good friend of Fred Egloff, editor of the Chicago Region SCCA newsletter, so let's hear Fred tell us about Roy Kramer.

"One of the true pioneers of the American sportscar movement was LeRoy Kramer Jr.," says Egloff. "Roy was an active member of ARCA, the prewar predecessor of SCCA.

Early on he became a close friend of Miles Collier, whom he had met while Miles was working in Chicago. Roy soon became the ARCA's Chicago Regional Executive. His first sports car, purchased from Studebaker Proving Ground, was an Alvis that S.C.H. Davis had raced at Le Mans.

"Roy himself raced an MG J2 in the Memphis Cotton Carnival road race in 1936. In 1939 he was listed as co-driver for Miles Collier's MG 'Leonidis' at the Le Mans 24-hour race. This was the first time the American colors flew at the Le Mans course since Jimmie Murphy won the French Grand Prix there in 1921.

"During World War II, he taught aircraft engine mechanics, eventually retiring as a Navy reserve lieutenant commander.

"Roy wasn't overly enthused when Fred Wacker proposed the start of the Chicago Region SCCA, feeling that he had already been through all that sports car stuff. Needless to say, he became an extremely active founding member of the region and eventually a life member of SCCA.

Longtime ARCA and SCCA racer and official LeRoy Kramer times the Arnolt Bristol team at Sebring in 1955. Roy was the team manager for Wacky Arnolt that year (courtesy Lee Kramer).

"Roy served as the region's third regional executive," Fred continues, "and editor of the region's publication *Piston Patter*. He organized the timing and scoring operations at the Elkhart Lake Road Events and served at chairman of SCCA's National Contest Board. He was among those instrumental in the design and building of the Road America race course.

"Roy was also team manager for the Arnolt Bristol Team at Sebring, winning a team prize while Rene Dreyfus was among their drivers. He was also a very active rallyist, with a room full of ribbons and trophies. He was responsible for setting up much of the far northern routing of the National Lake Michigan Miglia.

"Roy had long resided in Highland Park, Illinois, but upon retirement from the General American Corporation, he moved to Harbor Springs, Michigan, where he had spent his summers growing up.

"Other than cars, Roy had a lifetime interest in boats, especially sailboats. He received the honor of being named an Old Goat, having sailed more than 25 Chicago to Mackinac races. He was also one of the best, if not the best, experts at compensating and repairing compasses. Yachtsmen from around the world sought his services."

Roy Kramer enthusiastically flags the finish of a race at Wilmot Hills, Wisconsin, in 1955. He was the 3rd Regional Executive of the Chicago Region of SCCA (courtesy Lee Kramer).

According to son Lee Kramer, "Dad had a machine shop at Harbor Springs and he used to make steam engines. He made quite a few of them. He also made a canoe of fiberglass, using coated Styrofoam as a mold."

"In addition to SCCA," notes Egloff, "he was a member of the Great Lakes Cruising Club, the Society of Small Craft Designers, the Chicago Club, the Union League Club and the Society of the Cincinnati.

"Roy passed away in June 2004. He was 89 and was preceded in death by his wife Betty. He is survived by his daughter Margaret and two sons, LeRoy III and Frederick. Each of his offspring, on separate occasions, have said, 'I hope I can live up to the example he set.' What a tribute to a father. Roy was a gentleman, sportsman and a great example for all."

❧ Haig Ksayian ☙

"Hemp Oliver was a good friend of mine," says Haig Ksayian. "I'd known him since I was 15 years old. One day he called and said, 'I'm going to Watkins Glen — you

Haig Ksayian in the #8 MG TC pursues Bill Milliken in the #21 Bugatti Type 35 at the 1948 Watkins Glen race. Shortly afterward, this location would be called Milliken's Corner, as Bill rolled his car trying to outdistance the MG entered by Briggs Cunningham. The car was supercharged and race-prepared by team mechanic Alfred Momo. "It was very fast," Haig recalls (courtesy William Green Motor Racing Library).

should come too.' When we got there, he introduced me to Briggs Cunningham and he said, 'Briggs needs a driver for his extra car. Are you interested?' I said, 'Sure I am.' So he took me over to this MG.

"When it was time to race, I got in the car. I had never seen it before, and I had never driven one. I mentally made a note that I was not going to press it but I changed my mind during the race. The car was extremely fast. Alfred Momo from Inskip prepared the car. Briggs told me the car had 8-to-one compression and the supercharger had a 12-pound boost. The rev limit was 6500 rpm."

Haig won his class in two races that day. The Watkins Glen we're talking about was the first race of the postwar era, the 1948 race that young Cameron Argetsinger took a gamble on. Would there be enough entrants? Would there be enough spectators? Could it continue into another year and another race? All of these things were unknowns at the time.

Up to then, Haig Ksayian had only driven a hillclimb in his Alfa. But he was an intuitive driver and a natural athlete. There were two races in 1948, the Junior Prix (4 laps of the 6½ mile course) and the Grand Prix (8 laps). Haig and the MG were entered in both of them and won class B in both, and took 3rd overall in both. The only cars

The person who got Haig Ksayian the ride in Cunningham's MG was Hemp Oliver, a real figure in the sport in the early days. He was involved in organizing races, running races, announcing races, etc. He is seen here in Montlhery, France, while on a trip to photograph the Cunningham team at Le Mans in 1950. Standing next to him is Louis Wagner, winner of the 1906 Vanderbilt Cup Race (courtesy Hemp Oliver).

ahead of Ksayian were Briggs Cunningham in the Bu-Merc—2nd overall and 1st in class D, and Frank Griswold in the 8C 2900B Alfa—1st overall and 1st in class C. The classes then were set up the reverse of what they are now, that is, the smallest cars were in class A. A stock TC would be in that class, as was the class A winner in each of the races, namely Phil Stiles. The achievement of Ksayian in taking the class 1st and overall 3rd was amplified by the number of cars entered—23 cars in the Junior Prix and 15 cars in the Grand Prix. That was the last race for him. "After the race I never kept in touch with Cunningham. He wrote me a letter and expected a reply, but I never wrote back. I was busy with my family. Cunningham asked about it six months later: 'Why didn't you write back?' he asked."

Apart from the racing, Haig Ksayian had an interesting road car, an 8C 2300 Alfa with a Zagato body. This is the classic Alfa from the '30s (starting 1932 with the magnificent Vittorio Jano straight 8 engine) with the flat radiator and fenders as high as the long-louvered hood. "I bought my first Alfa," says Ksayian, "in 1943. It was a Castagna-bodied 4-passenger, 2-door with the same engine as the Zagato—a straight 8 with double overhead cams. It's in the Simon Moore book on Alfas."

Haig isn't doing too much with sports cars these days. "I just sold my car—it was a 1958 Giulietta Veloce that I bought from Alec Ulmann. I was active up to the turn of the century. I was a member of SCCA — the 37th member. I had SCCA license #1, from Watkins Glen."

Another thing I asked Haig about was whether Hemp Oliver ever raced his MG, or any other car. He said he did not. That's too bad. I had been told that he had, and wanted to write something about Hemp since he was a friend of mine, too. If I had I would have written about the person that Haig described as a "crazy enthusiast who loved cars." But Hemp was a lot more than that and someone should say so. He was a multifaceted Renaissance man with a very wide range of interests and capabilities. He was a very pleasant and engaging person. During World War II, his technical interests led him to do an analysis of the German machine guns, with their high rate of fire — more rounds per minute. These he passed on to the U.S. Army and they were used to give our machine guns, likewise, a high rate of fire. For many years, Hemp was the director of the Smithsonian Institution in Washington, D.C. He was an expert in the automotive field, especially the great American classics of the 1930s. He was the photographer for the Cunningham team at Le Mans in 1950.

Hemp and his equally personable wife Barbara moved from the north to Bellaire, Florida, in the panhandle, and quickly integrated into their new surroundings. Hemp would urge friends to send him canceled postage stamps from England, Italy, France, Spain and other nations to hand out to the neighborhood children and educate them about places around the world. Hemp and Barbara had a pair of Jack Russell terriers and were dog lovers to the core. Nancy and I had a golden retriever-black Lab mix named Cooper and we would trade dog stories for hours. Hemp and Barbara had hundreds of friends all over the country. Hemp died a few years back. They were both memorable people. You can't go into one of these little car clubs like Cal Gleason's "Friday Morning Club" or Tom Saal's "Third Thursdays" without hearing the names Hemp or Barbara Oliver sooner or later. They were real figures in the sport.

∽ BOB LARSON ∽

Like some of the racing drivers of his era, Bob Larson was a World War II veteran. "I flew with the 305th Troop Carrier Squadron," Bob says, "which was based in Capodichina, Italy, just north of Naples. We flew C-47s. At the time we shared the base with a British Fighter Group of Spitfires.

"When I returned home, I worked for a local bodyman, who took me under his wing and taught me metal finishing and painting. In subsequent years it became evident that he was one of the most talented bodymen I ever met. I realized this later, when I went to work for the Fisher Body Division of GM. I trained as a GM Training Center Instructor and became a Home Office Instructor.

"I had always been interested in cars. I built and raced Soap Box Derby cars at the age of 12. I built a gasoline-powered car, which is now known as a go-kart.

"After spending time learning the body trade, my interest led toward foreign cars.

Top: Bob Larson as a young man, in a training plane in the Army Air Corps during World War II. Bob flew C-47 troop transports during the war. *Bottom:* Bob Larson in his MG-TC as repaired after the road accident. Ahead of it were many years of rallying and racing activities in the MG Car Club and SCCA (courtesy Bob Larson).

Shown in a 1953 race at Offutt AFB, Bob Larson's TC corners flat in a high-speed turn out on the tarmac of the SAC-base airfield (courtesy Bob Larson).

My first car was an Austin A40. Not much of a sports car. However, at the time it seemed that any foreign car was a 'sports car.'

"The first sports car race I attended was at Elkhart Lake — not Road America. The second race was Watkins Glen, the original street course. My interest in foreign cars was building. I joined the North Shore Car Club and soon became secretary. I also, around the same time, went to work at a small foreign car shop in Evanston, Illinois. By this time I'd met many SCCA members.

"As often happens, my path took a turn and I bought a gas station in Chicago. Many of the sports car people became customers, so the flame remained lit.

"I received a call one day advising me that there was a totaled MG TC that could be bought: 'Right.' I bought it, to many people's horror. The car belonged to Dolph Nelson, who was producer/director of the Dave Garroway Radio Show in Chicago (prior to his moving to TV). Dolph, as it were, 'got behind in his steering and drove into the rear of a parked car.'

"The gas station provided the perfect space so after working hours I attacked the MG. Many friends helped find the parts I needed. They were all used and some were damaged, as they came from other wrecks.

"When it was completely repaired, my wife and I began to participate in as many

Bob's son Bill Larson, at speed in his Ralt RT5 Formula Atlantic at Waterford Hills north of Detroit (courtesy Bob Larson).

events as possible. I first joined the MG Car Club, which was sponsored by S.H. Arnolt, the distributor of MG, Morris and Riley cars. Shortly afterward I became an officer in the MG Car Club. Then I applied for membership in the SCCA and was accepted.

"The first SCCA event we entered was the 'Vernal Venture Rally.' There were fifty or more entries. The rally ended at a National Guard Armory for a Concours and a buffet dinner. My wife and I were unknowns at this point. When award time came, it was announced that the winner had a perfect score. The winners: 'Bob and Verna Larson.'

"It was time to try racing. The first race I entered was at Chanute Field in Rantoul, Illinois. I had three pit crew members— Bob Krasberg, Jay Brennan and Fred Egloff. As far as I remember, Fred was still in his teens." Bob's car was modified with 16-inch Borrani wire wheels, cycle fenders and a Shorrock supercharger. That put him in the E-Modified class with the real sports-racers including Ferrari and Maserati.

"I went to work for Fisher Body Division of GM late in 1954," Bob continues. "At the time, racing and working for GM didn't mix. After it became known I was still racing, the Big Boss sat me down and gave me a choice: either drive race cars or work for GM. Though not racing, my interest never slowed. For several years I packed my two sons up and we would go to the Grand Prix at Watkins Glen. I think my son Bill was only three or four when we first went.

The Bill Larson RT5, again at Waterford, hits the apex just right to keep ahead of a competitor following closely (courtesy Bob Larson).

"After motorcycle racing, sailboat racing and competition skiing, he came home from college and expressed an interest in driving race cars. After much discussion, Bill was off to England and the Jim Russell School at Snetterton. In addition he did a race series.

"When he came home we bought a '79 Van Diemen Formula Ford, which he raced for two years. He then went to a '79 March Super Vee car, which raced as Formula Continental. Moving up we went to a Ralt RT5 and finally came off the porch to run with the big dogs in Formula Atlantic.

"Bill was SCCA Northeast Formula Continental Champion and ran at the Runoffs at Road Atlanta five times. In a letter from the SCCA, Bill was advised he was the Formula Continental lap record holder at Bridgehampton. Bill raced for twenty years in both National and Club races. In 2000, Bill developed a brain tumor and passed away. Bill's favorite tracks were Lime Rock and the long course at Watkins Glen. When Bill was racing, I served on the Northeast SCCA board.

"Back to my racing, I raced at most of the air bases but my favorite was Wilmot Hills. I was very successful at hillclimbs and won many. Though not the fastest in Class E, I was able to bring home many trophies."

Drivers with whom Bob Larson raced include Jim Kimberly, Briggs Cunningham, Bill Spear, Charles Moran, Masten Gregory, Carroll Shelby, Fred Wacker, Hal Ullrich,

Norm Patton and Burdette Martin. Larson was in the sport at the same time as its legends were. He shared the paddock with them, said hello to them at the drivers' meeting and went to the trophy presentations with them. After his racing years and his son's racing years, Bob accumulated a number of Corvettes and he later had a pilot's license and owned several airplanes.

∽ ED LICHT ∽

As he began his interest in sports car racing, Ed Licht (pronounced "Light") was a corner worker in RCA, the pioneer organization that Fred German created after World War II. He was at the fateful workers' meeting in 1952 at the first Watkins Glen course, in town. "I was a flag marshal then," he recalls, "and we all went to the courthouse for a meeting Saturday morning. Fred Wacker got up in front of the group to speak on the safety of the event. Then, during the race, the family of the child who was killed kept putting a Coke case out in the street. The police would tell them to move back and, when they were gone, the Coke case would go back in the street. Then the cars came through three wide in front of the Glen entrance — at the turnoff from Franklin Street to the Seneca Lodge, where they sell tickets— and that's when the accident happened.

In the paddock at the 1954 Brynfan Tyddyn, in the dark green TC #36 FM, is racer Ed Licht. The car has been extensively lightened, with an aluminum hood, side panels removed, no windshield, no bumpers and cycle fenders front and rear (courtesy Ed Licht).

The #36 modified MG of Ed Licht waits for its race at the 1954 Brynfan Tyddyn event, with an F-P MG TD (#35) beside it. The production car has to race with full road equipment including bumpers (courtesy Ed Licht).

"I started racing in 1953, with a Mark II MG TD. I raced it at Watkins Glen in 1953. That was the second course, up on the hill in Dix Township, before the permanent course. We called it the 'inter-course.' It was September 19. I had driven the Labor Day race at Thompson a couple of weeks earlier. The Mark II had a higher top speed and an engine with more compression and inch-and-a-half carburetors. A most interesting thing about the course was going downhill. The wind blew from the west across the course and, when you were behind the barn, you were OK but when you came out, the wind could take you off the road. Cars that did not make the turn at the bottom would end up in the apple orchard at the base of the hill." Licht finished 10th in class F and 11th overall among 32 cars starting the race, in the #26 TD. On September 6, 1953, Ed ran at Thompson, Connecticut, as car #61 in the first race, finishing 6th overall in the 'TD.

"In 1954 I bought a wrecked TC from a Cornell student named Cunningham. He was driving home from school, fell asleep at the wheel and hit a guardrail. That somehow

Ed Licht, in the #39 MG TC, is on the pole at the start of the MG race at Watkins Glen in 1954. Next to him is TC #8 and behind him is TD #40 (courtesy Ed Licht).

reminds me of Gordy Morris, an MG dealer in Maryland, New York, near Oneonta. He had a terrible accident at the Callicoon race in '53. It was a bad course. The next day Spankey Smith and I took the car apart in his back yard as he sat in a rocking chair. The MG was twisted up pretty badly and Gordy was sore all over. We hid all the damaged parts and his mother never knew he had an accident.

"Another friend of mine, Fowler Wilson, was a 6th-grade school teacher in Binghampton. He had been an Army major stationed in Germany after the end of World War II and had somehow acquired a Glockler pre–Porsche VW. It had a pushrod engine and was before the Spyder. Another friend, J.D. Vogwill, tuned that car. Anyway, I raced the TC in '54 and then I went into the Army." Licht raced the car as #122 in the Queen Catharine Cup at Watkins Glen in 1954, in the F-Modified class. It was a tough race, with the first four places taken by OSCA Mt-4s [Frank Bott 1st]. Ed was sandwiched between the Siatas of Tony Pompeo and John Bentley, in 14th place in a field of 23 cars.

A close-up of the "Bogus Lotus" with Ed in it, apparently trying to shield himself from rain. Ed couldn't buy a Lotus at the time so this was the best he could do (courtesy Ed Licht).

According to Bill Green of IMRRC, Ed also drove the 'TC at Westover AFB on Chicopee, Massachusetts, where he took a 2nd, and at the Brynfan Tyddyn road races.

"I was in the Army in '55 and '56," he notes. "I lived in Binghamton, New York and came home on furloughs, so I was at Watkins Glen in '56. A guy from Rochester, New York, a father-and-son team, built a car out of a Crosley Hot Shot, with an aluminum body. The son was Gary Morgan. They took it to the race and presented themselves to tech inspector Les Smalley. He looked the car over and said, 'Which one of you is licensed to race?' When they said, 'Neither,' he replied, 'I think I can help you.' He said to me, 'Ed, would you like to race this weekend?' Of course I did. The car was not too bad. I was doing well in my class, for most of the race. Then a lap and a half from the end, the car started sputtering. I ran out of gas. The tank had not been completely full at the start." Ed got a DNF in the #145 Crosley Special.

Ed Licht in his red Elva Mark 1, car #282, at speed at Watkins Glen in 1957 (courtesy Ed Licht).

"By 1957 I was out of the Army and I started driving an Elva. Dominic Ravisi was a cam grinder I knew from Boston. He had an Elva Mark IB. It had an 1100cc Coventry Climax engine. He tuned it so it got 127 horsepower at 8700 rpm. It was very fast but it didn't have good brakes, only Triumph drums. (This was before the discs and it had small drums.) Even so, I was often faster than the F-Modified cars with 1500cc engines.

"I raced that car from 1957 to 1963, at Watkins Glen, Thompson and Bridgehampton. It wasn't always easy because I had six kids to take care of. He would call me Thursday evening and say, 'Want to drive at Thompson this weekend?' Then I would jump in a plane and come up."

Ed was seen in the record books at the August 31, 1958, National race at Thompson, in the #51 Elva, a DNF. In 1959, according to the IMRRC records, he drove three cars: the MG-TC at Watkins Glen, a Porsche at Cumberland, and an Elva again at Watkins Glen, in the Queen Catharine Cup race.

Ed was later the regional executive of the SCCA Glen Region. He's known a lot of people in the sport including Cameron Argetsinger, Millard Ripley, Bob Bucher, Etceterini importer Tony Pompeo, racing photographer Alix Lafontant and his wife Nicole, who would time and score the races, as well as Bill Wonder, who flew a Corsair in World War II. Ed worked at Westinghouse, at one point on the Lunar Lander. And he had an Irish setter named Ross.

"I was out of racing a long time and then I got a Lotus 11 in 1988 and started racing it in vintage events in 1990," he concludes.

Otto Linton

"I raced an MG in 1948 at Watkins Glen," says driver Otto Linton. "It was a J4, the only one in the United States, and it's now back in the UK. " As described in the book *The Story of the MG Sports Car*, the 1933 J4 was "too fast for most drivers." The car had essentially the same body that would cover MG frames until 1955, except no doors. Mechanically, it had a 4-cylinder OHC engine of 750cc displacement, supercharged, with one large SU carburetor and a four-speed transmission with a remote shift lever and lock-out reverse. It was built in 1933 in a special production of only 9 cars, at the same time as the more famous K3 Magnette with the same design engine but of 6-cylinder configuration — 30 of these were built and only sold to customer competition drivers.

Like many other drivers in that first race of the new sports car era — Bill Milliken, race organizer Cam Argetsinger, Denver Cornett and George Weaver, Otto posted a DNF in the event, with Haig Ksayian going on to take the win in the MG class. "I just had that one race in '48," says Otto, "plus a couple of hillclimbs in 1949."

"I drove all of the street races at Watkins Glen," notes Otto, "except for 1950. That year I built the car that Denny Cornett drove. It was a DuPont Indianapolis car with a B Type engine. But we didn't get all the engine parts so I installed a Mercury V-8, the full-size one, not the V-8 60. It raced as the Speedcraft Special in 1950 and I was in his pit crew."

In 1951 Otto drove Tony Pompeo's Siata. The Siata Otto is talking about was the prototype of the Siata Spider. As such, it had a tubular steel frame instead of the heavier platform frame. It was lighter by 200 pounds but it had a somewhat more curvy body, compared to the production Siata Spiders, which looked like Type 166 Ferraris in miniature.

This car, originally called the Siata "Amica," was renamed the model 300BC for its short production run. Both cars had aluminum bodies and a Siata-tuned suspension. Linton drove the car for Pompeo at Watkins Glen and Elkhart Lake in 1951. Then he bought it minus its Crosley engine, replacing it with a Crosley engine he had modified, built and tuned. Otto raced it at Vero Beach and Sebring, Florida, and his English mechanic wrecked the car at Bridgehampton in 1953. It was sold and later rebuilt.

Otto Linton at age 92, wearing his SCCA Philadelphia Region cap at the Watkins Glen vintage races (courtesy Otto Linton).

Top: In the #20 J4 MG at Watkins Glen in 1948 is driver Otto Linton. *Bottom:* Stretching out a lead on the #49 Jaguar is Otto Linton in the #58 Siata 208CS. It had a beautiful-sounding 2-liter V-8 engine (courtesy Otto Linton).

In 1952, Siata was building a beautiful new car with a 2-liter V-8 engine and 4-wheel independent suspension, and Otto ordered one. It was a 208CS coupe with a Stablimenti Farina body and whale-tooth grille. "My 208 was the first one to come into the United States because I went to Torino pick it up and have it shipped as personal belongings, arriving just a few days before the 1952 Glen where I had it entered." His car, #114, never raced there. Like all the other cars it was stopped after the fatal accident that year. Then Linton drove at the 1953 Bridgehampton and Watkins Glen second course, handily waxing all of the Jag XK-120s and winning his race. "For some reason, they always put me in with the Jags," Otto laments. The 208 was always driven to and from the races like a real sports car. That included most of the SAC races, earning a few 2nd places to Lunken's Ferrari race car. Driving the 1953 McDill AFB race at Tampa, Florida, Linton took 2nd to Lunken and co-driver

For several racing seasons, Otto Linton raced the ex–Giulio Cabianca OSCA. This is the famous Alix Lafontant photograph taken from a tree branch above the course at Brynfan Tyddyn in 1955 (courtesy Otto Linton).

Chuck Hassan in the E-Modified class, with Linton driving the 6 hours solo.

For 1954, he acquired the well-known early OSCA owned and raced by the famous Italian driver Giulio Cabianca, who was appointed to the Ferrari team but was killed before he could race for them. This OSCA was a little different from the Mt-4 models we usually see. It had headlights inside the grille and two-tone paint scheme of dark blue on top and red between the wheel wells. It was in class F but not up to the 1500cc limit — only 1342cc. Nevertheless, he won the Brynfan Tyddyn races of 1954 and 1955 with it. Alix Lafontant, the great racing photographer, took a wonderful picture of the car by crawling out on a tree branch overhanging the course, pre-focusing his Leica IIIF and setting the shutter for 1/1000th of a second. In this picture, which graces the cover of the September/October 1955 issue of *Sports Car*, the SCCA magazine, we see

Otto Linton also drove the larger OSCA models, including this 2-liter racing car seen at Virginia International Raceway (courtesy Otto Linton).

that Otto's tach is at 7000 rpm. In the 1956, race Otto had to settle for 3rd place because Carroll Shelby and Jack McAfee were 1st and 2nd, driving a 2-liter Ferrari and a 1500cc Porsche 550-RS Spyder.

From 1957 to 1963, there followed a number of wins, 2nds, and 3rds driving the 750, Mt-4, TNS and 2-liter OSCAs at Sebring, Watkins Glen, Marlboro 6-Hours, Vineland 4-Hours and regional races. "The TNS was the new version of the Mt-4," says Otto. "It had the same chassis as the Mt-4 but it had a 1498cc engine with a different head. It had twin ignition and more power. It was a real, real good car. We ran that at Sebring and we won the Marlboro race overall." In 1957, the TNS was a factory entry in the 12-Hour race, with Otto, Harry Beck and Hal Stetson driving. They finished 3rd in the 1500cc sports racing class, after two Porsche 550s. In 1958, again with a factory entry, Linton, Beck and Stetson finished Sebring 1st in the 1500cc class and 13th overall. Otto had joined in a business relationship with Lou Flink, who was continually selling off cars. The OSCA TNS had come from Jim Kimberly and it went to a fellow who was going to put a Ford V-8 in it. When the car was later restored, the special dual ignition head was missing. John Milos originally owned the TNS and all the trophies went to him. He's since died and no one knows where the trophies are. In 1964 at Sebring, Otto and co-driver Thomas Fleming placed 1st in the GT8 class with Fleming's 2-liter Abarth Simca, and 24th overall, right after A.J. Foyt and John Cannon in the Corvette Gran Sport. Linton also scored wins at Watkins Glen and the Bahamas in this car.

In 1967, Otto began to phase out of racing. "I was expanding my business," he says, "and I was getting a loan from the Small Business Administration. I had to turn in my license to SCCA or they wouldn't issue insurance. So after that I could only do local races that didn't require a license. I bought a Bobsy with an OSCA engine from a guy in Wyoming. But there was something about it that would seize up the main shaft of the transmission. We later concluded that the bronze pilot bushing should have been a needle bearing. I stopped racing after I sold that car."

∽ Bill Lloyd ∽

As Ferrari mechanic George Jasberg notes, Lloyd was another of the "Connecticut Crew" led by Briggs Cunningham and Bill Spear. Lloyd operated the Southport Body Shop in Connecticut. Best known for being the co-driver with Stirling Moss for the win at the 1954 Sebring race in an OSCA, he drove his first speed event at Mt. Equinox in July 1950, where he took 2nd in class E with a supercharged MG. His first car-to-car race was at Watkins Glen, September 23, 1950, in the #9 stock MG TD. In '52, at the 'Glen, he moved up to an Offenhauser-powered MG TD and took a 5th overall in the Queen Catharine Cup. And he drove it at Bridgehampton.

Bill Lloyd in his new Maserati 300S at Beverly, Massachusetts, in 1955. Lloyd is best known for his win at Sebring in 1954, co-driving an OSCA with Stirling Moss. The emblem on the side of the car is that of the exclusive Road Racing Drivers' Club (courtesy Alix Lafontant © Carl Goodwin).

A crowd gathers to see the Maserati 300S of Bill Lloyd, at the Beverly, Massachusetts, airport race in 1955. Pirelli Stelvio tires gave the car a grip on the road (courtesy Alix Lafontant © Carl Goodwin).

Also in 1952, he drove a Porsche America roadster at Thompson in October. By 1953, according to Jim Sitz, he had his own 2.7 Ferrari (which he later sold to Briggs Cunningham Junior). With the 2.7, a Touring-bodied barchetta, he placed 1st in D-Modified at Lockbourne AFB. At the end of the '54 season he was the Class D Modified national champion. The following two years he was in a Maserati 300S. He achieved a series of high finishes at venues such as Beverly, Massachusetts, Watkins Glen, Thompson, Hagerstown, Maryland, and Elkhart Lake with a string of class 2nds and 3rd^s, plus a 1st at Cumberland.

In 1955 he was 2nd in the C-Mod championship, behind Phil Hill, and in 1956 he won his second national championship, in D-Mod with the Maserati. This was the car that he loaned to Stirling Moss, who won the feature race at Nassau in it, in 1956. Lloyd is proud of his membership in the exclusive Road Racing Drivers Club, to which he was elected in 1954.

～ BOB LOSSMAN ～

"Bob Lossman was an early millionaire in Lakewood, Ohio," says racer Art Brow, "and an excellent plumber." His father was a plumber and had a hardware store at about 130th and Lorain Avenue in Cleveland, across from Halloran Park. His brother Ed was a plumber too, finally taking over the family plumbing business. They used to go boating. They had a rich friend they knew from boating, who wanted an MG. He was George Weber. They went over to Jag-Cleveland on the east side and they didn't have any. They were all sold out.

"Then they called the importer, Inskip in New York. They said, 'If you buy six we'll make you a dealer.' So Bob started selling them from the plumbing store. Then the city told Bob he couldn't sell cars from the plumbing store. A former dealership became available — it was Burkhardt Studebaker at Webb Road and Detroit. The building had been built by Baker Towing Company — I worked on the building, it was the first job I had right after I got out of the Navy. Lossman bought the building and sold MGs there. Jim Dever worked there as a mechanic and he suggested that I apply for a job there. Bob Shea was the service manager. He had come back from Europe and had a Willy Jeepster. But it wasn't like the ones he saw in Europe and he liked those. He bought an MG and hung around the shop until Bob Lossman hired him."

In the Cleveland car scene, Bob Lossman was best known for the role he played in organizing the famous Put-in-Bay road races. He had a cottage up there and knew all of the local people. He greased the skids to have the races there. As soon as they started, the local merchants made so much money they couldn't count it. Bob drove

Bob Lossman, proprietor of Lossman Motors and the best sports car service shop in town, waits on the starting line at Put-in-Bay. He was racing his MG TD in 1954 (Art Brow collection).

in the races, in both an MG and a Triumph. He also financed the first of the Akron Airport sports car races, in 1954. Skipping the cancellation in 1955, they were also run in 1956, 1957 and 1958. The Bay races ran from '52 to '59. There was also an "outlaw" event in 1963.

"Lossman was selling other cars, too," Art Brow continues. "I remember he sold a couple of gullwing Mercedes and several Volkswagens. After awhile, VW wanted their dealerships to sell only Volkswagens, so Bob had to find another building. He bought one at 16000 Madison Avenue and Hilliard Road and moved the MGs over there, with the VWs at Webb Road and Detroit. Besides the MGs, he sold Triumphs, Hillmans, Morris and Renault. Above the showroom at Madison Avenue was a pool room with a refrigerator for the beer. Then Fairchild Chevrolet built a larger building and he bought their old one to sell Renaults. Bob had two fancy cars: a Rolls-Royce that he let Jack Uhr drive when he got married, and a green Mercedes-Benz convertible that the Kennedy family had owned."

"Bob Lossman was a nice guy who took care of his people," says Dutch Brow. "He used to take us out to lunch, take us up to Put-in-Bay, and he had a party at his house for us on Christmas Eve. One time a self-important little man from Volkswagen told Bob to fire three of us, including me. Bob gave me a job at the MG store and I handled the warranty paperwork at the VW store. Bill Douglas was made the manager of the Renault store with some other responsibilities at the Volkswagen store. Bob treated us like a family. When Art wanted to buy an MG, he didn't have quite enough money. Bob said, 'I'll advance you the rest.' Later on, a bill came in from MG and Bob said, 'We will absorb that.'" At one point, the four dealerships owned by Lossman employed 80 people. All of his employees were former customers. By the late '60s he was selling 900 cars a year. When he first started out, it was hard to get financing. "Foreign car dealers generally were regarded as people with an extremely limited future," he once said.

"With Lossman, everything had to be level, plumb and true," recalls Art Brow. "They were building a new lift at one of the dealerships. I told the workmen, 'I think that lift's going to be too high.' They told me, 'We know how to build lifts.' Then Lossman came in and said, 'Art does, this look too high to you?' I said, 'Let's measure it.' It was two inches too high. The cement was already in and Bob said, 'You're going to have to tear that out.' On an addition at Webb Road, a support beam was off. I mentioned it. They said, 'Nah, that's OK,' and then 'Ahh, don't tell me.' Lossman came in and said, 'OK, let's get this thing plumb.'

"He had a part of the building he called 'the transporter store.' He later turned that into the body shop. Dutch was the first woman to work in a west side car dealership. She worked at both the MG and the VW stores and sold parts.

"Bob bought a speedboat with an engine that was seized. He had it over at Cleveland Yacht Club in Rocky River. I took some oil, a hammer and a punch. We removed the cylinder head — it was a flathead — and tapped on all the valves. I would oil them and hit them with the punch. Pretty soon we had all the valves working. We put the head back on and started it up. Bob had a big boathouse with two wells over on Put-in-Bay. He built a cottage inside the boathouse and put in electric lifts. He would pull into the slip and lift the boat out of the water."

Bob and his Lossman Motors were fixtures in the cultural life of Cleveland's west side, and in the Ohio Islands. The company operated well into the nineties and then closed for lack of a succession plan. Bob died, his wife Julie died in June of 2004, and his stepdaughter Ann died in 2008. The Lossmans are gone but they are still remembered.

✎ Karl Ludvigsen ✎

"A Chicago suburb," muses automotive author Karl Ludvigsen, "was where we found the MG TC that I raced and rallied in the early Fifties and drove throughout the eastern states. When I say 'we' I mean that my father generously bought the car for me, black with green trim, from its original owner after I graduated from high school at the age of 18 in the spring of 1952. As a rock-ribbed Republican family we subscribed to the *Chicago Tribune*; we may well have spotted the TC in the small ads.

"Why a TC?" Ludvigsen asks, and then answering his own question, "I'd started to follow the world of cars in the mid-forties and was a passionate fan of the TC model. I did rather well to beat all the TDs at Thompson in 1954 with a 1949 TC! I believe I'm right in saying that with the chassis number of 7032 and engine number 7587 she was relatively late in the production run. When I look back at those race results above I see that I was a lone TC racer among shoals of the new TDs. In fact I recall that I was seen as something of a TC die-hard at a time when the TDs were widely triumphant."

Ludvigsen was an undergraduate at M.I.T. studying mechanical engineering. He was a freshman there when Chuck Stoddard was a senior. Stoddard, also bitten by the sports-car bug, would later become a three-time national champion in Alfas.

With a race-ready TC, he attended a Sports Car Club of America driver's school at Thompson Raceway, the first permanent road racing course in America. There he experienced the hospitality of track managers George and Barbara Weaver and learned how to drive in competition from racer Hal Stetson. However, he never competed in SCCA races. He ran under the aegis of the Motor Sports Enthusiasts' Club (MSEC), with which M.I.T. in Cambridge, Massachusetts, was affiliated.

In other races at Thompson, he was second in class in the time trials in November 1952. He scored another second place in the same month a year later. In May of 1954 he placed third twice and at the end of October '54 he won the Stock M.G. race at Thompson outright. The reward for this finish was a little silver cup that he keeps to this day.

The Ludvigsen family lived in Kalamazoo, Michigan, midway between Detroit and Chicago. Spending summers there, Karl was able to run several events with the local sports car clubs: the Holland, Michigan, Sabot Rally of the M.G. Car Club in August of 1952 and the Club's Allegan Forest Rally of 1953, in which he was third. Then he went back to the Allegan Forest in September for the time trials, in which he placed third. He was a member of the Western Michigan Sub-Centre of the Overseas

Karl Ludvigsen gets ready on the starting line at the Allegan Time Trials, held in Michigan's Allegan Forest in 1953. This was an MG Car Club event. A Cromwell helmet and a seat belt are his safety equipment. Roll bars were not to be mandatory until five years later (courtesy Karl Ludvigsen).

Midwestern Centre of the M.G. Car Club. At the end of all these adventures, Karl's wife Annette made up a frame on the wall displaying the ribbons won.

Ludvigsen adds, "The TC became my transportation between Kalamazoo and Cambridge during my two M.I.T. years and then subsequently to New York when I changed to industrial design studies at Pratt Institute. These trips were sagas of endurance for both car and driver in those pre-expressway days in America."

"To light the way on my nighttime odysseys," he notes, "I found and fitted a massive American Trippe driving light, the 'flamethrower' of its day. Usually found on Duesenbergs and Packards, the Trippe was wired to come on with the high beams. I also installed a vacuum gauge, one of the 'in' accessories of the era. An accelerometer could be installed as well to help with tuning for racing.

"For regular maintenance I trusted the TC to Ernie Woodworth at Newton Corners, Massachusetts. Ernie and I tackled the challenge of the TC's legendary steering box. I had ordered and fitted a Tompkins cover, with its tapered-roller thrust bearing (screw-

Entering a double-apex turn at Thompson Raceway, Thompson, Connecticut, in 1953, Karl Ludvigsen takes a neat line in his MG-TC, to make a single apex turn out of it. Sometimes it's faster (courtesy Karl Ludvigsen).

adjustable, as I recall) replacing the standard cover. Ernie had the idea of reaming out the drop-shaft bore and fitting a bronze bushing; a Ford gudgeon-pin bushing fit perfectly.

"Ernie Woodworth also overhauled the engine at one stage. Finding generous piston skirt-to-wall clearances, he recommended 'Knurlizing' the skirts. This process knurled the aluminum, pushing the valleys into peaks that reduced the effective clearance. The knurling also helped hold oil on the skirts, said Ernie. Made sense to me.

"From Perry Fina in New York I obtained and installed one of his special cast-aluminium silencers. The normal silencer was removed and a straight pipe was fitted almost to the rear of the chassis. There sat the Fina silencer, shaped like a three-tined fork. The outer two tines had perforated caps holding in the steel-wool packing that did the silencing. In the centre tine was a butterfly valve worked by a T-handle on the floor. With a pull of the handle the exhaust was straight-through!

"With the Fina silencer the TC's race preparation was simple. I just pulled the T-handle and — presto! — I had a straight open exhaust. Off came the windscreen. Its wind wings served as aero screens, Allen-screwed to mounts on the cowl. Shell Rotella oil

Ludvigsen's #11 MG-TC at the start of a race at Thompson in 1954. Race preparation consists of removing windshield and bumpers, using a wind-wing for a racing screen, and taping the headlights (courtesy Karl Ludvigsen).

was poured in; I used Shell because Ferrari did. My favoured Bosch spark plugs were checked and installed. Italian Fren-Do brake linings were riveted on. The micrometer adjustment of the ignition advance was clicked just so.

"These modest preparations seemed to transform the TC. With the tonneau cover in place, tyre pressures raised, exhaust crackling, she took on a delightful urgency. I hadn't even prepared her when, after the stock car races at the Galesburg, Michigan, quarter-mile track, I slid her around for a few laps—turning left for a change. Afterward a well-dressed chap gave me his card and said, 'If you're serious about driving, look me up.' Who knows where that might have led?

"When I was at an SCCA drivers' school at Thompson, a personable young man (older than me!) was introduced. 'I'm writing a book about a TC,' he said, 'and I'd like to refresh my recollections of it. Would you mind if I drove a few laps in your car?' I was agreeable and thought little more of it.

"Surprisingly soon thereafter I received a copy of *The Red Car* by Donald K. Stanford, published for the younger market by Funk & Wagnalls. In it on 28 September 1954 Don Stanford wrote, 'For Karl Ludvigsen, with best wishes and thanks for the use of a good TC at Thompson.'

"In *The Red Car* Stanford described the crimson hero, a TC, as 'lean and racy and angular, with fenders that made no attempt to curve or blur into the body lines, but

Karl Ludvigsen in the #16 MG takes the checkered flag at Thompson with the grandstand in the background. This was an event put on in 1954 by the Motor Sports Enthusiasts Club of the Massachusetts Institute of Technology (courtesy Karl Ludvigsen).

stood out in a clean sharp sweep over the wheels. The wheels were enormous; they were almost ludicrous, at first glance. They were gleaming silvery wire wheels, standing high and narrow with the rakish scarlet body of the car between them, looking even now as if it were crouched close to the ground ready to spring forward.'"

"The car looked almost alive," Stanford wrote. "It had a personality all its own — an arrogant, insolent, challenging way of looking you right in the eye and saying, 'Drop dead!'"

"I think he captured well the special appeal of M.G.'s TC," Ludvigsen concludes.

"Handsome to be sure," he continues, "those big wheels were at best a mixed blessing. Once at Thompson I had one give way on me in a bend with a wobble that felt like a flat tyre. That was a wheel that had previously been repaired; I shouldn't have been using it for racing.

"Tyres weren't that easy to find either, although both Pirelli and Dunlop could still provide them. I took advantage of the fact that Sears, Roebuck could sell me 5.00-section tyres made for the Model A Ford and 4.50-section casings, artfully curved, made for motorcycles. Using the big Model A tyres on the rear gave longer-legged highway cruising but took its toll in acceleration — as I found to my dismay on the race track.

"Fuel pumps? I thought you'd never ask. I became reasonably competent at cleaning the points of the S.U. electric pump but it was never a device that could be relied upon. One summer evening I drove a gorgeous and adventurous Swedish lady, the mother of my friend Axel Rosenblad, from Princeton, New Jersey, into Manhattan. Where did the pump decide to quit? In the middle of the Lincoln Tunnel under the Hudson River! In the end-weekend rush hour!

"They're equipped for that sort of thing; they towed me out before I could get to grips with the pump. I can't recall if I fixed the S.U. or replaced it with one of the Autopulse and Stewart-Warner pumps I carried in the toolbox; I was always experimenting with pumps. Anyway, we got going again. Fortunately Mrs. Rosenblad considered the whole thing an utter hoot.

"A New York lady friend never tired of telling one story on me. We were driving cross-town in Manhattan when the TC hit a jouncing bump and I said, 'Oh!' She said, 'That's all right,' and I replied, 'No, I was worried about the car!' No wonder I never got to know her all that well.

Karl's friend Irene waves a cheery hello while they are driving around in the paddock after the 1954 event at Thompson Raceway in the #16 TC. This is probably the October race because they are dressed for fall weather (courtesy Karl Ludvigsen).

"In fact it was the ride that finally got me down. Slamming and banging over the unkempt roads and bridges of Brooklyn and Queens eventually lost its peculiar appeal. Some time in 1955-56 a dealer on the south side of Long Island accepted my TC in part exchange for a white long-door Triumph TR-2. It gave me a lot of pleasure, but I never raced it as I had the TC.

"I have many lovely memories of my first car. Putting my finger on the rear-view mirror to stop it from shaking so I could check for police cars. An indelible association in my mind, ever since, between 4,000 rpm and 60 mph. Zipping up the tonneau cover and sleeping under it to watch the races the next day. With Boris Said and Jim Hill (how did we seat three?) visiting all the foreign-car joints in Greater New York, Said urging me to greater speed. On a night in New Hampshire, switching off the headlamps and driving the back roads by moonlight.

"My TC experiences came in handy in 1957 when John Christy agreed to write *The MG Guide* for Jae Greenberg's Sports Car Press. John, my boss at the time at *Sports Cars Illustrated*, hadn't time to write it all so he asked me to contribute some chapters—

including the one on the TC. That began my involvement with car books that still continues more than four dozen years later.

"I just took a look at my file copy of the 1968 updating, *The New MG Guide*. It's autographed by John Thornley and Syd Enever, both of whom I met when I interviewed them for a major *Motor Trend* story on M.G.'s 50th anniversary.

"Come to think of it, I could do worse than to end these recollections as I did our book's chapter on the unforgettable TC: 'Just climb into a humble stock TC. Strip off the windscreen, shed the muffler and snap down a ¾ tonneau cover around you. Glance down at the big tach ticking impatiently between the spring spokes, then up at the headlights, radiator and the road ahead. Are you Dick Seaman, straining for the starting flag at Berne?' Could be!"

∾ Ebby Lunken ∾

Ebby Lunken was of the Cincinnati, Ohio, family that owned Lunken Airport. According to son E.B. Lunken, also a racing driver, the family had a succession of interesting cars even before World War II. "There was the '41 Packard limousine, complete with divider window and intercom, which we called 'Granny's Red Racer,'" E.B. recalls (it's pronounced "Ee Bee"), "and then there was the 1928 GMC station wagon, which I am slowly restoring now — that also belonged to my mother's mother, Grandmother Bachus. New floorboards and a tailgate have been made and we've re-done the side wood. All I have to do now is assemble it! I vaguely remember a convertible Buick during the war, though I was pretty little."

Ebby reportedly did a bit of racing before the war. While a student at Yale, he built a road-racing car on the chassis of the popular Willys model 77 car. He was racing it as an ARCA member with the Collier brothers when he had a crash that was featured in the newspapers. This came to the attention of his father, who telegrammed the stern message, "Get that thing back home!" So that was the end of Ebby's racing, at least prewar.

"As one of the few aviators who had plenty of flying experience before World War II," E.B. notes, "he had applied for combat assignments but was more valuable guarding the Canal Zone. Also stationed there were Chinese from the Chiang Kai-shek regime. At the same time that he was patrolling the Canal, he would teach the Chinese how to fly, in P-40 fighter planes. Later, at Waycross, Georgia, he instructed in P-51 Mustangs, and, at one point, tested the new P-59 jet plane, observing, 'It will do everything the P-51 will do, but not as well.'

"After the war, dad drove his father's 1941 fastback Cadillac. Then my dad got a '37 Cord Phaeton. It was a brand-new car, built in 1948 out of spare parts that were bought from various dealerships. Dad also got an MG-TC, a black one with red upholstery. I think he bought it from Chuck Hassan — he helped Chuck get started in business. I remember the car. I rode in it. It came in handy in the spring of '48 when the airport flooded. We used it to tow the Cord to a place where we could dry it out and get it started.

Rear three-quarter view of the Ebby Lunken MG-TC shows two conventional 19" wire wheels mounted for spares. The actual road wheels are 17" Borranis so, as Lunken's son E.B. notes, you have to change the tires on both sides in the event of a flat (courtesy Herb Kromholz, E.B. Lunken).

"During that time he also competed in air races. He bought P-51Ds war surplus. He bought three of them. I remember his brother-in-law Bud Marks got one from an Air National Guard unit and paid $1 for it. Dad raced in the 1947 and 1948 Bendix Cup (4th) and finished 3rd in '47."

The TC came in at the end of racing planes. It never saw competition, but soon after the war, Lunken became interested in sports car racing and bought two Aston Martins, both DB2s. "One of these, a right-hand-drive coupe, was purchased in 1951. I remember that we all drove up to my grandmother's house at Grosse Pointe in that car. I was supposed to watch for oncoming cars so we could pass. Later dad raced it at Vero Beach in 1952—his first race," notes E.B. "It spun a rod bearing because he ran the engine at 7000 rpm when the redline was 6500." The coupe was red. A favorite color of Lunken's was black with a red interior. The other Aston Martin, a convertible, was bought in 1953 and was not raced. It was just to go to the grocery store.

The next car Lunken got was a Ferrari—a 166 Barchetta (s/n 0054) bought in March of '52 from Bill Spear. At Vero Beach, Spear asked if he would like to buy it and he said, "I don't think I can afford it." To which Spear replied, "Maybe you can." In it, he accumulated enough points in the 2-liter class to be the national champion.

"In the summer of 1953," E.B. continues, "Dad bought Bill Simpson's Ferrari Barchetta s/n 0010 ex–Kimberly for about $500—Simpson was always having trouble with it." Then Ebby had Don Campbell rebuild the engine. He never raced it, and it was sold not long afterward. After the 166, he bought a 2.7 Ferrari 225 from Jim Kimberly in September of '53. By '53, Ebby Lunken was an official in the Ohio Valley Region of

Ebby Lunken's #43 Ferrari 166 leads an Allard at Elkhart Lake in 1952. This is the early street circuit and the car is on the main road that led to the town of Elkhart (courtesy E.B. Lunken).

the SCCA, and a competition driving instructor. In the 1953 race at Stout Field, Hassan drove the #0054 Barchetta and Ebby drove the Ferrari 225 #0220 2.7 liter that he bought from Kimberly.

Then, in the spring of '54 he bought Kimberly's Vignale-bodied 4.1 Ferrari; it was s/n 0204. Ebby and Walt Rye stripped the car down and color-coded the hydraulic lines. He also scalloped the area behind both the front and rear wheel wells, just as Kimberly had done on the 4.5. "Sundquist dished the fenders," says E.B. "Then it went to a guy named Doyle in Montgomery who did the paint — it was dark blue." Lunken put this Ferrari 340 #0324 on the pole at Road America in September of 1955 — it was an ex–Bill Spear car. At this race, Woody Johnston of the Cunningham team said to those assembled at Schwartz's Motel, "No one will ever get under 3 minutes on this course." But the next year, a Ferrari 500 TR turned 2 minutes 56 seconds.

When six of the area drivers began going to the races in their Ferraris, they became known as "The Cincinnati Gang." The men in this group were Edmund P. Lunken, John Quackenbush, Chuck Hassan, Howard Hively, Jim Johnston and Roger Bear (nicknamed "Cubby"). Over the years, they drove a variety of interesting cars including Hassan's Bandini and Ferrari Mondial, Hively's ex–Kimberly 4.9 Ferrari (s/n 0384), the two-liter Testa Rossas of Lunken, Johnston and Quackenbush ... as well as Lunken's 4.1 Ferrari (ex–Kimberly, ex–Chinetti Le Mans, s/n 0204), Roger Bear's 2.9 liter Vignale-bodied 250 (s/n 0390) and the Howard Hively/Richie Ginther 250 GT California (class-

Here Ferrari #70 is serviced during a 1953 endurance race at the McDill AFB. At the back, mechanic Don Campbell is putting gas into the 40-gallon tank with a 5-gallon can. There is another can next to helmeted Chuck Hassan, in the pit area getting ready to get into the car. Ebby Lunken is holding up the hood while fashionably wearing argyle socks and tasseled loafers (courtesy E.B. Lunken).

winning car at '59 Sebring). Bear's 2.9 was an ex–Hively car and he may have bought it new. Lunken's 4.1 was totaled when it came off the trailer on the way back from Lawrenceville. Then it was given to mechanic Walter Rye, who was able to rebuild it.

The Cincinnati Gang drove at Road America, Sebring, Nassau, Beverly, Akron, Lockbourne, Janesville, Lawrenceville, March Field, St. Joseph Airport, Smartt Field, etc. Three of them were aviators, notably Hively, who was a celebrated fighter pilot in the Eagle Squadron during World War II. Flying first Spitfires, then a P-47 and later a P-51, he scored 15 combat victories in the European Theater (Triple Ace) and received many decorations. Hively's racing cars were usually number 71 for the 71st Eagle Squadron, his old unit. Lunken, as mentioned, patrolled the Panama Canal and was a flight instructor, and Hassan was the personal pilot for Rear Admiral Felix Stump during the war, often flying him out to ships of the fleet in a Grumman amphibious plane.

A big season awaited Ebby Lunken and the group in 1956. But it did not begin auspiciously for him. At the Sebring 12-Hour race in March, he was supposed to drive the 4.4 Ferrari with Kimberly. But the 4.4 had a casting flaw in the head. It was only evident at racing speeds and it blew the coolant out. It could only be detected by watching the gauges and seeing the water temperature rise. So Ebby was out of a drive at

Ferrari #49 is seen at Sebring in 1953, approaching the hairpin turn. The Type 166 was driven by Ebby Lunken and Chuck Hassan to a class E first and 6th overall. This was the first year of the Sports Car World Championship, and the first points ever won for Ferrari. Walter Rye assisted in this win when a problem occurred with the battery connection. He took some solder that was used as a wheel weight and re-soldered the connection using the car's own battery as an arc welder, to keep it in the race (courtesy E.B. Lunken).

Sebring. "It was the first time I ever went to Sebring," says E.B. "I was 14 years old. My dad and I drove up from Miami airport with Walter Rye. Dad said, 'I'll bet I never get to sit in that car.' Well, other than sitting in it on jack stands in the paddock, he didn't. So the 4.4 didn't start. Dad did try a Lotus Eleven. It was Frank Baptista's car. He tried it for two laps and didn't like the car. Baptista drove it a couple more laps and then flipped it on the sand bank." Kimberly was a big Ferrari customer so they let him co-drive a factory car with Marquis de Portago. It was a new 3.4-liter 857 model. Their car went out after 137 laps. The exhaust system leaked and Kimberly was almost asphyxiated. The exhaust pipe had broken next to the foot well on the left side, burned a hole in the floor, and filled the area under the tonneau with exhaust gas. "In '56, Hawthorn and Fangio were there," E.B. adds. "So were Musso and Behra. Hively was there with the 4.9. He had Troy Rutmann as the co-driver. How did he do that? Hively may have picked up the phone and just asked him. But the 4.9 did not last."

At Road America 1956, in the event that would become the June Sprints, the third race was for F and E Modified. Ebby had his new Ferrari 500 Testa Rossa entered and so did Quackenbush and Johnston. Chuck Hassan was driving an older Ferrari Mondial.

Silly people do silly things: drivers with bowls on their heads include (left to right) Ted Boynton, Ebby Lunken and Porsche driver extraordinare Ed Crawford. In case you were wondering what could be done with a silver trophy, this is one suggestion. Carling's Black Label seems to be the beer of choice with this discerning crowd (courtesy E.B. Lunken).

There were six EM cars and four in the FM class. Unfortunately one of those was the new Porsche Spyder of West Coast pilot Jack McAfee, who had come east on a trip to get points toward the national championship. Then, too, there was the Porsche 550RS of Chicago ace Ed Crawford. These two took the lead immediately, followed closely by Lunken and Hassan in Ferraris. Hassan, in the older car, fell back in the pack while Quackenbush battled the 2-liter Maserati of Ted Boynton for 4th place. Lunken finished the race still 1st in EM and 3rd overall. "The finish of the Spyders," E.B. notes, "showed that a well-balanced car could be very fast."

On July 1, 1956, the Akron Airport sports car races were held (the 3rd annual). Race Seven was a 1-hour mini-enduro for F and E Modified cars and Chuck Hassan took the lead at the start, with Quackenbush passing him on the 7th lap. In 3rd was driver Don Sesslar in the Porsche 550RS sponsored by Cyrus Fulton of Lancaster, Ohio. Ebby Lunken was down in 4th place, ahead of Bob Fergus in a Porsche Spyder and Roger Bear in the Ferrari 250. Quackenbush held the lead to the end and finished ahead of Hassan by 18 seconds.

Smartt Field, near St. Charles, Missouri, had been a training field for the Naval Reserve during World War II. The Navy pilots would practice their take-offs and landings there so they wouldn't tie up the main airport, Lambert Field in St. Louis. The event was October 7, 1956. In Race Two, for over 1500cc modified, Lunken was leading until his oil sump plug came out. Fortunately, he spun out of the race, saving the engine. E.B. Lunken confirms the likelihood that his dad probably spun in his own oil. This was a special 2.5 engine that replaced the 2-liter engine that had swallowed a valve at Road America. When he called Luigi Chinetti to get a replacement he was told, "I'm terribly sorry, Mister Lunken, we do not have a spare two-liter engine. We only have a two and a half liter Grand Prix engine, but it will fit right in." Lunken ran again in Race Six, handily winning the event. With the larger engine, he was now in the D-Modified class.

As the final event in the '56 season, Lunken went to Nassau Bahamas Speed Week in December. Nassau had a huge number of races, 14 to be exact. In the 2nd Governor's Heat Race for classes B, C & D, Lunken's Testa Rossa finished 9th behind Maquis de Portago's 860 Monza. In the 3rd Governor's Trophy Race, also December 7, Lunken just edged out Jim Jeffords in his factory-sponsored Corvette. Jeffords finished ahead of six Ferraris and noted: "I remember the Cincinnati Gang. They were a fun group. In those days, people who ran those cars—the Ferraris—had the money to buy one. If you didn't, you had to put on an important drive. You had to blow off those Ferraris. So we in the Corvettes were more motivated." Of the three cars fielded at Nassau by the Cincinnati Gang, all had good finishes in their class, not only Lunken but Chuck Hassan and particularly Howard Hively in his new 500 Testa Rossa, who beat Ken Miles, Ed Crawford and Masten Gregory in one of the races. Ebby Lunken was running up with Stirling Moss in one race, until something broke on the Testa Rossa.

High-angle photograph of Ferrari #14 at Sebring in 1959. It's a pontoon fender 250 Testa Rossa. The unknown driver in the foreground is wearing the patch of the Scuderia D.O.M. "Dirty Old Men" Racing Team (courtesy E.B. Lunken).

Lunken's bad luck at Sebring continued in 1957, as the 2-liter Ferrari 500 TRC that he co-drove with Chuck Hassan went out on the 143rd lap. "They lost the clutch early on, drove without it," says E.B., "and then something else went." Earlier in the race he had been helped by the crew of Jim Kimberly's retired Maserati 200S, as flood lamps and other equipment were lent to the effort. Late in '57 he had a much better finish:

3rd in class and 7th overall in the September 7 Road America 500, with Chuck Hassan as co-driver in the Ferrari Testa Rossa.

"Dad's 500 TR was sold to Jimmy Johnston early in 1957," says E.B. "It had swallowed a valve in the 2-liter at Road America in '56 and then the 2.5 engine was put in it. Dad got a 500 TRC in '57. He kept that until the fall of '57. Then he sold it and got out of racing, at least in his own cars. Johnston got a 250 Testa Rossa in '58. Dad drove that car at Road America with Jimmie Johnston and they did well, with a 1st in D-Modified, 2nd overall and 3rd on Index of Performance. His last race was in '59 at Sebring in the same car with Jimmie, Augie Pabst and Gaston Andrey. Johnston had a back problem so he didn't drive." The car was 7th overall and 4th in class.

Meanwhile, in 1957, Eb Lunken had become more involved in the SCCA organization, and was elected Contest Board Chairman when Jim Kimberly was the president. Like Kimberly, Lunken was very safety-minded. Not everyone knows that Kimberly worked with the Snell Institute to get safer helmets, mandated roll bars and tightened up on licensing requirements. That year they visited Tony Hulman at Indianapolis. "Back then," Lunken said, "they had the pits right on the track. So I said, 'Tony, why don't you move the pits back away from the track? It would be a lot safer for everyone.' By the next time they ran the 500, the pits were moved back, with a wall between the pit road and the track."

After the one race in 1959, Ebby Lunken wrapped up his eight years on road courses. "Didn't he get back into airplanes then?" we ask. "He never got out of airplanes," says E.B. "He had several P-51s." Besides driving race cars, Ebby Lunken loved to fly. Then after the planes, it was back to cars in the early '80s with a 275 GTB/4, a 365 GTC, a 500 Superfast, a 365 GT 2+2 and a 400i. He also had some classic cars: two Aston Martin Ulsters, a 1934 and a '35; a '31 Invicta — "the low one," says E.B., "the epitome of the English sports car of the '30s"; a Lagonda and a 1937 Cord Replica. The first of his father's cars that EB drove was the '57 Ferrari TRC. It was at the Lawrenceville Airport. "I mistook my father's instructions to drive 'over 3000' and drove under 3000 rpm — I fouled all 8 plugs in the twin-plug engine." Which were his favorites? "I liked the 275 GTB/4 and I liked the '31 Invicta."

∞ Sandy MacArthur ∞

As Fred Egloff notes, "Ed 'Sandy' MacArthur raced at the early Chicago Region races. He was eventually RE of the SCCA Indianapolis Region. He organized the revival of the Wilmot Hills course with a fundraiser. He was very active in Class H — Nardi, Giuar, etc."

Henry Adamson, the Midwest racing historian, knew Sandy well. "He was in World War II in the Army," Adamson begins, "in the Solomons. He was in the South Pacific in Admiral Halsey's command. He took care of the IBM machines — their punch cards were used to track data. He went to Guadalcanal after it was neutralized, and to New

Sandy MacArthur brakes for a corner at the old Milwaukee Fairgrounds in the #89 Giaur. This make vied with Bandini for the title of the lightest 750-engined car. It was built for the Italian Formula 3 class (750cc, not 500). Twist a few Dzus fasteners and all the fenders come off, making it a formula car (courtesy Sandy MacArthur).

Caledonia. He was shipped to the Philippines in 1945 to be in General Stillwell's army for the invasion of Japan.

"After returning from military service," Adamson continues, "Sandy went back to college and got a degree at Lake Forest — he had started before the war at the University of Michigan. He bought a used MG in 1950. It was a TC but I don't remember whether it was red or black. He joined the Chicago Region about then, and he had a bunch of friends including Bud Seaverns, Dick Templeton and Baird Sheldon. They all knew Fred Wacker, who had a garage on Waukegan Road in Lake Bluff. They used to go over there on Thursday nights to lie about their driving exploits and pretend to work on their cars. Around this time Sandy put a supercharger on his MG. After a visit to his family's summer cottage at Desbarates, Illinois, or what we call 'Lake Forest on the Rocks,' he drove through the Upper Peninsula to go to Elkhart Lake, where he drove in the first event there."

MacArthur worked for one of his father's insurance companies. He didn't like the job and he wasn't interested in insurance. To use the MG as an everyday driver, Sandy removed the supercharger. Shortly afterward, he broke a crankshaft, but it was broken in such a way that it could still be driven ... at least for a short while before replacement. Besides working in insurance, he looked after his father's real estate interests. One of

Here is the Moretti-engined Giaur of Sandy MacArthur on the line for a run in the Blackhawk State Park Hillclimb in 1956. "The car, of course," says Sandy, "was MacArthur racing green!" The double-overhead-camshaft Moretti engine had four cylinders with two Webers and about 70 hp for 750cc (courtesy Sandy MacArthur).

these buildings had been a convent and an old Greek man was living in it. Seeing MacArthur in the TC, he said, "I don't know why anyone would want to drive a Jeep."

Adamson continues, "[MacArthur's] family owed some land in western Pennsylvania so he lived there for awhile. He met his wife there. Then he came back to Illinois and the insurance company for awhile. His grandparents let him have a small company that made surgical instruments, in Indianapolis. They made forceps, scalpels and scissors. They had a catalog of standard and specialized instruments—a good part of the business was in making special instruments for customers. The company was not doing well and Sandy brought it into the black. They did a very good business during the Korean War.

"About that time, in the early fifties, Sandy sold off the MG and got a Jaguar. But he didn't want to race a production car. That's when he built the first H-Modified Sparrow Mark I. There are two others, both partially complete. It had a ladder frame of chrome moly tube and a planar front end with the wishbone on the top and the transverse leaf spring on the bottom. It had a Crosley engine, MG transmission and Fiat rear axle. Joe Silnes, a circle track metal fabricator, made the body for the car. With five Dzus fasteners, you could remove the body."

To say the car was rugged is an understatement. The car was titled for the road

Here's Sandy MacArthur racing in the rain in his Bandini with a 4-cylinder-inline Mercury outboard engine. He's at Milwaukee Fairgrounds in 1955 (courtesy Sandy MacArthur).

and one spring morning while driving, MacArthur ran into a Cadillac. Luckily no one was hurt and, Sandy noted with pride, the frame wasn't even bent. After the Sparrow special, he got a Bandini and a Giuar with a Mercury outboard engine. It was followed by a 750 Stanguellini, also powered by a Mercury motor obtained free from Carl Keikhaefer. This was the Herm Behm car, and he drove it with Carl Haas in the 1957 Sebring race, placing 1st in class and 28th overall. The entrant was Behm Motors, Oshkosh, Wisconsin, same as the Stanguellini entrant for the 1958 race, which was an 1100cc Sports model driven to 4th in class and 21st overall by Carl Haas, Alan Ross and Suzy Dietrich. To enter the 1959 Sebring race, he bought a very nice envelope body G-Modified car and drove the #66 car with co-driver Rob Rollason. A collision with a bridge support instantly reduced the value of the new machine from $6000 to $600 when the wreck was sold to Lou Laflin.

"In 1958, Sandy went to Belgium with his family," Henry Adamson notes. "While in Europe, he went to the factory and met Mr. Stanguellini. There he bought the first Formula Juniors. He sold six of them in the Chicago area. Later, Alfred Momo was given the East Coast distribution for the cars. Mr. Stanguellini thought that Lake Forest was on the West Coast. These are in the John de Boer Etcetereni Register. The Giuar is now in Texas and the Bandini is with Cliff Reutter.

"Over the years, Sandy raced at Elkhart Lake, Road American, Put-in-Bay, Watkins Glen, Bridgehampton, Lime Rock, the SAC bases, Chanute — which was not a SAC base, Dodge City Airport in Kansas (1956), Sebring, Nassau Bahamas and Wilmot Hills. Wilmot is there because of him. In 1954, the racing surface was disintegrating. Sandy raised the money to have it repaved.

"Sandy MacArthur was a well-known Bugatti enthusiast. He owned three. One was a Type 35A that was imported as a Type 37 and owned by Clevelander Edsel Pfabe. It starts to get complicated when we note that this car was converted into a Type 35B. VSCDA founder John Kleen later owned that 35B and sold it three years ago. MacArthur also had two Type 40s. One was two cars put together into a configuration with some Type 57 features. In 1987, Sandy put together the first all-Bugatti vintage race, at Road America."

He was a great enthusiast. He had a lot of friends. He had some interesting cars. He had a good life. Nothing wrong with that.

∾ Henry Manney III ∾

Henry Manney became a ballet dancer on the advice of his doctor, for back pain. He remained one as a way of following his girlfriend around. He later married Annie. According to their daughter Cecilia, Annie Manney was a Russian-trained ballerina; she and Henry toured South America with a dance troupe. From 1947 to 1950 they lived in the Hollywood Hills and then moved to the house on the beach, where they lived from 1951 to 1953. Al Moss, a friend of his, remembers that Henry had an MG-TC. "It was early 1949," says Al, "about when I started my shop. He didn't race the TC. It had been repainted white — not cream." Shortly after that he had a Healey Westland, the 4-passenger roadster that preceded the Silverstone. He bought it from Donald Healey for the huge price of $7500. According to Jim Sitz, Manney ran this at the Sandberg Hillclimb and a drag race — Sandberg was on the old highway from L.A. to Bakersfield, California.

He joined SCCA in May of 1950. After that he got a Jag 120 that he ran at Palm Springs in 1951. Then he got a Crosley Hot Shot, race prepared by Ernie McAfee. "He ran it at Palm Springs," notes Moss. "He was missing for a couple of laps and then came into the pits. 'Better check the oil,' he told McAfee, as he explained that the car was rolled and then rolled back over."

"Somewhere in there," notes Jim Sitz, "Henry bought a Lancia Aurelia coupe from Bill Spear. Spear trailered it out to Offut AFB in Omaha and then Jack McAfee brought it the rest of the way. McAfee won the race with Tony Paravanno's 4.5 Ferrari. Manney was of a well-to-do family and soon bought himself a 4.1 Ferrari. He scared himself in it," Sitz recalls, "so he gave it to Ernie McAfee to sell, and they built a Crosley Special." Al Moss suggests this was probably the "George" car, named after the popular expression "That's real George." With a Murray Nichols fiberglass body, it was raced at Pebble Beach a couple of times.

After that he got a Ferrari 195 coupe. It was the famous ex–Cunningham "little blue coupe" that Phil Walters used to terrorize Erwin Goldschmidt at Bridgehampton.

This is not a racing car. Henry Manney occasionally enjoyed posing with an eccentric machine such as this home-market-only Renault R4L, styled by the local brick factory. Posing at the rear door is *Road & Track* staffer Dennis Shattuck (courtesy *Road & Track*).

Manney raced this at Madera and had many adventures including Al Moss's recollection of his blowing off a Jaguar on the long steep climb of California's Ridge Route. His last, and best, racing car was a Siata Spyder that he drove to 1st in class at Moffett Field and at March Field, both in 1953. Then he moved to Paris with Annie and covered races, first for *MotorRacing* newsletter and then for *Road & Track*. As one who learned Italian from listening to operas, says daughter Cecilia, his command of the language was amusing to the Italian mechanics, and it frequently had them in stitches. The last race he drove, Jim Sitz tells us, was the last Mille Miglia, 50 years ago, in an Alfa Giulietta Sprint.

    Manney was one of those rare persons like Alix Lafontant, who could take pictures and write at the same race, and come up with a cogent description of the event. He had a Mamiyaflex camera. He developed a freestyle language all his own with expressions like "Pheel Heel," which we all took to be a Frenchified "Phil Hill." It was a brave way of writing and many people found it refreshing; some thought he was the best auto writer there was. Yes, he fell into the class of really good writers like Antoinne de St. Exupery, Jack Kerouac and David Ogilvy. After Europe, Henry and Annie Manney moved to California in 1966.

Left: Leaning into the camera, pipe clenched firmly in his determined jaws, Henry Manney appears to be saying something. Perhaps it's about racing. *Right:* Few could master the furtive glance as Henry Manney could. In fact, this glance is very furtive (courtesy *Road & Track*).

Jim Sitz remembers, "I was at *R&T* when Henry arrived home to stay. He and Jesse Alexander and Phil Hill all came home from Europe at about the same time. Henry and Annie bought a nice little house south of Newport Beach in Corona del Mar. He told me at lunch in October of 1967 that he had a little problem — he had two Ferrari coupes and one had to go: a 330 GT road car, ex–John Surtees, or a 250 GTO, the Jean Guchet 3rd place Le Mans car. Take your choice — $6000 for either one." Tom Bryant says that the price was most of a year's salary then. According to Al Moss, they were thinking of going to Santa Barbara when Henry got sick ... but they never did. Tom Bryant would go to the VA hospital to read and play music. After that we lost Henry Manney.

∽ Don Marsh ∽

The highlight of Don Marsh's driving career was being the IMSA Camel Lights class winner of the Daytona 24-hour race with his son Kelly in a 2-rotor Mazda-powered Argo JM16, in 1985. He repeated the feat at Road America that year, but let's back up to 1952. Before wheel-to-wheel racing, Don competed at the Bainbridge, Ohio, hillclimb (1st CL, MG-TD) and then the Columbus Acceleration Trials (3rd CL E-Mod, supercharged MG). Then came racing at airports and road courses. "I went to Cumberland, Maryland, for my first novice outing, in a 'TC — I still have that car. I won the race and they gave me the *Auto Age* Trophy for the Outstanding Novice. That was all the encouragement I needed. On August 9, 1953, I drove at Lockbourne AFB in MG #24 and took second to Bob Fergus. Then I took Bob Fergus's MG to Stout Field near St. Louis. I was late and had no practice but they let me race anyway. Ralph Durbin from Detroit said, 'Follow me.' I did, and won that race.

"In the 1954 season, I got the Lester MG that I later sold to Chuck Dietrich. We

Bob Fergus (MG-TC #21) leads Don Marsh (MG-TC #24) at Lockbourne AFB, August 9, 1953. Fergus and Marsh were teammates and friends for over fifty years in racing (courtesy Alix Lafontant © Carl Goodwin).

took it apart and took the wood out of the body frame. We replaced that with a tube steel frame. Ray Leo in Columbus was a midget car builder and he did the work. He also built a new nose for it. The Lester was an original Monkey Stable car, on Meyer's team in England, built on a TB frame ... not the later one that Duncan Black had, which was built on a TD frame with independent suspension. It weighed about 1300 pounds. We changed the wheels to 15-inch wires, from 19" in the front and 16" rears. In '54 we raced it at Cumberland, Giants Despair and Brynfan Tyddyn, where we were 2nd but DNF'd. We never finished a race with that car, then it sat in my barn until we sold it to Chuck in about 1955.

"I did nothing in racing until 1977. Then we got interested in vintage. We had some cars so we went to Sebring with a GT40 and a J2X Cad-Allard. We broke everything we took. So we figured we'd better prepare the cars. We also had an Elva Porsche, a 910 and a 908. My son Kelly drove the GT40 and the 908 and I drove the Elva, the 910 and a Porsche 550A. Next we thought, 'It's hard to get parts for these old cars,' so in '83 we went into 'real' racing. We rented a car from Jim Trueman, a GTU Mazda, and then we bought one and then got the Argo."

⚘ JACK MCAFEE ⚘

Jack actually started racing in sprint cars, but soon found out that the professionals were not clean drivers. "There was too much of this 'You cut me off' business," Jack said, "and I just didn't want to race that way. After I started in sports cars, I would never go back to sprint cars." Longtime racing enthusiast Jim Sitz notes that McAfee went up and down the coast racing on dirt tracks before he quit.

When he switched to sports cars, he got a ride in a John Edgar MG. "It was a supercharged car with cycle fenders," says Sitz. "He started driving it at Palm Springs in 1950. In '51 the car was rebodied in aluminum by Emil Deitz. There was a rumor that, for the money Edgar had in the MG, he could have bought a Ferrari."

In 1950, Jack drove a 1949 Cadillac in the Panamerican Road Race, for Tony Paravano. He placed 11th out of 53 cars in the sedan class. Then they went to Palm Springs, where he drove the Cadillac in a production class. "Tony immediately realized he needed a true sports car to run in road races," says Rex McAfee. At Palm Springs, Paravano spied his first Jag XK-120. "We gotta get one of those," he said to McAfee. They got a red one and, according to Jim Sitz, paid a hefty premium for the popular car. Jack raced it at Santa Anna on June 25, 1950, the first day of the Korean War.

Jack McAfee flying up the hill in John Edgar's blown MG, number 88, during the Sandberg Hillclimb in 1951. Soon afterward, streamlined bodywork would be installed on the car, which greatly improved its top speed in future road racing events (courtesy Bob Canaan).

Jack McAfee was always a fierce competitor and always drove with precision. This special-bodied MG-TC is hard to recognize as such but its red streamlined body was a familiar sight at West Coast road racing events for many years (courtesy Bob Canaan).

He was towing Johnny Crean's MG Special back from racing at Elkhart Lake in 1952 when he stopped on the way at Aspen, Colorado. "Why don't you run the MG?" they asked. He did, and won the event, which was also entered by Danny Collins from Denver. After the MGs and Jags, he drove a Siata Gran Sport briefly and won a 1952 race at Palm Springs in it.

Then he moved on up to a 4.1 Ferrari and a 4.5. The 4.1 was fielded by John Edgar and raced mainly on the West Coast, the first event being at Stockton in August of 1952, where he placed 2nd to the Allard of Sam Weiss. He drove that car through the 1953 season and then drove a 4.5 Ferrari for Tony Paravano, winning important races at Golden Gate and at Offut AFB, the Omaha SAC base.

Jack was often confused with Ernie McAfee, but they were not related. Ernie was an importer of the interesting little Etceterini cars—Siata, Moretti, Nardi, Bandini and a few others as he was able to obtain them, often from Tony Pompeo on the East Coast. Ernie was also a top-ranked driver, but he unfortunately lost his life in 1956, at the wheel of a 4.4 Ferrari at Pebble Beach.

Jack was a Porsche dealer, and when the Porsche Spyders came out, John Edgar ordered one from Jack, for Jack. Edgar entered it in some races out east, along with a Ferrari for Carroll Shelby to drive.

At speed in the #88 Porsche Spyder is Jack McAfee at the 1956 Palm Springs race (Jack McAfee collection, courtesy Rex McAfee).

It was in this car that McAfee made his reputation. At Cumberland, Maryland, he nearly beat Walt Hansgen in a D-Jag and he posted an easy second place to Shelby at Brynfan Tyddyn. Among other things, he inspired Bob Holbert to get a Porsche Spyder. On the eastern swing, Jack also drove at the Giants Despair hillclimb, Lime Rock, the Beverly, Massachusetts, airport and Elkhart Lake. In 1955, Jack was 26th in the national points standing, with 500 points. In 1956, Jack was 1st with 7250 points and the SCCA National Championship in F-Modified, and the 2nd-place car had 2730 points.

In 1957 and '58, he did a little racing in a Porsche, but was definitely tapering off. As Rex McAfee, Jack's son, notes: "John Edgar wanted to go national again in 1957, but my dad said he couldn't — he was moving his dealership from Sherman Oaks to Burbank. Then, in 1958, Stan Sugarman, a Phoenix housing developer, bought the Porsches from John Edgar. My dad recommended bringing Vasek Polak from the East Coast to work on them. Dad drove the Stan Sugarman Porsche locally and won the West Coast Championship."

In 1959 he concentrated on building his dealership and his only race was Sebring. There he co-drove an RSK with Ken Miles to an 8th overall ahead of Richie Ginther and ex-fighter pilot Howard Hively in a Ferrari California. The RSK, which was 3rd in Class F, had been entered by Precision Motors of Los Angeles.

In 1961, Jack drove a Lotus 20 Formula Junior and had several wins, at Laguna

Seca, Pomona and elsewhere. The Lotus was owned by Harry Jones and, with it, Jack won the West Coast Championship in FJ. His last season of racing, according to Jim Sitz, was 1962, when he ran a Porsche RSK at Riverside and Pomona. He also ran the Lotus, including a race at Nassau, but the car burnt a piston and DNF'd.

After many years of racing, Jack retired to run his Porsche-VW agency. He was a popular figure at vintage races and writers' clubs like the Motor Press Guild.

❦ STEVE McQUEEN ❦

After three years in the Marine Corps, Steve McQueen became an aspiring actor in live theatre in New York, in 1952. He got a couple of bit parts and then he was able to afford an MG and he got a 'TC. It was white, or actually ivory. According to Matt Stone, who wrote the book *McQueen's Machines: The Cars and Bikes of a Hollywood Icon*, the actor found the car in Columbus, Ohio, sent in payments and later drove it to New York. There are some streets in Manhattan that will break the axle of a TC and, after busting three of them and an undetermined number of spokes on the 19" wire wheels, McQueen sold the MG.

By 1956, he had moved from off–Broadway up to Broadway, and at the end of the play, he went to Hollywood and got some parts in western movies and TV shows. He soon bought an Austin-Healey, which he had for a short time, and a Corvette, which his first wife crashed.

Then he bought a Siata 208S. This is as close as you can get to a Ferrari without actually having one. In fact, McQueen used to tell people it was one. It has a 2-liter V-8 that sounds better than anything you can name, plus four-wheel independent suspension, big brakes, Borrani wire wheels and a great-looking aluminum body. Siata 208s were a force in early SCCA racing and one later won a national championship. McQueen's car was silver when he owned it.

The Siata was followed by a black Porsche Speedster — according to racing photographer Jim Sitz, this was in 1959. It's still owned by McQueen's son Chad. The 1958 car had a 1600 Super engine and was raced in F-Production as #71 at Southern California SCCA events, at circuits including Willow Springs, Del Mar and Riverside, notching three wins in three events. For racing, he removed the bumpers, installed a cut-down windscreen and put in a roll bar. He bought, sold and repurchased this car.

Meanwhile, in 1959 he bought a silver Lotus 11 sports racing car, according to Beverly Chamberlain, wife of West Coast Lotus importer Jay Chamberlain. But McQueen didn't buy it from Chamberlain — he might have bought it from the factory, or even from Tony Pompeo, who was selling Lotus 6s, 9s and 11s on the East Coast. He raced the G-Modified car at Del Mar, on the north side of San Diego, and at Santa Barbara, in both events as car #33. At the latter, racing against Frank Monise in the #37 Lotus 11, he finished 4th; at Del Mar, he had a DNF.

Beverly and Jay also knew actor James Dean and she notes that after Dean's death in a racing car — even though it was not on the track — the studios really cracked down

The first sports car for Steve McQueen was this MG TC, which he found in Columbus, Ohio, and drove to New York City, where he worked as a stage actor (Chad McQueen collection).

on actors racing. In 1960, McQueen had a TV western series, *Wanted: Dead or Alive*, and filmed *The Magnificent Seven*. The studio insisted he quit racing, and he sold the Lotus.

As Steve McQueen got these bigger and better parts, he was able to buy a Jaguar XK-SS. This is the road version of the D-Type racing car that won Le Mans three times: 1955, '56 and '57. With the right gearing, these cars were good for close to 180 mph. Lucky for McQueen, the studio didn't know this. They just thought it was a stylish what-you-may-call-it. Construction of these great cars was a lightweight monocoque tub with tubular steel sub-frames at the ends. The engine was the traditional Jag six with racing cams and side-draft Weber carburetors. Road equipment included a full-width windscreen, folding top and luggage rack. The original owner was Jim Peterson, who built Riverside Raceway.

According to *Motor Trend* editor Matt Stone, McQueen used to exercise his cars, including the XK-SS, on Mulholland Drive, a popular place for "midnight practice." As Stone describes the view south, "All of Los Angeles lies before you, like a giant ant farm." The winding road goes for miles. Sort of like Chagrin River Road on an incline.

In 1961, McQueen went to England to film an obscure movie titled *The War Lover*. Out of sight of the studio brass, he raced a Mini-Cooper, finishing 5th at Oulton Park, not-so-well at Aintree and 3rd at Brands Hatch. Also in England, he bought a Cooper

Formula Junior (T52) from John and Charles Cooper. They are the people who really set the direction for the modern race car. The T52 is the first of four FJs that the Surbiton constructor made. After the filming of *The War Lover*, McQueen brought the Cooper back to the States with him and, when his TV series *Wanted: Dead or Alive* finished, he was free to race it, which he did at Del Mar (April '62; won two races), Cotati and Santa Barbara, where the fun came to a halt as the studio served him with a restraining order prior to filming of *The Great Escape*. This film classic has the motorcycle chase and the great jump scene. McQueen did the chase scene himself and cycle guru Bud Ekins did the jump. Later, there would be another good chase scene, in the film *Bullitt*.

He'd met Stirling Moss in England. Moss and John Cooper got him invited to drive at Sebring in 1962, as a member of the BMC team. There were two events: a 3-Hour race for production cars, and the 12-Hour event. In the first one, team cars were Austin-Healey Sprites. McQueen was teamed with Moss, Pedro Rodriguez and Innes Ireland. On a wet course, he finished 9th of 28 cars. Then, in the 12-Hour race, he drove a modified Sprite with fastback coupe bodywork. His co-driver was John Colgate of the toothpaste company. At the 6-hour mark, the car was leading its class. But at the 7th hour, the car threw a connecting rod with Colgate at the wheel and the car was out of the race.

After the filming of *The Great Escape* and *The Sand Pebbles*, McQueen discovered off-road racing though his bike friends Dave and Bud Ekins, who had been racing in the desert since 1962. He began to compete in a car called the Baja Boot. This machine, designed and built by well-known off-roader Vic Hickey, had a mid-mounted Olds V-8, full roll cage and big balloon tires. The first big race, notes Matt Stone, was the Stardust 7–11, June 13, 1968, in Las Vegas. The car was entered by Solar Productions, a company he had formed. But the racer DNF'd with a broken axle. Then it was a matter of "sitting in the desert until help came." In the 1969 Baja 1000, McQueen was in second, chasing James Garner, when a transmission part failed at about 300 miles.

With the making of *The Thomas Crown Affair* and *Bullitt*, McQueen was at the height of his career. Also in 1969, the Solar Productions team went to Le Mans in preparation for the filming of a movie. As noted in *McQueen's Machines*, Solar purchased the Porsche

Steve McQueen in his driver's suit during the filming of *Le Mans* (courtesy *Motor Trend* magazine).

908 that Brian Redman and Jo Siffert had driven in the race. McQueen intended to do his own driving in the movie and wanted to familiarize himself with a car of that performance capability. After a few warm-up races, he planned to drive at the 1970 12 Hours of Sebring.

Former Porsche dealer and national racing champion Chuck Stoddard has driven the 908 and describes it as "a wonderful car — handles very well — like a little roller skate. The first 908s were coupes. Then the factory decided to make a lightweight spyder, the second version. It was the 908/02 — the '02 cars won a tremendous number of races. Half of the races in Porsche's first 917 championship were won by 908s. Top speed, of course, depends on the way you gear them, but the 917 will go 235–240 mph at Le Mans and the 908 will not go 200, but close. On a track like Brands Hatch, a 908 will beat a 917. Horsepower was 120 per liter or 360, and it weighed 1300 pounds. Don't over-rev it — it'll zip to 9000 in a second. 8400 to 8500 is about right. They're very reliable and fun to drive. I think McQueen and Revson finished second at Sebring. Steve was no match for Brian Redman but he was a very good driver. They drove conservatively and finished the race."

We've all seen movies about racing that lacked the ring of authenticity. But McQueen wanted to make the ultimate in a realistic picture about our sport. He found a great appeal in the heroic long-distance races and decided to make a film about the greatest of them all, Le Mans. In an interview for *Motor Trend*, Matt Stone learned that McQueen wanted to give the audience the feeling of going 220 mph in a racing car. To this end, Solar Productions devised several entirely new methods of filming a race. They were not just at the apex of corner four, they were in the car, on the car, beside the car, with camera mounts that no one had ever thought of before.

The production company acquired its own fleet of state-of-the-art racing cars, namely three Porsche 917s, four Ferrari 512s, an Alfa T33, a Ford GT-40, a V-12 Matra 650, two Lola T-70s and a few others, a total of about 25, including the 908, which had been made into a camera car. The production was expensive and more difficult than anyone had imagined. McQueen himself did not do any of the driving, as he had hoped, except in post-race filming. If he were injured, the production of *Le Mans* would have been delayed or even canceled. There was another corporate entity, namely the Cinema Center Films, so it was not only the decision of Solar Productions. At the end of it all and now in retrospect, *Le Mans* stands as one of the greatest motor racing films ever made.

During the time that McQueen was making the movie *Le Mans*, he was driving an Allard around town. Beverly Chamberlain doesn't recall exactly which Allard, but she said it had cycle fenders. It was probably a J2X, Chrysler-powered. Oh, the list is long of wonderful cars one might buy with the taste and the money McQueen had: Ferrari Lusso, Ferrari 275 GTS, Ferrari NART Spyder, Mini-Cooper, Porsche 911S, Porsche 911E, Porsche 930, Corvette Sting Ray, Rolls-Royce Silver Shadow, Mercedes 6.3 and many more. And this doesn't include all the motorcycles. That's another subject for another time. Oh, and the airplanes, too.

There isn't much doubt that Steve McQueen would have done a lot more racing if not for the worrywartism of movie studio executives. And don't forget, these were the years of great advances in racing safety: not just roll bars and seat belts, but Snell Foundation helmets, Nomex driving suits, fuel cells, remote fire systems, improved barriers and track design. It was getting safer all the time. The great irony of it all is that the race car didn't kill him. The race car was his friend. It was cancer that brought him down. And he was only fifty.

✜ Ken Miles ✜

The builder and driver of the famous Miles MG Shingles drove a stock MG first then the R1 and R2 MG Specials, then a Porsche, then a Cobra and a GT40. Miles was born in 1918 and was a World War II combat veteran, a tank commander in the British Army. After the war, he tried to get into racing in England, with a Mercury flathead-engined Frazer-Nash. He called it "the 5-lap wonder." Then a school friend, John Beasley, offered him a job in America. Beasley was president of Gough Industries, the MG distributor on the West Coast. Ken would manage the service department for them. He was determined to assimilate and later became an American citizen. America gave him the opportunities he could not get in England.

Ken Miles in the #5 R-1 MG won every event from the April 1953 debut to March 1954. Here he is leading an October 1953 race at Reeves Field at Terminal Island. The event was put on by the Long Beach MG Club. Besides winning his class, he placed 2nd in the main event, to Bill Stroppe's Kurtis. This shot was taken by Jim Sitz with a 2¼ format Rollei camera (courtesy Jim Sitz).

Top: The #50 MG Special is Ken Miles's R-2, which won races from March 1955 to October 1955, finally beaten October 30 at Sacramento by Pete Lovely in the "Pooper," a Porsche-engined 800-pound Cooper. Here Miles is at the Santa Barbara Airport, May 29, 1955. This shot was taken by Jim Sitz with a 4 × 5" Linhoff studio camera (courtesy Jim Sitz). *Bottom:* Ken Miles in his MG Special soon was sweeping the rest of the 1500cc class away as he won most of the races he entered. Miles, because of his driving skill, more than once finished third in the main event, ahead of cars with double the power of his small MG (courtesy Bob Canaan).

Here's a great Jim Sitz photograph of Ken Miles in the #50 Porsche RSK Spyder, flying along at Laguna Seca in 1959 (courtesy Jim Sitz).

"His first race in the U.S.A. was at Pebble Beach in 1952, driving a cream-colored TD. Then on April 19, 1953, a wet rainy day at Pebble Beach, I had my first sight of Ken Miles, winning in a car built by himself and friends," says photographer Jim Sitz, "beating the best Italian and German cars. It was the first race for the MG Special and the car to beat was the OSCA. In 1955, after the Porsche Spyder came out, we all figured MG was washed up. Other fans thought it was the rain, and his ability as a driver in the rain, but as the year went by he just kept winning, and would do so the next year until finally, on the last day of October, 1955, he was beaten by Pete Lovely in a Cooper-Porsche. That was the final race for Ken in the MG at Sacramento Fairgrounds, and then he joined the Ecurie von Neumann to drive the Porsche 550.

"Ken could do it all — build the car, drive it to win and lay out a course like Willow Springs, carved from desert land with a bulldozer. He and Bill Pollack laid out the course, then an earthmover constructed it. Miles could run the Cal Club, organize a race or tech inspection ... and in his spare time operate a drivers' school with partner Sam Hanks and also write a column for *Competition Press*. This sort of versatile ability would be a valuable asset at Shelby American, where he finally found a home after drifting from job to job. His own effort to run a shop failed but many afternoons in 1961 I would drive my beat-up 356 Porsche and enjoy a cuppa with Mr. Miles. Most any story he would tell would be funny, no matter. I still miss him."

Miles figured heavily in development of many Shelby cars, including the 427 Cobra, and played a major role in the 350GT Shelby Mustang and the GT40, which

Ken Miles in Cobra #33 leads teammate Dave McDonald in #97 at the June 30, 1963, USRRC Manufacturers' Championship Series, Watkins Glen (courtesy Alix Lafontant).

Shelby took over from John Wyer—Miles and Lloyd Ruby won at Daytona in the car's first race. Ken Miles, sadly, was killed testing the Ford Mark IV prototype at Riverside Raceway in August of 1966, at the age of 47. That was after the production people at Ford took over the racing program and failed to magnaflux a suspension part. There's no telling what he could have done had he lived—possibly a Formula One drive, but no one will ever know.

∽ Bill Milliken ∽

"Did you start out in an MG, Bill?"

"Yeah. I did. I was down in New York City, at the Lexington Hotel, where I usually stayed. It was early autumn, in 1945, and I was enjoying the weather. All of a sudden an MG showed up. It was a postwar car, an early TC. I looked it over and I decided that was the car for me. I asked the owner, 'What would you sell it for?' Then I wired home for the money and bought the car.

"I was driving it up to see my cousin Ed Waterhouse, near Albany. He saw my new car and said, 'There's a group you should join. It's called the Sports Car Club of America.' I looked them up—they were in Boston. I decided to drive out there and I attended a meeting in Boston. Russ Sceli was the president then and he had a Bugatti.

Then I thought, 'This is the car I'd really like to own.' So I asked Russ if he would sell it. He thought about it and said, 'Give me your MG and $1000.' So we worked out a deal. It was a Bugatti Type 35A — not the hottest one. That was the only car I owned. I drove it to work, and I drove it summer and winter.

"In those days, everyone wanted to race but there was no place to race. I knew of Pikes Peak and decided I would race there. I had my car shipped out by Western Auto Transport, going to Denver. I soon discovered that, at Pikes Peak, you've got all these winding roads. It wouldn't be too smart to go off. My first race there, I got a 6th place, which I thought was good. The real problem was coming down the mountain. The turns were so sharp that you would have to hit the throttle and break it loose to make the turn. That was dangerous.

"I went to Pikes Peak four times after that. In 1948, I went there with the 4-wheel-drive Miller. Later in 1948, I went to the race at Watkins Glen. I had just come back from Pikes Peak. I was hoping to drive the 4WD Miller but it had been damaged up at the mountain. So I had to drive the Type 35A Bugatti. I really drove pretty hard. I got up to 3rd place. But I lost it on the corner that is now called Milliken Corner. I rolled the car. I raced at that course for years. It was a pretty complicated course — 6.6 miles. I got to know it well — all the difficult places like Stone Bridge. I enjoyed it very much."

In 1950, with the running of the first Sebring race, Milliken co-drove the #3 MG-TC entered by Frank O'Hare of Rochester, New York, to a very creditable 6th overall and 2nd in class F.

This is Bill Milliken's T-35A Bugatti before the race (courtesy Don Snelbaker).

Then, the car begins to get squirrely

Finally, it hits the hay bales and rolls, at a location thereafter termed "Milliken's Corner." His car was narrowly missed by the supercharged MG TC of Haig Ksayian, who stopped his car just before the overturned Bugatti. Haig was able to drive around it and resume racing without losing his position (courtesy Don Snelbaker).

In the 1950 race at Watkins Glen, Bill and Doc Scher's Bugatti Type 54, with a Dynaflow transmission, were on the front row with Tom Cole in the Cad-Allard next to him. In the row behind them were Fred Wacker in another Cad-Allard and Bridgehampton race founder Bruce Stevenson, in the Cadillac-engined Meyer Special. Back in the pack was Sam Collier in Briggs Cunningham's Ferrari Type 166 Corsa Spyder, as well as Erwin Goldschmidt in his Cad-Allard. After an action-packed start, the second lap saw Cole in the lead, Milliken second and Sam Collier in third. The leaders were lapping at nearly 70 mph. Then Cole left the road just after the Seneca Lodge. After White House Bend, Collier passed leader Bill Milliken and pulled away at a speed estimated at 120 mph. It was then that Collier got into gravel in the right-hand bend before School House Corner.

"Sam Collier passed me at the beginning of the back straight," Bill recalls, just before the railroad underpass. On the Friday before the race, I actually walked the whole course before the race — it was six miles. So I knew there was gravel on the inside of the fast corner to the right, at the end of the straight. Sam got into that and threw up a sheet of rocks and sand — it was hard to see what was happening. I did see him go end over end at the apple orchard. He would have been all right if the seat belt anchorage had not broken. He was thrown out and the car landed on him.

"The accident did not look that serious from what I could see. I was finally passed by Goldschmidt and then Wacker — I don't remember seeing Stevenson at all. After I re-passed Wacker and got back into second, I lost it at Seneca Lodge. It was a tricky corner. When the tail came around, I jammed on the throttle, sprint car style. But with the Dynaflow you don't get an immediate response. When it did, that drove me into the inside of the corner and I was out of the race.

"There are other courses I liked. I raced at Bridgehampton several times when I raced for Doc Scher. It was another Bugatti, a Type 54. We had trouble with it at Bridgehampton and tried to fix it out there but we couldn't, so we brought it back to Buffalo and fixed it."

Doc Scher is remembered as a racing patron by Barbara Fleming, wife of SCCA official Bill Fleming: "Sam Scher was a plastic surgeon from Texas," Barbara says. "When he got out of medical school, he didn't have any money. He fell into a lease on Park Avenue in New York. His first patient was a lady who needed a nose job. The operation turned out very well. She spread the news and he became rich. His wife was a lawyer, and his hobby was collecting cars. He lent some of these to drivers including Bill Milliken and Otto Linton."

Bill raced from 1945 to March 26, 1960, at Sebring. "Cam Argetsinger was going to run at Sebring but his friend talked him out of it. He always felt bad about not driving at Sebring so he invited me to drive. It was in an Alfa Giuietta Veloce. It was the last race for both of us." The Argetsinger/Milliken #48 Alfa finished 27th overall in a field of 65 cars, and 4th in its class, completing 156 laps of the 5.2-mile course during the 12-Hour race.

During and after his stint at the wheel, Milliken was an SCCA race official. He authored the first set of SCCA General Competition Rules. He was on the first SCCA board of directors. He was a club vice president and contest board member as well.

From 1958 he was the chief steward of the Formula Libre events at Watkins Glen and then he was the chief steward of the U.S. Grand Prix from 1961 to 1970. His most memorable event was at the 1965 Formula One race when it was raining so hard no one wanted to go out. Bill was the Clerk of the Course when Dan Gurney got up and said, "We came here to race. We have to practice to race. Let's go."

"Dan suddenly became a good friend of mine when he said that," Milliken notes. In fact, the foreword of Milliken's most recent book is authored by Dan Gurney. And what book would that be? *Equations of Motion*, a 658-page volume published by Robert Bentley. That's in addition to the book written by Bill and his son Doug, titled *Race Car Vehicle Dynamics*—it is required reading for all automotive engineers, both of racing machines and passenger cars.

∞ CHARLES MORAN ∞

An early president of SCCA (1954–1955; joined in 1949) and friend of Briggs Cunningham, Moran was the first American to race at Le Mans, in 1928, in a DuPont car. After World War II, he raced a Bugatti and then two MGs. Charles's son David notes: "Dad had an early history with motorcycles: as a young man, he was a test rider for the Indian Motorcycle Company in Springfield, Massachusetts. His association with mechanics Alan Carter and a man named Jack from Wilmington, Delaware, dated from his DuPont automobile racing days. The DuPont team was based in Wilmington."

As son Charles Moran III recalls, "It is true that Dad raced a TC when he returned to racing in the late '40s. He had been, in 1928, the first American to race at the 24 Heures du Mans; in 1929 he'd also won the Bol D'Or at Baldoux, in France, driving a Rallye for the full 24 hours himself, without relief. He'd raced a DuPont at Indianapolis in 1932, qualifying at 89 mph and completing 22 laps before an accident."

George Jasberg notes, "The DuPont was stock based, had a 322 cu. in. straight 8-cylinder engine and was entered by the factory. He qualified 19th in the 38-car field at 89.7333 mph. The lap-22 accident which ended his race involved three more cars."

"He returned to racing after the war," Charles III continues. "His first car was a Bugatti T35A; in it he DNF'ed at Bridgehampton (1949) and Watkins Glen. Then came the TC, which he raced at Bridgehampton in 1950 (don't know his finish, but he did finish) and DNF'ed at Watkins Glen."

"My memory of the MG TC," says Charles, "was that it was green, that we balanced the wheels by wrapping wire solder around the spokes, that the car was hugely loud. My memory of the blown TD was that it had a Roots-type blower—and was yellow and was even louder. Very exciting. It lived, as did all of Dad's cars before the Cun-

Opposite, top: Charles Moran, president of the Sports Car Club of America, presents a trophy to Jim Kimberly at the 1955 Beverly, Massachusetts, race. Kimberly received the prize for finishing 2nd to Phil Hill's Ferrari Monza in the feature race, in his 4.5 Ferrari. *Opposite, bottom:* Charles Moran thanks a race worker at the 1955 Beverly, Massachusetts, event (courtesy Alix Lafontant).

ninghams, in our house's garage in Rye, New York, and we'd tinker with it — most often rebuilding the SU carburetors, a delicate and tedious job."

Son Dave notes that the 1948 TC was purchased from Miles Collier and that his father also raced it at Wilkes-Barre and won his class, receiving "a wonderful trophy carved out of anthracite coal." After that he got a 1951 MG-TD. It had cycle fenders was painted school-bus yellow. He later added a supercharger. I remember going around the course with him in practice at Watkins Glen. You could have passengers then and you didn't have to wear a helmet.

"He then bought a Ferrari 212 and towed it on a trailer behind a Dodge Power Wagon. He raced SCCA and he was a friend of Alfred Momo, who prepared the car for him." Charles picks up the story here, noting, "In 1951 he finished 16th at Le Mans in a Ferrari 212, and 14th at Watkins."

Adding some detail, George Jasberg notes that Moran covered 1,913 miles at Le Mans with co-driver Franco Comacchia, finishing 7th in class at 79.75 mph — Moran's Ferrari was a Touring-bodied, 2.6 liter car. In 1952 he was 4th at Vero Beach in the Ferrari, raced it at Bridgehampton and DNF'ed at Le Mans (electrical failure).

"Moran was first at Giants Despair Hillclimb in 1951," notes Jim Sitz, "and at the Mt Equinox hillclimb, both in a supercharged MG-TC. At Watkins Glen in '51, he was 3rd in class in his 2.6 Ferrari."

"Then," Charles says, "he raced Cunninghams for the Cunningham team. Co-driving with John Gordon Bennett, he finished 10th at Le Mans in 1953, in the Cunningham C4RK coupe. Later, he bought all of the Cunningham racing cars from Briggs. Between 1953 and 1958 he finished 14 races in Cunningham cars. In 1957 he finished 9th in the Spa Grand Prix, driving Lotus XAR 11."

David adds, "When he raced the Lotus 11 in Europe, his tow car was a Bentley Continental. He bought the Lotus from Colin Chapman and painted it American colors. He drove it at Sebring in 1958. After the Eleven, he drove an AC Ace."

Moran stopped racing in 1959. In 1962 he divorced, and after he

Charles Moran, president of the Sports Car Club of America, presents a trophy to Lotus driver Len Bastrup, who won the First Race at the 1955 Beverly, Massachusetts, event (courtesy Alix Lafontant).

remarried, the new wife did not like the cars. So he auctioned off all the Cunninghams at Sotheby's and they were bought back by Briggs Cunningham. "He was executive secretary of the SCCA in 1952 and 1953," Charles concludes, "and president in 1954 and 1955. He was a member of the CSI (Commission Sportif Internationale) and of the American Competition Committee of the FIA."

❦ AL MOSS ❦

E. Alan (Al) Moss, the founder of Moss Motors, was a figure in the sport on the West Coast. While his actual racing was somewhat limited, he was involved in rallying, race officiating and maintaining the cars we all love. "I bought my MG," he says, "September 13, 1948. I still have it." Asked whether it is stock or modified, he says it has a supercharger. A Shorrock? "No, the one Moss Motors sells— the new ones are a lot better." A few months after getting his MG, Moss organized the first rally on the West Coast. "It was December 1948 and it went from Los Angeles to Santa Barbara — we had an entry of twenty cars," he notes. "I started my shop in 1949. We sold a lot of Lucas parts. A Lucas distributor rotor from Hoffman, for an Alfa Giulietta, was about $7. The same part, which fit an MG, retailed for 90 cents from Lucas." Shortly afterward, Al became interested in racing.

Since there weren't any road courses in California at the time, they raced at Carrell Speedway; even Phil Hill did that. In his first race at the half-mile track, Al decided to

Al Moss drives a red MG Special at Sears Point in 1986 (Al Moss collection).

High-camera angle picture of Al Moss in his MG-TC at Monterey in 1993 (Al Moss collection).

stay down low to make it harder for people to pass. When the yellow went out due to an accident, Al learned a racing lesson: "I slowed down at the yellow and everyone caught up to me. When it went back to green they all passed me." Where did he finish? "Let's say behind Phil Hill," Al quips. A later escapade yielded another lesson, when he flipped an Allard, also at Carrell Speedway. "It was a Cad-Allard on a muddy dirt track, and the story is too long to tell," he remarks. After a brief racing career, Al Moss settled down to his business and race officiating at California sports car events. In 1953, Al was appointed an MG service dealer by Ken Miles and then became the first factory-authorized Jaguar service dealer.

He names many of the MG drivers he knew: Paul Pedago—TC with a V8-60; Floyd Burt, with a TA, a blue one; Jack McAfee with the #88 John Edgar MG; Kjell Qvale and his brother Bjarne; Henry Manney and his TC and, of course, the famous and infamous Ken Miles. Bjarne Qvale, Sitz notes, won the very first West Coast sports car race in the postwar era: November 1949 at Buchanan field in Walnut Creek, California, home of Etceterini car guru John de Boer. The race was put on by the San Francisco MG Club and Bjarne won it in a TC.

Moss Motors later expanded to manufacture and distribute parts and accessories not only for MGs but for Triumphs, Austin-Healeys and Jaguars. Al sold the company in 1976. For 27 years—almost the time that MG had been in America—Al helped to keep those cars on the roads. And now, Moss Motors still does. Plus, Al still owns, drives and races his original TC.

ALAN PATTERSON

Alan Patterson has been racing 57 years and he still races three of the cars he started with: an MG-TC, an Allard J2X and an Elva Mark IV, which his grandson also races.

The first race he ever saw was the 1950 Bridgehampton event; he went to Watkins Glen the following year, 1951, with his TC.

He bought his TC from importer J.S. Inskip. It was a demonstrator, but it wasn't until 1951 that he first raced it, at Pennsylvania hillclimbs from Pittsburgh to Hershey. In 1952, he raced the TC at the 3.5-mile Brynfan Tyddyn road course, finishing somewhat down in the pack: "I had taken the sides of the hood off," says Patterson, "and the copper bleed tube on one of the float bowls broke off. During the race it poured gas on me. I wanted to stop but I couldn't. At the end of the race I was covered in gasoline. I don't think any of us cared where we finished. We just wanted to drive on that course. There was a big party on Senator [T. Newell] Wood's lawn after the race — he paid for everything."

He raced the #14 TC at Sebring in 1953, co-driving with Hubert Brundage. They were 28th overall and 7th in Class F. He drove the white TC up to the 1953 race at Put-in-Bay from the University of Miami. That's not Miami of Ohio, that's the one in Coral Gables, Florida. He pulled up to the dock just as the ferryboat was leaving. Luckily his brother Charles was already on it and he was able to persuade the captain into backing the boat up.

While racing the MG at Watkins Glen he borrowed a set of spark plugs from Briggs Cunningham. He was practicing for the race and his car developed a miss. He went over to the Cunningham trailer to see if they had a set of plugs. Briggs said to Alfred Momo, "Find Alan a set of spark plugs, will you?" The crew chief went into the cavernous trailer and came out with four plugs in the familiar red, white and black Champion boxes. "May I pay you for those plugs?" asked Patterson. "Not a chance," replied Cunningham.

In 1954, he became the first person to race the new Triumph TR-2. He was selling cars at night at the Jack Pry dealership to pay his way through college, and the new TR-2s arrived. Since he had driven at Sebring he was asked to drive one of the Triumphs. "We had five cars and we blew up the engines in all five. There was no hole at the bottom of the main bearings. The factory thought it would be OK but it was not. We burned up the cranks. The factory engineers came down and looked at them. They all had the same problem. We changed the engines at the track and still finished 3rd in class. We were doing the testing for Triumph. Think of how lucky they were that we did that. The car was manufactured at the end of the year and shipped to Florida, ahead of the European and English racing schedules, and before distribution to the public." Ever hear the expression "racing improves the breed"? If this problem had not been identified via racing, it would have ruined the Triumph brand in America. The Patterson car was #35 — the co-driver was a Mr. Hendrick, and it finished 24th overall, ahead of the George Moffet/Bob Said OSCA, and 3rd in Class E.

In 1958, Patterson went back to Sebring to drive an Elva Mark III with Charles

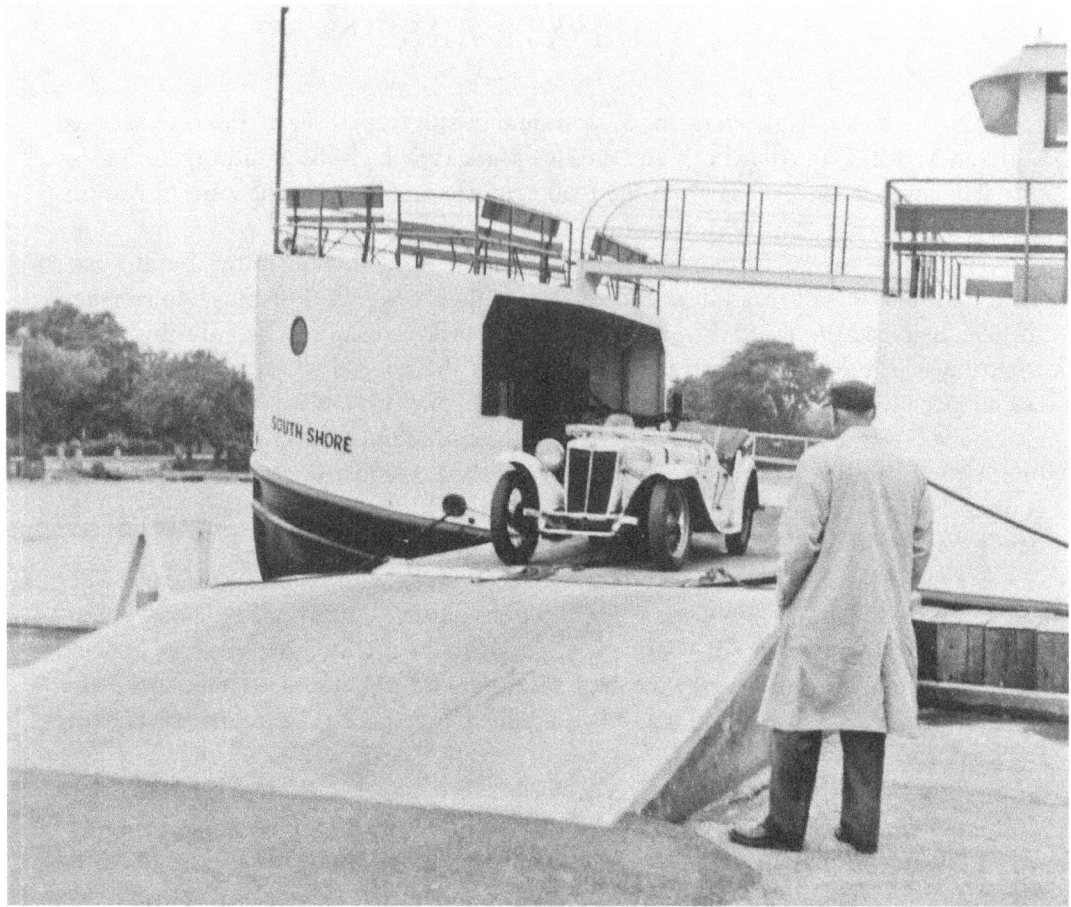

The #12 MG TC of Alan Patterson is about to disembark from one of the numerous Miller Ferries and roll down the gangplank onto Put-in-Bay, to race in the 1953 event (courtesy Joe Brown).

Kurtz and J. Karmer. The car, entered by Avant Corporation of Pittsburgh, was #77 and it DNF'd on the 68th lap.

Other cars he has raced include a 1959 front-engined Formula Junior, which he raced with Frank Nichols in England, and the Elva Mark II, III and IV that he raced in the States. There was also a rear-engined Lotus 22, with which he won the SCCA Northeastern Division title in the Formula Junior class, in about 1963. "I did not buy it from Fred Stevenson at Lotus East; I bought it directly from Colin Chapman. Tim Meyer, Stevenson, Revson and I were trying to get one. But when they drove the Lotus 22, they changed their minds and decided to stick with Cooper. I won the championship with a Lotus. We drove at all the East-Coast courses — Lime Rock, Bridgehampton, Watkins Glen, Vineland, Marlboro, Cumberland and one that was down south, maybe Atlanta."

Alan Patterson is still racing. He raced his Allard in Europe during the past two years prior to this writing, at Silverstone, Pau, France; Monaco, Porta in Portugal, Donnington and a few others. He describes vintage in Europe as "very fast racing, very serious." He goes to Monterey every year and has raced at Watkins Glen fifty times. Patterson is the racing founder and organizer of the Pittsburgh Grand Prix, the Schenley Park races put on by the VSCCA and Steel Cities Region of the SCCA.

"Pittsburgh is the only street race left in the country that is a stand-alone race," says Patterson. "The race is free and yet it has raised $2.5 million for autistic children, all from sponsors."

BILL POLLACK

Bill Pollack is not only famous for the black Cad-Allard with red wheels and white sidewalls (per the title of his book), he drove lots of other big-bore equipment, too: Kurtis-Buick, Lister-Chevy, Corvette, HWM-Chevrolet, C-Type Jaguar and Maserati 300S. Of the one-time drive in the Maserati, he said it was the first car he had ever driven that had no faults. He drove from 1949 through 1958 and it all started with an MG-TC. Prior to road racing at Palm Springs, notes Jim Sitz, Pollack ran as a novice in the Goleta Time Trials, September 1949.

Before owning an MG, Bill drove a Chrysler sedan with Fluid Drive. Then he saw the red MG-TC in a store window on Ventura Boulevard in Studio City. Shortly afterward, he bought a Shorrock supercharger from John von Neumann, who told him

Allard #14 leads the Don Parkinson Special at a Reno, Nevada, race with spectators watching from in front of scenic Virginia Lake (Bill Pollack collection).

Bill Pollack on the starting grid in the #4 Alfa Spider, at Santa Barbara in March 1956. On Saturday he won the under 1500cc production car race; on Sunday he placed 2nd in the under 2000cc production race (Bill Pollack collection).

about a race at Palm Springs, April 16, 1950. As William Edgar notes, Pollack won the first sports car road race in Southern California with his TC in the novice event. Then, in the main, he finished 3rd, just behind Sterling Edwards in a V-8 special and E. Forbes Robinson in a modified TD. "As a result of that performance," says Pollack, "Ernie McAfee asked if I would be interested in driving an MG for John Edgar. Of course I was interested. Ernie lived in my area and we all dropped by his shop to find out what was new on the sports car scene. The Edgar #88 MG had an Italmecannica supercharger and a Crosley radiator mounted in the door as a cooler for the supercharger. Early in the race, the first Pebble Beach race, the radiator leaked, the electric motor pump filled up the engine, and water spurted out of each exhaust stack." On November 4, 1950, he was driving an MG, and in less than a year, he had moved up to a Cad-Allard. Alan Moss had mentioned that a meat-packer in Tacoma had an Allard and was looking for a driver. In the second Pebble Beach, May 27, 1951, he won at the wheel of Tom Carsten's #14 Allard and drove the big cars for another four years. His races with Phil Hill were legendary. Phil would be in a prewar supercharged Alfa, a Ferrari of some kind, or a C-Type Jaguar. And Bill's wins at Pebble Beach, Reno, Golden Gate Park and Madera airfield are memories of contests with a friend.

Bill Pollack poses with the Tony Paravanno Ferrari 212 at Torrey Pines, July 20, 1952. Not a racing Ferrari, the car DNF'd in the race (courtesy Bob Canaan, Bill Pollack collection).

The following years would produce drives in other interesting cars, including the Baldwin Mercury Special, Clem Atwater's Alfa Giulietta and the Corvette of Richard Gess. In the mid-fifties Pollack drove a couple of Maseratis, a 3-liter for John Edgar, and a 2-liter for Lance Reventlow. "That was at Sebring in '57," Pollack recalls. "It was my first time at Sebring and I loved it. We were a private entry with a Maserati and the factory adopted us. At that time, Sebring was not developed and we were a long way from anything. We stayed in a rooming house out there. We went to dinner with the whole Maserati crew, including Behra and Fangio. He was a gentleman, a nice man, and he had a very high voice that didn't go with his image as the world champion. It was a lesson to me that he was so fast. I learned I wasn't as fast as I thought I was. We were leading our class. Reventlow was driving with Richie Ginther right behind him in the 2-liter Ferrari. We had a higher top end but they had better brakes. There was one corner with a washboard section where you couldn't get a bite under braking. I was going through that and Fangio came up in the 4.5 Maserati, drove around the outside, looked over at me, waved, and drove on. Chevy had several cars there, including 2 or 3 Corvettes totally trashed. They asked some of the English drivers if they would

The J2 Cadillac-Allard (#14) of Bill Pollack has the pole position on the starting grid at the first Reno race, November 21, 1951 (Bill Pollack collection)

like to drive one they called The Mule. They did, but they were not impressed. Then they asked Fangio. He had just set the lap record in the Maserati. He got into the car and took off out of the pits like a rocket. He did the first lap so fast that all the suits from GM couldn't believe their stopwatches. He set a time that was 2 or 3 tenths off the record. He got out of the car, thanked them and left.

"Our car did not last. It went out when Lance was driving. A warning light came on and he had to bring the car in. It had a dry sump system. The crewman only looked into the tank but did not use a stick. We were burning a lot of oil because we were driving the shit out of the car. Lance was very angry about that because we were leading our class. After we went out, I walked out to turn one to watch the cars at night. It was a fast left-hander. Visibility was not good, so most of the drivers would exit the turn in the middle of the track. When Fangio came through he would go all the way out to the edge, every lap."

After Sebring, Bill drove a couple of races in Coopers— an FII and a Bobtail—for Lance Reventlow, and then another big-bore machine. In May 1957, he drove the Kurtis

Buick of Bill Murphy at Santa Barbara and led easily. "I raced until 1958. I drove the Times GP in Dean Van Lines's Lister Chevrolet and then Laguna Seca, the next race, was my last one."

∽ BOB SAID ∽

Boris "Bob" Said's MG-TD drove at Linden Field, New Jersey, in 1950, but he wasn't in it—David Ash was. As noted by his mechanic, George Jasberg, Said would race at Thompson April 22, 1951, and win his class at the July 1951 Giants Despair Hill-climb in the same 'TD. By this time, the TD had been modified and it finished ahead of Bob Fergus in a 'TC. That fall, October 28, 1951, he drove a Jag 120 to a Class III 4th at Mt. Equinox Hill Climb. The next year, he drove Cisitalia #7 at the companion road race, Brynfan Tyddyn. Shortly afterward, Lex DuPont introduced him to the Formula III class ("I engaged the clutch and all hell broke loose"). Bob entered an Effyh FIII at the 'Glen in '52. George Jasberg recalls, "We got acquainted in 1952 when I was working

Bob Said, towing from Zandvoort to Modena, August 16, 1954. The location is a restaurant on the Autobahn, north of Munich. Note tubular trailer frame, master cylinder visible and '53 Ford station wagon with "Ecurie Yankee" on the door (George Jasberg collection).

Top: Ninian Sanderson (left) and Bob Said at the wheel of the Ecurie Yankee Ferrari Mondial in the paddock at Zandvoort, August 15, 1954. *Bottom:* Before the Trullo d'Oro on August 22, 1954. Bob Said and the English-speaking daughter of the president of "Automobile Club Bari" (A.C.B. had organized the race). This was just two years after Bob drove a borrowed stock MG-TC in the Allentown MGCC event — he won a narrow victory over Dick Thompson (George Jasberg collection).

Ferrari mechanic George Jasberg with the #106 Bob Said Mondial just before the Trullo d'Oro on August 22, 1954. The scene is in a courtyard in Castellana, near Bari. Jasberg is on leave from the U.S. Air Force (George Jasberg collection).

for Momo. In 1953 I would find myself face-to-face with Bob, the first time at Bergstrom AFB and the next time at the Dundrod circuit outside of Belfast."

In April of 1953, Said scored a dramatic win at Bergstrom AFB, in the badly wrecked OSCA of George Moffat. He and airmen from the base worked all night to pound out and fix up the damaged car. Owner Moffat asked Frank Bott, "You know anyone who can drive it?" Frank replied, "I can't, because I'm on Rees Makin's team." Then Bob said, "I'll drive it." And he really did. Bergstrom was a 100-mile, under-1500cc race, and that year it was noted for Bob Said's race-long dice with John von Neumann's special Porsche. Later that year, Ecurie Yankee was formed and equipped with the OSCA that Jack Frierson had brought to Le Mans in 1953, with which Said won at Rouen (where he set a new lap record) and captured an overall win at the Crystal Palace in England.

For Said to win three major events in '53 — Bergstrom, Rouen, Crystal Palace — was what Jasberg calls a "1500cc Triple," and it did a lot for Said's reputation. For Ecurie Yankee's 1954 season, a new 2-liter Ferrari Mondial was delivered, but not until August. With a '53 Ford station wagon, a unique tube frame trailer and mechanic Jasberg, he raced the Mondial. Results: a 3rd at Senegallia, DNF at Zandvoort, 2nd in the Trullo d'Oro at Bari, and 2nd in CL (to Luigi Musso) at Tourist Trophy (and 9th OA). There at Dundrod, Masten Gregory co-drove with Bob, but brake fade prevented a higher overall finish. In 1955 Bob took the ex–Ascari Indy Ferrari to Daytona Beach and set a record at 174 mph, driving the flying mile on the beach. Bob retired from racing after a crash while running second at the 1955 Sebring 12-Hour event ... racing only occasionally, at Nassau in the late fifties and the inaugural American Grand Prix at Sebring in 1959.

Beyond the racing, he was a colorful person who had been an Olympic bobsledder at Lake Placid and kept a cheetah in his house at Pound Ridge, New York.

ART SEYLER

Art Seyler is the backbone of SCCA club racing. A 53-year member of the Sports Car Club of America (Neohio Region) and former member of the MG Car Club, he started racing in 1954 in a borrowed MG-TD, then moved up to a Jaguar XK-120 from 1954 to 1957, then up to a C-Type Jaguar, which he raced in 41 events from 1961 to 1965 in SCCA and USRRC. Then he did 35 races in a Lang Cooper Cobra (a Monaco with a Peter Brock–designed body and a 289), '65 to '71, and afterward brought back the C-Jag and went vintage racing from '71 to '85. From there he decided to race in Historic Can-Am, O2L and U2L, Group 7 and bought a Chevron B23, racing it from '86 to '92, and then leased a Chevron B-34 Formula Atlantic, initially with a C-Sports body (1993 to 1994) and later in open-wheel FA configuration at the end of his 42-year driving career, in 1996, with 125 races logged. Well, not quite the end, because in 1998 he started going to Nelson Ledges lapping events, "Run What You Brung," or Friday Test Runs, now called Fun Days. He drives a Mitsubishi Lancer Evo-VIII at Nelson Ledges. He was out there twice in November 2009 and shaved five seconds off his best time. Arthur is over 80 years old and he hasn't gotten enough of this racing business just yet.

Art's interest began in 1953, at the Put-in-Bay road races, the island races offshore of Sandusky, Ohio, in Lake Erie. Art had an MG-TD but his wife was leery of letting him race, so he went up just to spectate. He promised her he would not race. He did, however, participate in "night practice." During the race he worked a flag station right at the kink into town. "The cars were coming right at me," Art recalls. "Chuck Dietrich sped by in his supercharged MG, about three feet away. I was completely absorbed in watching the races but I began to experience the symptoms of Rose Fever, which I am

Opposite, top: Longtime Neohio SCCA stalwart Art Seyler stands next to the modified MGTD that he borrowed from Hank Becker for the 1954 Akron Airport Sports Car Races. With cycle fenders and a louvered hood, it's a nice-looking car but Art recalls that it had virtually no oil pressure. "In the first practice session," Art says, "Jim Kimberly roared by at 135 miles an hour in his Ferrari, two feet away, and I said to myself, 'What am I doing here?'" *Opposite, bottom:* Here's Art Seyler in the beautiful C-Type Jaguar that he raced for so long, seen racing at Mid-Ohio, June 16, 1963. Art drove the car to, and raced in, 41 SCCA events and 1 USRRC race. All of the race preparation was done in the garage and driveway of his home in Cleveland Heights, Ohio (Art Seyler collection).

This is Art Seyler's #93 Lang Cooper at the 1967 USRRC race at Mid-Ohio. The car was a rebodied Cooper Monaco with a Ford 289 in the back. Though it was light and fast, Art says it was the poorest-handling car he ever drove. Since the standard Cooper Monacos handled well, it may be possible that the new body affected the handling (Art Seyler collection).

susceptible to. It took me several minutes to realize I was standing next to a bed of roses." Later that summer Art bought himself a Jaguar XK-120.

The following year — it was June 12, 1954 — he again went to Put-in-Bay, this time with his brother Al, and again ran a few laps of night practice, in the Jag. "Then someone said to me, 'If you really want to see the race, go to Cemetery Corner. You can see the back straight, the corner and the straight into town all from the same spot.'" And that's just what Art did. "It was a pretty good day of racing at Put-in-Bay," he recalls. "Afterwards we took the ferry boat back to Port Clinton, drove back to Cleveland and I dropped my brother off." Like a few others, Art couldn't get the idea out of his system, so he decided to start racing in 1954.

"A little later that year I was entered at the Akron Airport sports car race, in a borrowed and very tired, modified MG-TD, which my good friend Henry Becker wisely passed up to race a 1500cc Kieft."

∽ Bob Shea ∽

Bob Shea was a one-of-a-kind character and a figure in the sports car scene of northeast Ohio during the early 1950s. He was employed as the service manager of

Here is Bob Shea and the Lossman Motors gang at the Akron Hillclimb. They're sitting on the Jaguar XK-140 of Bo Miske and the Triumph TR-3 of Charlie Barber. From left to right, they are: Art Brow, Ralph Cadwallader, Bernard Miske, Dutch Brow, Ann Lossman, Judy Cadwallader, Red Cowan, Charlie Barber, Jack Uhr and Jack's friend (Art can't remember his name, but Bob Shea called him "Homer Chop"). Behind Ann Lossman is Bill Staufer and Jim Schwarz, with Bob Shea in from of Cowan (Art Brow collection).

Lossman MG. Lossman's was on the west side of Cleveland and was one of the first MG dealers in the state. Bob Lossman figured prominently in the organizing of the Put-in-Bay road races and also sold Triumphs and VWs. Two weeks before the Bay race, he would bring in a transporter loaded with TR-2s, and every one of them would be sold by the time of the event.

As Fred Troyan notes, Shea was involved in the Put-in-Bay races as both a tech inspector (along with Joe Kovach, Ron McConnell and Walter Jarmain). Their approach was to help the drivers pass tech rather than keep them out for some trivial thing. Bob was also a racing driver. He had an MG-TC that he drove for several years. He was car #51 in the Put-in-Bay MG race in 1953. He was car #36 in the Put-in-Bay MG race in 1954. He was #5 in a 'TC in 1955 and #15 in 1956. He was entered in '57 as #12 but did not drive. "He had bursitis in his shoulder that year," says Dutch Brow. "He was sick during the race and went back to the place where he was staying. He let Chuck Dietrich drive the #12 TC, and Chuck won the race with it. Art ran the same car in the G-Production race. Shea also raced at the Akron Airport sports car races in #28, the familiar TC. He was a good driver," says Dutch, "but he had to quit. He had shrapnel in his back. His doctor thought it was moving, and the racing could shift it closer to his spinal

Art Brow in Bob's TC at the hillclimb; Ralph Cadwallader in the background (Art Brow collection).

cord and paralyze him." As Art Brow notes, Shea had been an Army infantry lieutenant in World War II, serving in combat during the Battle of the Bulge. He once gave a bag full of pistols and swords to co-worker Fred Troyan. He had no love for Germans, and during a less-than-pleasant exchange with one at the dealership, he said, "I think you're one that we missed."

Walter Jarmain worked with Shea beginning 1958. He had immigrated to America from The Mother Country. "I was a mechanic in England and I thought I could do that in America. But Lossman wasn't hiring mechanics and so I started in sales and later was in the MG parts department. I knew Bob Shea very well. He was one of the best. The dealership's reputation was built on Bob Shea. People would come over from the east side of Cleveland to have their sports cars serviced: Dick Henn and his black Jaguar, Walter Halle and his Halle green MGs, Sam Sheppard and his family, Reed Andrews and many others. The attraction was Bob Shea. Most people would bore a TD block 120 over. He would bore it 160 over. He'd be standing over the boring machine himself, making sure it was right. Bob was a gem. He was a hard-drinking character but it never interfered with his work. He was always square with people. You could ask him for anything—he lent money to people at the dealership. He was one of the most generous people I ever knew. He hired some good mechanics, including Quay Barber, except

Basil Jagovdik and Bob Shea at MG Motors with an Austin taxicab (Art Brow collection).

that nobody ever called him Quay — it was always 'Charlie' or, if he wasn't near, 'Fats.' Barber was very temperamental. He prepared and drove his Triumph TR-2 well enough to win races from Put-in-Bay to Akron to Lockbourne Air Force Base. As the dealership expanded," Jarmain adds, "they added Fiat, Jaguar, Porsche, Borgward and Hillman. Shea could fix any of those, and so could Art Brow. Bob and Art would work at the shop on the racing cars until 2 or 3 in the morning. Once Bob got a Speedwell engine and took it apart to make sure they had done it right."

"After being service manager at Lossman's," says co-worker Fred Troyan, "Bob ran the body shop. He was an interesting man. He had nicknames for everyone. 'Hagsnower' was a customer, and 'Snagglemouth' described a salesman at the dealership. Women were 'Dollies.' A feline who frequented the dealership body shop became 'Cosmo Cat.'" Co-worker Bill Staufer was "B. Roy Snavely" and Walter Jarmain was 'English.'" Dutch Brow adds some more: TC driver Ralph Cadwallader was "Larson E. Cadwallader," Jack Miller was "Sneadbee" and his wife Dolly "Mrs. Snead." Dutch herself was "Dutchess," Art was "Arter" and Tommy Hind, a Scotsman with an undecipherable brogue was "Scotty," of course. Bob put him on the service phone at Lossman's to cure his accent.

"Shea was an unforgettable character," says Dutch Brow, longtime Formula Vee racer and wife of Art Brow. "You never knew what he'd do next. He'd walk into your house and yell, 'Glorp, where's the mud?'—that was one of the Shea-isms and it meant coffee. He'd go into a restaurant and eat all the butter — he said it was because he was poor when he was a kid." Bob and Dutch used to go to lunch at the same diner and

Left to right: Bob Shea, Art Brow, Charlie Barber and Bill Staufer, at Put-in-Bay with trophies. Each wears the distinctive Glengary cap that identified the cognoscenti in the sports car crowd (Art Brow collection).

one time the waitress looked at Bob and remarked to Dutch, 'That's not your husband." "No," Bob explained, "she needs two of them." Dutch recalls, "Bob and Ralph Cadwallader were thinking of going to Palmina's Italian Restaurant. But they didn't know if they'd be welcome back. The last time, the service was poor and while they were waiting they ate some candles and a snake plant."

Dutch was interested in racing so Bob and Art taught her how to drive. Bob let her drive his MG-A, but she didn't like the car — it didn't handle as well as the T-series MGs. Art taught her how to speed shift Bob's MG-TC. That was the one that later went to the Akron Drag Strip at Derby Downs. It was supercharged and ran on alcohol. Art remembers: "We put a Shorrock supercharger on and I drove it at Akron in 1956 when Art Arfons broke the 150 mile an hour mark with a Ranger-powered Green Monster. We had the TC on 15-inch wheels. I took it down the strip, I was wrung out in 4th gear when the carburetor started icing up. So I just put it in neutral and coasted the last 150 feet through the traps. It went 90. The Olds 88 drivers were laughing at us when we first got there, but they didn't laugh after that because none of them could do 90." The car later went 100 in the quarter mile.

Back to Dutch and racing. Next, Dutch decided to do some hillclimbs. Bob, Art and Dutch took various cars out to events put on by the Pennsylvania-Ohio Sports Car Club. At the Sewickley Hillclimb near Pittsburgh, they took the supercharged TC. They went to Old Smokey Hillclimb in Pennsylvania just across the line from Youngstown, Ohio, where Art took a 2nd in one class and a 3rd in the other. They raced at Donora,

Jack Uhr with Bob Shea's Sprite and Art Brow with his Turner at Akron Airport (Art Brow collection).

Pennsylvania, just south of Pittsburgh, which also has a nice roller rink. And they went to the Mohawk Hillclimb, also near Youngstown. It was Dutch's first race, and she took a 3rd, driving the Turner. Planning for the next event, Shea said, "We've only got one girlie driver so we've got to put her in the fastest car." That would be the MGA Twincam, except that Dutch didn't care for the handling of the machine. But she did drive Bob's Sprite at Dragway 42. They put her against Charlie Barber in a TR4. He said, "I'll give you a sporting chance — I won't use overdrive." But he changed his mind when she started to pass him during the race.

Former Put-in-Bay corner worker Bob Satava also remembers seeing Shea at the Bellville Hillclimb near Mansfield, Ohio, an event sponsored by the Mid-Ohio Sports Car Club during the fifties, and suggests that he also raced at the Lowellville Hillclimb off River Road near the Boston Mills ski area. Satava remembers seeing a Corvette at this event ("too fast") and a Keift-Norton Formula III ("a wicked car, very loose"). Dutch Brow says that one of the Lowellville hillclimbs was June 23, 1957, put on by the

Penn-Ohio Sports Car Club; another event was the Akron Sports Car Club time trials, at the airport February 10, 1957. At Lowellville, there were six drivers who worked at Lossman MG or VW, in addition to well-known local competitors such as Barnie Burnett, Lorrain Holder, Jim Eichenlaub and Roger Penske. At Akron, there were also six Lossman people, and Art Brow was the fastest MG, at 5:31.6.

After quitting the racing scene as a driver, Shea owned a few cars that he let others drive. "In 1959, Jack Uhr drove Shea's Sprite at Put-in-Bay," says Art Brow. "Positions on the grid were drawn out of a hat so Jack was on the back row and I was there in my Turner. I went from second-to-last to 3rd in 3 laps. Then I brushed a hay bale and when I looked back, my helmet visor flew off. I tried to get a pair of goggles that was in the side pocket. While I was trying to get them on, I buzzed the engine on the Airport Straight, I had low oil pressure, and the camshaft seized. Jack Uhr was 3rd but he overheated. Ron Miller's intake manifold blew a plug out, and Whitey Tyrone's exhaust system fell off. What a race." Uhr also drove the Sprite at Akron. Somewhere in that timeframe, Shea had a Morris Minor pickup truck, which he let Bob Lossman race at Put-in-Bay. "It was modified," says Walter Jarmain, "and it had a straight pipe — it was very fast."

Shea later owned a Lotus Formula Junior that was driven by Ron Miller, one of his drinking buddies. After the TC's racing days were over, it was used for two things: driving around with a collie named George in the passenger seat, and rallying. Art and Bob went on the MG Picnic Rally once. It started at Linsay's Tavern, where the precise Greenwich Time was available via shortwave radio. Shortly after leaving the start line, Art asked Bob, "Did you write down the mileage? How about the time?" Neither had been done, so Art did his best to stay equidistant between the car ahead and the one behind. The car ahead put on its brake lights as it missed the last left turn. Art and Bob turned in to the checkpoint and won the rally.

After Art Brow started racing a Formula Vee, Shea said, "You need a professionally-built racing engine," and he gave him the money to get one. With a little innovation, Art stretched that to one engine and a spare. "He helped a lot of people," says Art. In June of 1975, during the Formula Vee era, Art and Dutch took Bob with them to a Trans Am race at Nelson Ledges, where Art was driving a Camaro. In midafternoon, Ma Beasley, the queen of Neohio SCCA, asked Dutch, "How did you like the donuts?" "What donuts?" said Dutch. "The dozen donuts I left at your table." It turned out that Shea had eaten all twelve of the chocolate-covered morsels.

Bob Shea's wife Gladys worked as the head handbag buyer at Taylor's department store in downtown Cleveland. He once explained why they didn't have children: "Because somebody would have to quit their job." Bob had a hat fetish; he loved hats. He came over to Brow's one time and threw his hat on the floor. Spooky the cat promptly ran over and barfed in it. Once Shea and co-worker Bill Staufer were talking and the subject was good things made in Cleveland. "Name one good thing made in Cleveland," said Staufer. "I was," said Shea. "You were an act of God," was the retort. "No, my parents meant it," was the reply. Bob adopted Art Brow as a son, and Art stuck with him till the end, which came at a west side Cleveland nursing home after Gladys died.

Carroll Shelby

Shelby is famous for so many things it's hard to know where to start. Is it the 1959 Le Mans win for Aston Martin? Or the Cobra? Or race-preparing the GT-40? Or his role in the Chrysler comeback? Or his children's foundation? One thing's for sure — he's a man of many accomplishments whose racing career started in a borrowed MG. Actually, they were all borrowed — Shelby never owned any racing car he drove. According to expert Jim Sitz, the TC seen below belonged to Ed Wilkens and was raced, in the early spring of 1952, to a 2nd place at Norman, Oklahoma. His next race in the same TC was at Caddo Mills, Texas, on May 2, 1952, where he took a 1st. He then ran at Caddo Mills, July 5th, 1952, in a modified MG-TD — he DNF'd. After that he borrowed a Jaguar, followed by the Cadillac-Allard owned by Roy Cherryhomes.

George Jasberg believes that his first overseas race may have been the January 1954 1000 km of Buenos Aires. At Sebring in March of 1954, he was paired with Charlie Wallace in a works DB3S. They ran as high as 3rd but were out in the 6th hour when the rear axle failed. He went to England on May 29, 1954, and impressed all at the inaugural Aitree meeting, driving a private DB3S in heavy rain. In an early big-league finish, he was second to Phil Walters and Mike Hawthorn at Sebring in 1955, with co-driver Phil Hill in a Ferrari Monza. On August 27, '55, Shelby was a DNF at Oulton Park in Tony Parravano's temperamental 6-cylinder 4.4-liter Type 121LM Ferrari. On Sept. 17, '55,

The number 12 MG-TC was originally raced in 1952 by Carroll Shelby at Norman, Oklahoma. It's now owned by Syd Silverman, pictured here driving it at the VSCCA Lime Rock Vintage Festival in 1995. Behind him are Jim Donick in the Allard and Jeff McAllister in the BMW (Jim Donick collection).

he and Masten Gregory won class F in a Porsche 550 Spyder, in the R.A.C. Tourist Trophy at Dundrod in Northern Ireland. They were 9th overall in the race won by Stirling Moss and John Fitch in the Mercedes 300SLR.

From there he joined up with team owner John Edgar to post a series of wins in Ferraris. One of the most dramatic of these was his win at 1956 Road America in the hard-to-control 4.4 inline six-cylinder car — one that only Castelloti, Maglioli, Phil Hill and few others were able to drive. He beat the D-Jaguars of Lou Brero (2nd) and Ernie Ericksen (3rd) after Walt Hansgen and Sherwood Johnston crashed their Cunningham entries. This was followed by a first at Le Mans in 1959 driving a factory Aston Martin with Roy Salvadori. Faced with a health problem, he decided to stay in racing by building a car. The first Shelby Cobra was completed in 1962 and began winning

Shelby waves the checkered flag after a win in the 4-hour endurance race at Road America in 1956. In the OSCA Mt4 with him are co-driver Jim Kimberly and Carroll's wife (courtesy Alix Lafontant). *Opposite, top:* In the excitement of mixing it up with the D-Type Jaguars of Walt Hansgen and John Fitch, Carroll Shelby went off the road in his Ferrari and up on a sandbank at Thompson Raceway, September 3, 1956 (courtesy Alix Lafontant). *Opposite, bottom:* Shelby greets his team as he pulls into the paddock after winning the 1956 race at Brynfan Tyddyn. Driving a 2-liter car provided by Luigi Chinetti and sponsored by John Edgar, he finished ahead of Jack McAfee, also in a John Edgar car (courtesy Henry Wessels).

B-Production events immediately. Then Shelby converted some Cooper-Monacos into V-8 King Cobras, to win the big-engine sports racing class.

When Ford could not succeed with the GT40, they turned it over to Shelby, who won at Daytona, Sebring and Le Mans. Ford Mustangs were remade into Shelby Mustangs, which won in the Trans Am Series and B-Production. In the eighties, Shelby did some performance work for Chrysler, including promotion of its new racing program and development of the twin-cam engine. Now he is active in the Carroll Shelby Children's Foundation, which funds heart transplants for children.

Left: **Carroll Shelby, the driver from Texas, wearing his trademark bib overalls (courtesy Alix Lafontant).**

～ BILL STAUFER ～

Bill was a well-known driver and SCCA member in the Neohio Region who was exclusively an MG driver. During World War II he was trained at the Great Lakes Naval Station in Chicago as a gunner and radioman in a Navy TBF torpedo plane. He served from 1943 to 1945. After the war, he worked for MG Motor Sales in Lakewood, Ohio, as well as two other dealerships later on, Bedford Porsche Audi and Bedford Metro Lexus, both in the Cleveland area.

The owner of MG Motors, Bob Lossman, started the dealership when he wanted to buy an MG. According to Art Brow, who also worked at MG Motors, they wanted to buy a car, but Jaguar Cleveland didn't have any MGs. When they called New York they were told, "If you buy six we'll give you a dealership." Lossman purchased a store at West 133rd and Lorain in Cleveland and started selling those six MGs. As soon as they were gone, he ordered some more, moved to Webb Road and Detroit Avenue in Lakewood, Ohio—a location that was formerly a Studebaker dealership—and hired Staufer.

Bill Staufer was a salesman for the dealership—he got a yellow 1953 MG-TD and started entering hillclimbs. Art Brow recalls that some of these hillclimbs included Sewickley, near Pittsburgh, and the Ohio hillclimbs at Milan, Lucas, Youngstown, Boston Mills and Akron (which ran from 1955 to 1958). As Pat Staufer recalls, Bill also competed in the 2nd and 3rd Annual Old Smokey hillclimbs in Pennsylvania, and in the Mohawk 1st, 4th and 5th annual hillclimbs, both of these in the Youngstown, Ohio area. "They are housing developments now," says Art Brow. Other events included the Akron Sports Car Club speed trial in 1957 and the Akron SCC time trial on March 15,

Top: Bill Staufer jumps the pale yellow #14 TD at what appears to be the Lucas Hillclimb in northwestern Ohio. *Bottom:* Cornering the #3 MG-TD briskly in 1956 at Put-in-Bay is well-known Neohio SCCA driver Bill Staufer. Bill just passed the escape road at the corner going out to the airport here (courtesy Chris Staufer).

Top: Bill and Pat Staufer pose with their MG-TD at MG Motor Sales. This is about 1956. *Bottom:* The sign in the window of MG Motors in 1958 says it all. Usually before the 'Bay races the sports car dealers would get a truckload of cars, which would all be sold by the time of the races (courtesy Chris Staufer).

1957. Both were held near Derby Downs, on a ½-mile country road that later became the Akron drag strip (where the gang from Lossman MG took a Shorrock-supercharged MG-TC fueled with alcohol and ran 100 mph in the quarter mile, to the amazement of local Olds 88 drivers).

In 1956 he began racing at the legendary Put-in-Bay races. He also raced there in 1957, 1958 and 1959, the last year. Bill ran a race with the Mid-Ohio Sports Car Club, June 22, 1958, at Mansfield Airport. After the 'Bay raced ended, he competed a couple of times at Mid-Ohio in the H-Production class with his MG.

Pat Staufer holds the checkered flag after Bill's win in the MG class at Put-in-Bay in 1959. Most of the cars entered by Lossman employees, including Art Brow, had those checkered number panels and neat numbers — a step up from masking tape! (courtesy Chris Staufer)

∽ Bruce Stevenson ∽

If you're in the sports car scene out east, you know the name Bruce Stevenson. He started the racing at Bridgehampton. First he organized racing in the streets, and then he got behind the drive for a permanent road course — some say it was the best in the country. Bruce was also the founder of the MG Car Club, which sanctioned the Bridgehampton race and which fueled the growth of the Sports Car Club of America. "I had a system for grid position that Miles Collier suggested," Stevenson recalls. "The drivers reached into a grab bag and picked their grid position out of a hat. I drew my position in the middle. I was moving up steadily when a spark plug lead fell off. I went into the pits and Jim McGee spotted it right away. I got back in the race and was working my way through traffic again but the pit stop had cost me too much time."

He drove his #2 MG-TC at those races in 1949 and 1950. After that he moved up to the Meyer Special, a Cadillac-powered sports racing machine that was competitive with the Cad-Allard of Erwin Goldschmidt and the Chrysler-Allard of Tommy Cole. A most interesting man, the Wall Street financier went to prep school with Briggs Cunningham, in the prewar era (1937) he was a motorcycle racer, in the war he was a fighter pilot in a P-40 in North Africa and then flew a P-47 over Germany, and he was a sailing champion in the Star Class, all before Bridgehampton and the black #2 MG-TC.

Top: Bruce Stevenson in the #2 MG-TC charges around the course at Bridgehampton in 1949 (Don Snelbaker collection). *Bottom:* Coming off Bridge Lane onto Ocean Road is the #2 MG-TC of Bruce Stevenson, at Bridgehampton in 1949 (courtesy Tommy Weber, Bruce Stevenson collection).

Right: The 1951 Bridgehampton race featured a great battle between the Cad-Allards of Erwin Goldschmidt (#98) and Tom Cole (#87), as seen from the cockpit of Bruce Stevenson's Meyer Special. *Below:* Bruce Stevenson poses at the wheel of the Meyer Special at the inaugural Bridgehampton race in 1957. Stevenson organized the first race at Bridgehampton (Bruce Stevenson collection, © Carl Goodwin).

~ Chuck Stoddard ~

When he was a student at MIT, Chuck Stoddard got an MG-TD. In his senior year of college he raced it several times at Thompson Raceway in Connecticut. He liked it, but it wasn't quite the car he wanted, so in 1956 he got a Siata, a racing car, from a distributor in New York named Tony Pompeo. This was a lightweight machine, with no engine, that Chuck finished off with a tuned Crosley engine and a set of Stewart Warner gauges.

The little black car was decorated with a Tweety Bird cartoon and successfully raced at the Put-in-Bay and Akron Airport sports car races. He drove to a first in H-Modified at the 'Bay in both '56 and '57.

Then Chuck became a car dealer and his carlines did not include Siata, so he began racing an Alfa Romeo, which is what he sold — a light blue Giulietta Spider. In an early race in '58, at Put-in-Bay, he won both the G-Production race and the Blow-up Trophy. Rounding the last corner of the last lap, his engine blew up in a cloud of white smoke. Fortunately, Chuck thought to stick in the clutch and coast over the line.

He soon came around to the view that it was extravagant to be racing a car he could be selling, so he sold the blue car. Then he got a red Veloce. It was a 1956 car with serial number AR 1495 00298 — in other words, the 298th Giulietta Spider made.

Here's Chuck Stoddard as a young man when he drove his green MG-TD up to Thompson Raceway in Connecticut and raced it (courtesy Chuck Stoddard).

Chuck Stoddard's TD is in racing trim with the windshield and frame taken off and a Plexiglass screen substituted. He notes that he still has that jacket, which he bought at the MIT student union. Waste not, want not (courtesy Chuck Stoddard).

It may have been the earliest Veloce Spider built. "The red Veloce," Stoddard says, "was a derelict that I got for next to nothing. It was a junker. I was young, I was starting a business, and I didn't have much money."

Stoddard prepared the car to the limit of the SCCA rules and generously shared this with his competitors in two articles in *Sports Car* magazine, April and May 1961.

Campaigning for the 1959 national title, Stoddard drove at Indianapolis, Meadowdale, Elkhart, Mid-Ohio, Lime Rock, Watkins Glen, Cumberland, Marlboro, Dunkirk, Akron, VIR and Mosport.

"The people I raced with," says Chuck, "included Barry Budlong, Norm Webb, Jack Crusoe, Bob Grossman, Ed Hugus and Bob Parsons. Grossman was a very aggressive driver. He was the only one who would hit you. The officials didn't notice, or if they did notice, they didn't care. If someone finished ahead after hitting a competitor, that was not really winning. For many years, you didn't hit people. The trick was to drive better. Of all the good drivers like Jimmy Clark or Jackie Stewart, none of them hit anyone."

Stoddard's racing record was compiled by former employee Bob Kendall, and by Bill Green of the International Motor Racing Research Center at Watkins Glen. In 1959, Stoddard raced to three firsts, two seconds, a 4th and a 6th in SCCA National Races, for a total of 70 points, to win the G-Production Championship.

A victory lap for Chuck Stoddard at Mid-Ohio in the #5 Alfa GTZ, in 1965. Carrying the checkered flag is Stoddard Imports employee Bob Nikel. Stoddard won three national SCCA championships in Alfas, two in Giulietta Spiders and one in the GTZ coupe (courtesy Chuck Stoddard).

In the 1960 season, Chuck cut back on racing to concentrate on building Stoddard Imported Cars, his Alfa and Porsche dealership in Willoughby, Ohio. Though the Veloce had been moved up two classes, Chuck was able to finish 4th nationally with a light schedule.

Starting 1961, the remarkable little 1300cc Alfas were still too fast for E-P, so SCCA moved them up to D-Production. Stoddard ran Marlboro, VIR, Cumberland, Dunkirk, Road America, Meadowdale, Bridgehampton, IRP and Watkins Glen. He chalked up two firsts, three seconds, three thirds, a 4th and a 6th, for a total of 62 points and his second SCCA National Championship.

In 1962, Stoddard again shifted back into the business mode to promote his dealership. "You have to make a living," he notes.

In '63, Stoddard did a few races in his new 550-RS Porsche Spyder. His car was the ex–Millard Ripley machine, with a 1600 engine for E-Modified. This, unfortunately, put him in a class with the new RSKs of Bob Holbert and Joe Buzzetta.

In '64 he went back to Alfas with a factory ride in a GTZ. A 1965 championship in another GTZ was the last season for him in SCCA racing. Later he vintage-raced until year 2000, notably in his Porsche 917.

Driving the #2 Porsche Spyder for all it's worth is Chuck Stoddard, at Elkhart Lake, June 1963. The car serial number, for those interested, is #550A-141. A beautiful car from the era of aluminum racing Porsches (courtesy Chuck Stoddard).

The red Veloce was sold in 1964. "I sold it after I made the deal for the Alfa GTZ," says Stoddard. "I bought the GTZ for $6000 from the factory. After nearly 3 racing seasons, I sold it for $6000 and I thought that was a good deal."

After ten years in SCCA racing, Chuck Stoddard left the sport with three SCCA national championships and transitioned into vintage racing with Porsches he had acquired over a period of years, including a 907 and a 917. He stopped racing in 2000 after a competitor hit him hard and deliberately spun him out. "That's one reason I backed off racing," he notes. Stoddard's car, the red Veloce, was sold to a string of owners and then Ed Merhar of North Ridgeville, Ohio, bought it in 1983. Ed gave the old car another 13 years of racing, running 43 SCCA Regionals, 25 Nationals and three SCCA Runoffs.

∽ John Tame ∽

John is a club racer like you and me. In the mid-fifties he got a gray MG-TF 1250 and, at first, rallied the car successfully, in events from the Ohio 24 to the Chateau

Top: John Tame hustles the #19 gray MG-TF around the course at Put-in-Bay in 1957. Note the absence of a roll bar. The next year they were required. Later in the summer of '57, John raced at Watkins Glen. *Bottom:* Cruising his TF through town at Put-in-Bay, John Tame may have noticed the broken hay bales, mute testimony to errors in judgment, at speed (courtesy Joe Brown).

Kicking up dirt at a time trial in the field next to the Akron, Ohio, airport in 1960 is MG TF driver John Tame. Now there's a stout roll bar in the car, as well as the insignia of the Funny Face Auto Racing Team on the side of the car (courtesy John Tame).

Chevalier, Photo Rally and Red Leaf Rally near Kane and Bradford, Pennsylvania. "I navigated and Bob Meyer drove — he was a classmate of mine from Case Tech," John notes. Then he entered the TF in some races. The Kirtland, Ohio, resident joined the Cleveland Sport Car Club and raced at Put-in-Bay in 1957. He raced there in '58 as well, then came back in '59 to post a solid 2nd place in the usually tough MG class at the 'Bay. "The last year I couldn't get past Bill Staufer's TD. I had more top speed because the TF was more streamlined, but he had more acceleration." John was the archetypical amateur driver: "I drove my race car to the track, stripped off mufflers, bumpers, windscreen, etc., raced, put the car back to street condition, drove it home and drove it to work on Monday."

He also ran at the Akron Airport sports car races in '57 and the last year, 1958 ... plus Watkins Glen, which was an eight-hour drive from Cleveland on Rte. 20. Other venues for Tame were Dunkirk, New York, Harewood Acres, Ontario (3rd place in 1958); Louisville, Kentucky; Stout Field at Indianapolis; and Cumberland. He remembers meeting Briggs Cunningham, Jim Kimberly and Roger Penske at the Cumberland Nationals. In addition to CSCC, he was active in the MG Car Club (meeting at Linsay's Tavern to watch the Shell Oil movies about the Mille Miglia and other classic races) and Neohio Region SCCA. Tame was an engineer for Brush Development Corporation, which later became Clevite, from 1956 to 1989. While there, he worked on torpedoes, including the MK48 "and other things for the U.S. Navy."

John was among the sports car racers sailing at Mentor Harbor Yacht Club — Charlie Ellmers, Fred Steger and Pat Black included. John had a wood-hulled Thistle-class boat, a lightweight 17' speedster with way too much sail area that could easily change sailors to swimmers with a bit of a puff. He also crewed on bigger boats in the long-distance events on Lake Erie. "John sailed with us on *Merdeka*—which is the Malay word for freedom. It was my father's 41-foot Alden sloop built in 1936," says Pat Black. "He bought her in 1956. John sailed a Port Huron Mackinac race with us, I think in 1961." Pat's first sailboat regatta was 1949, in a Thistle-class boat named after his mother, *Julia B*, and he later owned an aluminum-hulled 42-foot Sparkman & Stephens boat named *Tortue*. Now, many years later, John recently sold his TF to Pat Black. The car couldn't be in better hands.

❧ Dick Thompson ❧

Thompson, a dentist from Washington, D.C., won 7 national SCCA championships over the years. So many were won in Corvettes—in the era of Grady Davis, Don Yenko and Bob Mouatt—that he is now in the Corvette Hall of Fame. He also drove for Briggs Cunningham, a rear-engined Cooper Monaco with a Maserati engine. But he started in MGs, that is, after first sampling a Pennsylvania hillclimb in his father's Nash-Healey. In 1951, Dick got a Mark II TD and began racing in nearby Maryland.

Early in 1952, he decided to race at Sebring. He and his friend Bill Kincheloe drove down to the 12-Hour race, flat-towing the MG with Dick's station wagon, with a pit

The #2 MG-TD of Dick Thompson and Bill Kincheloe soldiers on at Sebring in 1952, pursued by the #51 Bandini of Chuck Hassan and Beau Clark. The TD finished 8th overall and the Bandini DNF'd on lap 55 (Bill Foster collection).

crew of three dentists and a car full of tires. At Sebring he pulled up in front of a card table with a AAA sign on it. "Can I sign you up for the race?" the man asked. All went well until the first pit stop. "When we pulled in for our first stop, nobody moved a muscle," Thompson recalls. "They said, 'What's the hurry? It's a 12-hour race.'" Thompson and Kincheloe had the highest-finishing stock MG: 8th overall and 3rd in class.

Thompson won regularly with the MG, at road courses up and down the East Coast, in 1951, '52 and '53. During part of that time, he was in the U.S. Navy, serving as a dentist at the Marine Corps Recruit Depot at Parris Island. Then, for the 1954 season, he bought a Porsche Cabriolet to race in F-Production. The Speedster model had not yet been introduced and a cabriolet was lighter than the coupe. He always raced it with the top and side windows

Top Corvette driver Dick Thompson smiles for the camera at Cumberland in 1957 (courtesy Alix Lafontant, © Carl Goodwin).

up. In pictures of this car racing, it looks as though he is out for an afternoon's drive. Asked why the top was up, Dick replied simply: "It was faster that way." Apparently so, since it won him a title in class FP.

Also in 1954, Corvette owner Bob Rosenthal brought his car to the sports car races at Andrews Field outside Washington, D.C., where Thompson lived at the time. Dick drove it for him and set times comparable to what the Jaguars were posting, despite the limitations of the 6-cylinder pushrod engine and automatic transmission. That was before the brakes faded and the seal blew out of the trans.

For the 1955 season, Thompson went into the C-Production class, with a Jaguar XK-140MC. He placed 3rd in national points, ahead of 27 other Jaguars. He planned to do another season in the 140, until he talked with John Fitch, who told him about an opportunity to drive a Corvette for the factory. Fitch had declined the offer due to his responsibilities in designing and managing the Lime Rock race course.

"I set it up for Dick Thompson to drive," Fitch recalls. "Dick was ideal for it. He was an excellent driver, with a business that allowed him to do the schedule." By then, Thompson had a private dental practice in the D.C. area. He notes: "I started driving

Driving his A-Production Corvette Sting Ray, Dick Thompson makes an outside pass on a B-Production Porsche Carrera at Marlboro in 1963. Thompson was first in the SCCA AP-class national point standings in '63 (Bruce Jennings collection, © Carl Goodwin).

a Corvette because John Fitch told me it was a good car. John said they wanted someone to campaign the car seriously and go for a national championship."

Thompson and the Corvette started the 1956 season at the famous Pebble Beach race. In practice, the lap times recorded by the Corvette came as a real surprise to the drivers of 300SLs and Jaguars. This was the second year of the V-8 engine in the Detroit car. It delivered what western racer Danny Collins called the "explosive acceleration" of the small-block V-8 and the "unexpected good handling" of the chassis. Thompson won his class and finished 2nd to a 300SL. As the season wore on, the success of this car influenced many other drivers to switch to Corvettes. And by the end of the season, the Corvette had won the SCCA national title. For '57, the car was bumped up into a newly-created class, B-Production. There were a number of improvements, going from a 3-speed to a 4-speed transmission, fuel injection and handling improvements. The only things it didn't have were good brakes. Thompson did have help from the factory. Frank Burrell was the mechanic, one of the best in racing. Even the Corvette product manager, Zora Arkus-Duntov, was on the team. "He was the master negotiator between the racers and the company," says Thompson. "He didn't let them know any more than he had to about the racing operation." And then there was Barney Clark, from Campbell-Ewald, Chevy's ad agency. "Barney was a big help to me in the early days," Dick said, "because he knew the hierarchy at Chevrolet and could get things done."

With this team the 1957 national championship was won. It was ready to take on another when Chevy unexpectedly dropped out of racing. Thompson quickly found another ride, with Austin-Healey, behind the wheel of the new 1958 100-6 model. By season's end, he had notched his 5th SCCA title.

The 1960 season began with a trip to the Le Mans 24-Hour race, as part of a 3-car team of Corvettes entered by Briggs Cunningham. His car and another one went out, but John Fitch and Bob Grossman finished the third one 8th overall and 1st in class, a production car ahead of several sports racing machines. For the balance of the season, he drove a C-Modified car made up of the '57 Sebring practice car with a Bill Mitchell body on it. They called it the Sting Ray and it won yet another Sports Car Club of America championship, his 6th.

In 1961 he drove part of the season in the Sting Ray and part in a production Corvette entered by Grady Davis. Thompson also did some development work on the new 327 engine and in the 1962 season won yet another championship with the new A-Production Corvette, for a total of seven. His racing career began to taper off in 1963 when he drove the Corvette Grand Sport. "It's the fastest car I ever drove," said Dick. "It was extremely light: about 1900 pounds. It had a tube frame, aluminum transmission and differential; everything was lightened up. The car had tremendous potential and it's unfortunate that this was never realized." Also in '63 he did a lot of driving for the Cunningham team and then later switched sides, as it were, and drove a variety of Fords for Carroll Shelby, including Cobras, Mustangs and the GT-40. He finally got out of the sport after Le Mans in 1967.

"I left racing," he says, "simply because I had done it for over 15 years and there were other things I wanted to do."

∽ LAKE UNDERWOOD ∽

This well-known Porsche driver with multiple national SCCA championships began racing on a motorcycle, an English 500cc Triumph. But he soon caught the sports car bug and bought a couple of MG-TCs: a '47 and later a '49. He raced them everywhere he could, including the obscure race at Callicoon, New York, and Brynfan Tyddyn near Wilkes-Barre, Pennsylvania. After that he got a couple of Jags—a 1949 XK-120 with an aluminum body and later an XK-120MC. He and his business partner, Bengt Soderstrom, set up a Porsche dealership in Maplewood, New Jersey, on April Fool's Day, 1954.

They began racing one of the early Speedsters in 1955, then continued in '56 and '57. After racing every weekend, they decided to rest for awhile, polish their trophies and count their national championships—four of them. Lake also drove a Porsche 550RS Spyder borrowed from Briggs Cunningham. At Lime Rock, June 9, 1957, he beat Walt Hansgen's D-Jag, finishing second to Shelby's Maserati. Shelby called him one of the ten best drivers in the country. At Sebring in 1959 he drove Cunningham's Lister Jaguar.

Top: The #64 MG-TD races along at Brynfan Tyddyn with Lake Underwood at the wheel in 1953. The car is in F-Modified, with bumpers, fenders and hood panels removed. He had driven the same car in the stock MG class in 1952. *Bottom:* In addition to driving pushrod and four-cam Porsche Speedsters, Lake Underwood also drove this #37 Porsche Spyder, a racing car with an aluminum body and tubular frame. The car was lent to him by Briggs Cunningham and finished 3rd in SCCA national points in 1957. Underwood later drove a Porsche 904 and a Porsche 906 (Lake Underwood collection).

Later, in 1963, he went back to racing with his own Porsche and was 30 seconds ahead of everyone else in his first race at Lime Rock. He drove a Porsche 904 to a class win at Sebring 1965 with Cunningham and then piloted a Porsche 906 to an 8th place overall at Sebring 1966 with Ed Hugus, and that was his last race.

Lake Underwood, in his Porsche Speedster. Lake won three SCCA national championships in Porsches and also drove the Spyder, the 904 and the 906. In the Spyder he dominated the FM class in 1957 and was 3rd nationally with just a few races. Carroll Shelby called him one of the ten best drivers in the country (courtesy Norman Menard, Lake Underwood collection).

～ GEORGE VALENTINE ～

Valentine was one of the premier MG racing drivers, and he won the SCCA national championship in 1955 driving his TC in the G-Production class.

Bill Green of the International Motor Racing Research Center at Watkins Glen put together a racing record for him that includes a 1st in class with his MG-TC at the 1955 Beverly, Massachusetts, race, a 1st overall at the 1955 Thompson race on Labor Day, a 5th in class at Watkins Glen in '55 and a 1st in class at Hagerstown, Maryland, in '55 in the 'TC ... then, in 1957, an 11th overall at Montgomery, New York, in an MGA, a 3rd in class at Watkins Glen in '57, a 5th overall at Watkins Glen in '58 and a 1st overall at Dunkirk in '58, also in the MGA. In 1959, Valentine drove to a 4th overall/1st in class in the D- and E-Production race at Berwick, Pennsylvania, in a Morgan. Morris Wheat recalls that Valentine also ran at the July 19, 1958, race at Berwick, which was a replacement for the Brynfan Tyddyn race. "At the race in Berwick, Pennsylvania, where he drove the Morgan," says Tom James, "he used Wards Riverside Tires and lapped everyone in the field. His tires were down to the cords at the end." And Dave Nicholas adds that Valentine's black MGA also ran at Montgomery in 1958 and at Lime Rock that year.

Tom James was a classmate of Valentine's and notes that George graduated from Oswego State College in 1953 with an industrial arts major. Before that he was a Navy veteran. Tom notes that George was always buying and selling cars, most of which were Model Ts that he found around the countryside. Then George raced jalopy cars at the Oswego, New York, track. He drove the cars to the track until the police stopped him. Then he had a friend tow him there on a rope. "Most of the time he just drove the police up the wall with his antics," says Tom.

When he got his MG TC, he drove fast around town and the police could not

On the big runway at Beverly, Massachusetts, in 1955, George Valentine in the #46 MG TC dodges a wobbly Siata driven by one of those easterners (certainly not an Ohio Siata driver!). George would go on the win the SCCA national championship in G-Production that year, probably the last year that could be done with the coming onslaught of Alfa Giuliettas in that class (courtesy Alix Lafontant).

catch him most of the time. When they did, the dean of the school would bail him out — he was a car enthusiast. He later married the dean's daughter, who was the exact opposite to George. He spent one year as a teacher in Sidney, New York, and then worked for an auto dealer.

Another episode in his bouts with the police was that he had a set of imitation parking tickets and would check to see what the police were using in each town he visited. He would get one out of his supply and put it on his car at the parking meter.

Ed Licht knew him well. "George was from Oneonta, New York," says Ed, "between Binghamton and Albany. He was in the Binghamton Region of SCCA that was started by Bob Bucher, Spankey Smith, Gene Osborne, Jari Fitch and myself. George was an automotive shop teacher in the high school there. In the early races, when I was racing in the production class, we raced together. I used to race his car and he would race mine. He was a wild character, a very fast driver and a little unsafe."

According to Joe Tierno, "After the MG, George had a red Morgan with a square ugly roll bar. He won a race at Berwick with it. He was killed in the Morgan coming off a cloverleaf in Syracuse, in the tri-cities area of New York, in about 1959. It was a highway accident, not racing."

George Valentine picks up the checkered flag to drive the victory lap in the #111 black MGA after winning 1st overall and 1st in F-Production at Dunkirk, New York, June 1, 1958 (courtesy Alix Lafontant).

Frank Kovarick recalls, "Just a short note on George Valentine and his activities in the southern New York region. At one time SNYR was one of the most active in the Northeast: rallying, autocrossing, race workers, drivers and crews. I can recall a couple of stories he related to us at some gathering. He was returning from some race in the Northeast and driving his MG TC through a village where Colgate University was. He saw a speed reading pneumatic tube across the road and stepped hard on his brakes. Since he knurled the drums, the brakes locked up and tore the tube away from the recorder, to the dismay of the officer who stopped him. Some sweet talk from George left him off with a warning.

"One last one for the moment is that he occasionally lent his TC to one of the two brothers who raced a TD. This brother was known to be a fast shifter and his shifts sounded like those of an automatic. The problem was, when George got the TC back, he had to rebuild the synchronizers in the transmission."

On the changeover from the TC to the MGA, David Brown notes: "George raced his own MGA while he was service manager at Millard Ripley's Ithaca dealership. He owned at least one MGA after the TC, prior to his purchase of Woody Young's Morgan.

I recall a late-night high-speed drive from Watkins Glen to Ithaca in the fall of 1957."

Another New York enthusiast who knew Valentine was Morris Wheat. He notes, "My memory of George Valentine started in probably 1957. I had been in the service up until November of 1956 and so missed some of the exploits of George. I remember meeting him in Sidney, New York, while with Spankey Smith. I believe that George was a teacher in Sidney at the time. He had raced Spankey Smith's black MGA at Watkins Glen in 1956. I know when I got back from Alaska that Spankey had the MGA in a body shop for some work — probably damage from racing. It seemed that there may have been some disagreement between Spankey and George as to his future racing Spankey's MGA so that was the end of that association.

"They still remained friends and George was a regular at the road rallies of SCEC in that geographical area of New York state. He was friends with Sherm Decker, who also raced [MGA, Cooper-Ford, etc.], and lived in Oneonta, New York, while working at the Morris Garage in Maryland, New York. He was friends with Gordy Morris, who owned the Morris Garage where a lot of us bought our MGs. I remember him at a lot of races in the '57 and '58 time-frame. He eventually got into a Morgan, which I think he obtained from Woody Young in Pennsylvania. I think he raced the Morgan at Berwick, Pennsylvania, in 1957 or '58.

"George was a one-of-a-kind person for sure," Morris Wheat concludes. "I think one of his expressions or sayings was 'going like the hammers of hell,' and that may be the best description of his life."

∞ BILL VICTOR ∞

Bill is a longtime race driver from Chicago who raced for ten years, mostly in a Jag 120 and Mercedes 300SL. But he started in an MG. "I drove it down from Chicago with a friend one time. It was one below zero when I started. It was a TC and there was no heater so we wrapped ourselves in copies of the *Chicago Tribune*. I learned about an event while I was down there, a race at Davie, Florida, airport. There was a ballgame there and this race was put on for a little excitement during the intermission. I laid my windshield down to look like a racer but the cars in front were kicking stones up. I think I finished about third. There were a lot of well-known drivers at this event — George Huntoon, Sam Collier and Briggs Cunningham."

After racing for many years in a Jaguar XK-120 and a Mercedes 300SL at Road America, Meadowdale, Janesville Airport, Blackhawk Farms and other courses, Bill got out of it and assembled a nice car collection. "Between 13 and 16 cars," he notes, it had several Packards, including a 1938 V-12 convertible sedan, three E-Type Jaguars, his original MG-TC and an XK-120. A highlight of earlier years was first place at a hillclimb in his 300SL. This was a combined event of the Chicago and Wisconsin SCCA regions. It rained so heavily that a Ferrari went off and rolled. What was it like in a swing-axle car in the rain? "I just kept my foot in it," says Bill.

Top: This is the MG-TC that Bill Victor first drove in a race at Davie Airport in Florida in 1949. Bill still has the car, and here he is pictured in 2007. Notice how young the TC makes him look. *Bottom:* Bill Victor's red 1949 MG-TC is the same car he drove the year it was new. He raced an MG before moving up to a Jag 120 and a Mercedes 300SL. A longtime member of SCCA's Chicago Region, he and his family owned Victor Gasket (Bill Victor collection).

Bill Victor is seen here with his #101 Jaguar XK-20 coupe, at the Janesville, Wisconsin, airport race in 1953 (Bill Victor collection, © Carl Goodwin).

❧ John von Neumann ❧

John von Neumann was one of the most prominent people in American sports car racing, especially West Coast racing. He was a car dealer, driver and team owner. Racing photographer Jim Sitz knew him and has this information for us: "Von Neumann was from a wealthy New York family. His father was a doctor. So he had a number of interesting cars including a Mercedes-Benz 540K and a Lagonda V-12. Then World War II started and von Neumann went into the Army. Since his family had been of Austrian descent, he knew German quite well and served as an interpreter during the interrogations of Nazi prisoners.

"After the war," Sitz continues, "von Neumann went to California and began working as a car salesman for International Motors. In 1947, von Neumann started racing with a Talbot. After that he got a Jaguar SS100. Then, in 1950, he bought an MG-TD. He had the engine and chassis prepared by Warren Olson, who worked at International Motors. He used to race the MG against Roger Barlow in the Simca Special. He would usually lose, because the Simca was a pure racing car — it only weighed about 1100 pounds. I saw von Neumann race the MG for the first time at Palm Springs in 1950. The group at International Motors decided it was time to form an organization that would encourage speed events, and this became the California Sports Car Club.

Prominent West Coast car dealer (Competition Motors, Los Angeles) and Ferrari driver John von Neumann corners his Special MG during the Reno Road Race in 1954. Not many years later von Neumann would be driving Ferraris but, like so many owners and drivers, he started in an MG (courtesy Bob Canaan).

"Von Neumann and the dealership owner, Roger Barlow, would compete for who could sell the most cars. But von Neumann was not getting his commissions. One day he complained about this to a customer and the customer said he would back von Neumann in a dealership of his own. It was Secondo Gausti, a collector and enthusiast who owned the Tazio Nuvolari Alfa Romeo that had raced on Long Island in the late 1930s."

Von Neumann was a popular and dynamic man. As he successfully built the new dealership, Competition Motors, he continued to race. "In September of '54," Sitz notes, "he bought a Ferrari Mondial, a 2-liter 2-cylinder car — it was dark blue and had been owned by Porfirio Rubirosa. He raced this and he raced the special lightweight Jaguar XK-120s that had been built by the Hornberg Jaguar dealership. Von Neumann was a good driver and did well with these cars. In 1955, he became a Porsche dealer. My wife Dorothy loaned him the money to get the Porsche dealership from Max Hoffman. She was a good businesswoman and she kept telling him 'the money is in VWs.' But, at first, von Neumann only wanted Porsches to race. He had the only 550 Spyder on the West Coast. Even before that he had an aluminum Porsche coupe, a factory racing car. He cut the top off and won many races out here.

In the 1956 season, John von Neumann ran a team of Porsche Spyders dubbed "Ecurie von Neumann," with drivers Ken Miles and Richie Ginther. Here Ginther exits a corner at Pomona in 1956 in the #211 silver Spyder (courtesy Jim Sitz, Int'l Motor Racing Research Center).

"Then he formed a team. The first driver was Ken Miles. Miles had raced MGs in '54 and '55 — his own Flying Shingle specials. Von Neumann had two Spyders — a new 1956 car with a 4-cam engine and an old one with a pushrod engine from the Mexican road race. In January 1956 at Torrey Pines, Miles went out and flipped the new car on the first lap. They ran back to the dealership and brought back 'old faithful' and Miles still won. This did not make a good impression on von Neumann, but still he expanded the team to include both Miles and Richie Ginther. The only car that ever beat Miles was the Cooper chassis with a Porsche engine, nicknamed the 'Pooper,' that was built and driven by Pete Lovely. It was an 800-pound car. Von Neumann himself was running the Ferraris, with a 3-liter Monza. His daughter Josie was by then driving the MG in competition.

"Three years after buying his first Ferrari, von Neumann became a Ferrari dealer. In November of 1957, he ordered a new 12-cylinder 250 Testa Rossa. He had the factory paint it silver and ship it direct to Nassau for the Bahamas Speed Week. John painted his Porsches red and his Ferraris silver — he was a contrary kind of guy. But he had trouble in Nassau, in January he shipped it to Argentina and had trouble there, he didn't do well at Sebring in March and did not win a race until July 1958 at Vacaville.

By that time, both he and Richie Ginther had 250 TRs to drive. Later on, von Neumann acquired the ex–Phil Hill/George Tilp Ferrari 335S."

At the time of acquiring the 335S for himself, von Neumann also ordered a special Ferrari from the factory, according to Jim Sitz. Before the 1958 racing season, Californian Lance Reventlow had commissioned the construction of the Chevrolet-powered sports racing Scarab cars. These were powerful and dominant machines. So von Neumann asked the factory for a 4-liter, four-camshaft car to beat the Scarabs. It was called the Ferrari 412 MI and only one was built. The showdown between these cars was October 12, 1958, at the First Annual Los Angeles Times Grand Prix. The race boiled down to Phil Hill in the 412 and Chuck Daigh in the Scarab, trading places on the new track at Riverside. Jim Sitz was there when the Ferrari rolled into the pits with fuel vapor problems on lap 24. He watched as the mechanics tried in vain to fix the problem and get the car back on the track. The Scarab went on to a popular and well-deserved win.

The 1959 season was von Neumann's last one. Von Neumann was racing his 500 TRC at the time. As Sitz recalls, he only ran one race and that was at Avandaro, Mexico, a road course where he had competed many times. The TRC was fitted with a 12-cylinder engine at the time and failed to finish the race. Things began to unravel in his life as he was divorced by his wife Eleanor, who won the Ferrari franchise in the settlement. In 1965, he bought the Ferrari franchise for Switzerland and in 1973 he sold the VW and Porsche dealerships back to the factory—he had retained these after the divorce. Then he started a business importing motor yachts from Italy, after which he formed a company to market Lear Jets to business executives. All of these ventures became successful, prompting Sitz to describe him as "the man with the golden touch."

At the end of a life well lived, John von Neumann was still out on the blue Pacific in his 75-foot Italian Baglietto yacht with twin 2610 engines, and driving the highways full speed in a Ferrari F40. Nothing could stop him but the man with the scythe, and von Neumann died December 25, 2003. He was truly a figure in the sport.

∽ FRED WACKER ∽

Anyone in the sports car scene knows this name—an early president of SCCA, hard-charging Cad-Allard driver, technical innovator (worked with GM on use of the Hydramatic transmission in racing). His battles with Erwin Goldschmidt and Bill Spear are legendary. He figured heavily in the creation of Road America—he and Jim Kimberly flew over the site and said almost in unison, "That is the place." Then they worked with Clif Tufte on building a course there. All of this car stuff started with the #8 MG-TC that he raced at Watkins Glen, September 17, 1949. According to Jim Sitz, he was 3rd in class and 6th overall—beaten by Tom Cole in an HRG 1500 and John Fitch in a TC.

In a story told by Fred Egloff, Wacker bought the MG early in 1948 when he found out that a dealer in Stony Point, Wisconsin, had two of them, a black one and dark blue. Fred and race organizer Bayard Sheldon arrived at the dealership at the same

Top: Fred Wacker gets ready to race in the #8 MG-TC at Watkins Glen, September 17, 1949 — he finished 6th overall and 2nd in class. By removing the fenders, side panels and windshield, Fred probably saved about a hundred pounds (Fred Wacker III collection). *Bottom:* This is Fred Wacker driving the #8 Cad-Allard in the famous race with Bill Spear in the 4.1 Ferrari, at Bridgehampton in 1952. Wacker lost by a whisker because his transmission faded. It was common to use a Hydramatic trans for its gear ratios, but when they heat up, acceleration suffers (Don Snelbaker collection).

Top: Fred Wacker in Arnolt Bristol #8 is passed on the inside by Jack Manting in the #74 Jag 120, at Lockbourne AFB, August 8, 1954. Wacker finished 2nd in class and 15th overall. *Bottom:* Fred Wacker accelerates the Cunningham C-4R coupe in a 1955 race at Watkins Glen. The car belonged to Charles Moran at the time (courtesy Alix Lafontant, © Carl Goodwin).

time, each worrying the other would get the color they preferred. But Wacker got the black car he wanted and Sheldon got the blue he liked. Wacker took the car home to show his family. His father was terminally ill and Fred thought a shiny new car would cheer him up. He parked it under his father's bedroom window. When his father shuffled over and looked down at the little car, he said, "You'll kill yourself in that."

In his business life, he managed his family's manufacturing plant north of Chicago. In his early years, he was a bandleader for a swing orchestra. But most do not know that Wacker was a naval aviation officer in 1944 and 1945 (after stateside training in '43) who participated in the battles of Luzon, Okinawa and Iwo Jima — bitterly hard-fought battles in the Pacific Theater of World War II. Though a military pilot, he was not in a plane at the time — he was on the deck of the aircraft carrier USS *Shamrock Bay* as the fighter director officer. It was the job of Lt. Wacker to coordinate the take-offs and landings of F4U Corsairs providing air support for the U.S. Marine infantry during those conflicts.

∞ Harley Watts ∞

Everyone in the postwar era was eager to put World War II behind them, especially since so many of the newly-minted sports car enthusiasts had been in combat themselves. This was true everywhere, including Columbus, Ohio. Harley Watts's brother Bob comments on the era: "The population of Columbus was about one-tenth what it was in 1997. With few exceptions, males between 17 and 30 had been directly involved in the recently-ended war. Everyone at home had been involved in the war effort, with rationing of most everything. Also the Great Depression was a very vivid memory of a not-very-distant past. Gasoline and tire rationing ended in late 1945 and a desire to take advantage of this was not fully satisfied by 1949."

The TCs started coming in the spring of 1948, with plenty more by the fall of 1949. By then, Harley Watts had found a green '48 TC in Dayton, Ohio, his brother Bob had a 1949 TC, and there was a group of these MG owners in Ohio who all knew each other: Chuck Dietrich from Sandusky, the Greiner brothers in Springfield, Don Marsh and Dave Lee in Columbus, Tom and Phil Miller ... about ten TCs in the area.

As Bob Watts notes, "Vehicles on the road around Ohio when the TCs were new were leftovers from the '30s. If not in fact, they were in design, just like the TC. Relatively new Fords had 85 hp flathead V-8s and torque tube drive. Chevrolets were straight-6 pushrod engines that recently had gone from 15psi oil pressure to full pressure of 35 lbs. Most others were flathead fours, sixes or eights. Standard transmissions were normal three-speeds on the steering column, which were very sloppy, even when new. Four-

Opposite, top: August 9, 1953, at Lockbourne AFB, Columbus, Ohio — Harley Watts Jr. and his MG TC with a reporter from the *Columbus Dispatch*. Note the row of Strategic Air Command bombers in the background. *Opposite, bottom:* Harley Watts's TC again, at a hillclimb in southern Ohio in 1953. It's the Bellfontaine Hillclimb (courtesy Bob Watts).

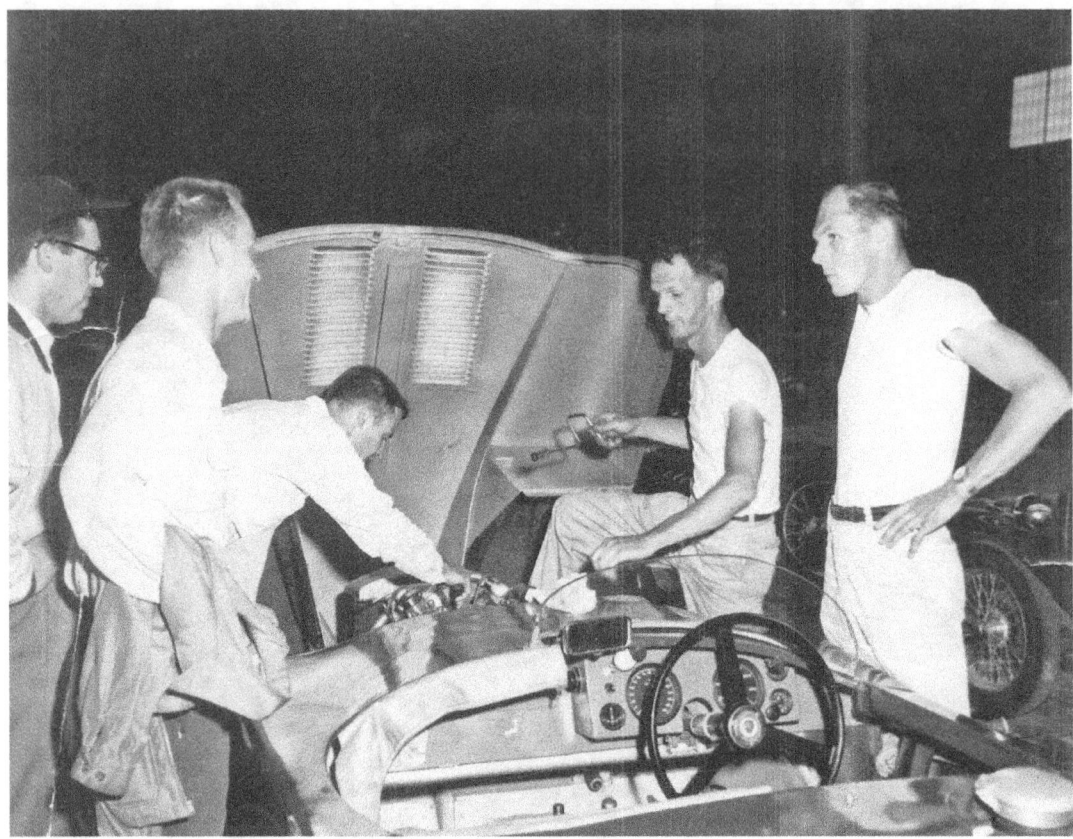

The crew works on Bob Fergus's C-Type Jaguar at Lockbourne AFB in 1953. There's Harley Watts with the wrench, and brother Bob Watts to the right of him (courtesy Bob Watts).

speed transmissions were unknown to the average driver. As a result, any well-driven TC or TD could out-drag and outrun many then-current American cars, even on straight roads."

The MG enthusiasts enjoyed driving their taut-handling cars on the winding roads of southern and central Ohio, and occasionally drag racing on the street. Bob Watts described the area's "Grand Prix." "Locally, a road course was set up southwest of Columbus on country roads. Traffic was light. The course had a number of bends, several of which were fairly tight, several long straights and some rolling bends. Good MG roads. The sheriff soon became aware of the 'fun.' Frequent efforts to catch the 'speeders' took place but the rolling bends were not 'Ford' roads. Police radio was not very good and attempts at roadblocks were always after the fact. Sitting at Harley's house and listening to the sirens was like listening to hounds chasing the fox."

Meanwhile, weekends were very active with hillclimbs, regularity runs, rallies and just finding MG roads and driving them. Harley went to Watkins Glen in 1949. While on Bob Fergus's pit crew, he went to Brynfan Tyddyn, Giants Despair hillclimb, Elkhart Lake, McDill AFB, Lockbourne AFB, Chanute Field in Illinois and others. The TC was driven to, during, and back from every race. Harley kept the Fergus TC running at its

Harley Watts, his 1948 TC and a young lady are props in a publicity photograph for the *Columbus Dispatch* at the Lockbourne SAC base races in 1953. Note the B-47s in the background. At the height of the cold war, these were ready to deliver a nuclear bomb to the Soviet Union on a moment's notice (courtesy Bob Watts).

best. Harley worked at Columbus Sports Car Co., owned by Bob Fergus. Late in 1950, after the first Elkhart Lake race on June 23, Fergus placed an ad in the *Columbus Dispatch* noting: "Now on display in our showroom: the winning MG of the Novice Class Elkhart Lake Road Race. This car was tuned at the Columbus Sports Car Co. by Harley B. Watts. If you want your MG to be rapid, bring it out to Harley."

"At Watkins Glen," says Bob Watts, "Reggie Ogilvie, the Postmaster General of Ontario, broke the crankshaft in his TC coming down the long steep hill into the north end of town. Bob Fergus did the same. Bob got to the 'spares truck' from New York first, and purchased the only XPAG crankshaft in stock, for $35. With no spare crank, Reggie removed the rod, piston and pushrods for the cylinder. Heavy gasket paper was wrapped around the broken throw and held in place with several hose clamps. The pan was replaced and the engine cranked up. It ran with a very bad vibration and was driven back to Canada."

Harley Watts's racing was primarily road races and hillclimbs. The one at Bellfontaine included the 1953 event. Harley took it up the hill with a very good time. And then a friend asked if he could drive it down. But a dog ran across the road. Fortunately he missed the dog, but unfortunately he rolled the car down the hill. The body was junked but the rest of the car was saved. Early in the 1953 racing season, Watts teamed with Bob Fergus at McDill AFB in Tampa, Florida, where they took 1st in F-Production. Another of the races Harley entered as a competitor from the Ohio Valley Region of SCCA was the '53 SAC-base race at Lockbourne near Columbus. There he raced against Don Marsh and Bob Fergus.

In 1954, Harley and Fergus drove down to McDill AFB in Tampa, Florida, raced Bob's TC in the 6-hour enduro, took a 1st place, and drove it back to Columbus.

Those old TCs are rugged cars, all right.

Herb Whiting

Herb Whiting was a typical club racer. He drove, at various times, a Jag 120, an MG-TD, a Siata Spyder, an Austin-Healey Sprite and a Porsche 550 Spyder. The Porsche was not raced. That was the car he drove to his law office in downtown Cleveland. Some people thought it was a pushrod-converted Spyder but, no, it was the full-blown 4-cam Porsche. Herb raced at only five venues: Put-in-Bay; Akron Airport sports car races; Watkins Glen; Dunkirk, New York; and Thompson, Connecticut. He wasn't the world's greatest driver and did not always have notable finishes, but he was a participant, the top rung in the continuum of "thinking about a parade, watching a parade, being in the parade."

Alfa national SCCA driving champion Chuck Stoddard came to know him in a roundabout way. "Herb was an attorney," Chuck says. "He bought an XK120 from Jaguar Cleveland, and he later had a problem with it. The dealership said it would cost $600 to fix. This was a lot of money considering that a new 120 was $3900. Through the Cleveland Sport Car Club, he heard about me. I had a small sports car parts and service business at my house, while I worked weekdays at Thompson Products.

"I had just gotten home from work when here comes Herb Whiting in his Jaguar. It was something special—something the neighbors would slow down to see. The car had a drivability problem. It just wasn't right—there was a funny noise in the engine. I told him maybe I can figure it out—leave it overnight. He got someone to pick him up and left it. So there I am with this wonderful Jaguar. As I'm walking around looking it over, I open the trunk. There's a very fat roll of tools, about six inches thick. I open it up and the kit includes spare parts like points, condenser, rotor and valve springs.

"The valve springs gave me an idea. I took off the cam covers and pushed on all the valves. One of them went down. A broken spring. So I took it apart and wired the chain driving the cams, removed one cam, kept the valve in place with compressed air, and replaced the spring. On the test drive it ran perfectly. The next day Herb came back. He said, 'Did you find anything?' I said, 'Take it for a ride and I'll tell you about it.' He brought it back and he was so happy. I charged him $50, which was very good

Herb Whiting in his MG-TD at Cumberland, Maryland, in 1954. Herb's daughter Pat Dillard notes, "I found a silver trophy bowl of Dad's with the inscription 'Watkins Glen Grand Prix, Sports Car Road Races, First in Class, 1958'" (courtesy Pat Dillard).

for one night's work, and he was pleased with that, too. He told me, 'Keep in touch,' and off he went.

"Two months later, Walter Terhune pulls into the drive. Do you know who he was? He was with the J.S. Inskip Company in New York City, which imported Jaguar, MG and Rolls-Royce. He said, 'I thought I'd stop and thank you for fixing our customer's car,' referring to Herb Whiting. He told me I ought to be a dealer. I didn't know how to do that. Later there was another phone call and it was from S.H. Arnolt Inc. (Wacky Arnolt) in Chicago. His sales manager, Jack Nakagawa, was trying to recruit dealers. Jack told me, 'I had lunch with Walter Terhune.' He then said I ought to be a dealer, an MG dealer. He said, 'If you want to do this, I'll help you.' He shipped me six cars and said, 'Send me the money when you sell one and I'll send you the title.' Very soon I was selling 100 cars a year and I had a real business. Just at that point, along comes Herb Whiting again. He did everything. He formed an Ohio corporation for me. He did all the paperwork with Columbus. Everything. When he had set it all up, I said, 'What do I owe you?' He told me, 'Nothing.'

"Herb was my first Porsche customer," Stoddard continues. "He bought a '58 356A coupe and became the founder of the Northern Ohio Region of PCA. It struggled in the beginning but now has over 700 members. In the mid–'90s I took him to a local PCA meeting as the guest of honor and he was really humbly impressed by how his baby had grown. I last saw Herb about four years ago when we went out to dinner with our wives. He joked about his current sports car, a genuine World War II Jeep."

As a sometime racer, Herb ran his modified MG-TD in the second race at Put-in-Bay, 1954, finishing 6th. He ran the same Mark II TD at Akron. Then in 1957, he drove a Siata Spyder in the second race at Put-in-Bay, and at Akron. The following year at Akron he drove a Sprite, which he also drove at Watkins Glen, Dunkirk and Thompson, Connecticut.

Besides being a car enthusiast, Whiting was a racing sailor. He sailed at Mentor Harbor Yacht Club, east of Cleveland, with his friend Don Whitaker, who later became the club's commodore. One of these races was with the writer — it was the Deepwater Race, an overnighter from Cleveland Yacht Club on the west side to Put-in-Bay, in about 1975, to kick off the start of Bay Week, the big regatta. Whiting was an excellent sailor — good on the helm, good at trimming sails, good at navigation and a very pleasant person to be on the boat with.

Toward the end of his career in law, Herb Whiting became a judge. Those who knew him will miss him.

∽ Bill Wonder ∽

In World War II, Bill Wonder flew a Corsair as a Marine pilot in the Pacific campaign and later was a commercial airline pilot for Pan Am. He worked for them during his whole career and retired after almost fifty years of service.

His racing started with an MG-TD owned by his friend Bill Wellenberg. The engine was blueprinted by "Little Joe" Giubardo, who ran an Esso station on Long Island. In March of 1953, Wonder and Wellenberg drove it down from Flushing, Long Island, to Sebring, Florida, drove the 12-hour race and drove all the way back. They placed 4th in class F and 16th overall, beating the lightweight Motto MGs.

Then, for the race at Floyd Bennett Field, August 30, '53, in Brooklyn, Bill Wonder and Joe Giubardo built a modified TD out of a wreck. It was the first of three MG specials, the next of which was an interesting tube frame TD-based car. It had a gusseted subframe and an airplane aluminum body with cycle fenders. It weighed only 1200 pounds. The engine was bored to 1330cc for Class F and featured a Harman & Collins cam, tube headers and Ford carburetors. Top three finishes for the car included a 3rd at the dangerous Callicoon race in upstate New York in 1953. A subsequent MG special featuring a TD engine and Porsche suspension was completed and then ignored as Wonder and Giubardo began racing Austin-Healeys and then a Frazer Nash. After the Frazer Nash, Bill bought an AC Bristol from a friend of his from the aircraft industry, Bill Woodbury in Valley Stream, who was the importer. "That was the last car you could drive to the races," Bill says. "I drove it to Lime Rock, Thompson and Bridgehampton. It never broke. Woodbury and I tried to keep the class honest, but we weren't able to."

After that, Wonder bought a Porsche 550RS with a broken engine. Undaunted by

Top: Bill Wonder gets into his modified #18 MG-TD at the Floyd Bennett Field race in 1953. *Bottom:* The Bill Wonder/Joe Giubardo MG Special, at Joe's Esso station in New Jersey. The car weighed about 1200 pounds, with about 70 horsepower (Bill Wonder collection).

Top: Lillian Wonder smiles at the wheel in Bill's Frazer Nash Mille Miglia Replica, at the Reading Hillclimb in 1955. *Bottom:* Bill Wonder in the #77 Porsche RS-60 leads Newt Davis in his #18 Lister Chevy at Thompson, Connecticut, on the second track, which was built about 1957. The RS-60 was not out until 1960, so it's probably more like 1961 or '62 (Bill Wonder collection).

Bill Wonder (left) poses at Daytona with his GT-40, which was the ex–Ken Miles/Lloyd Ruby car. Standing with him are Cal Bedell (middle) and Bob Parker (right) (Bill Wonder collection).

the complexity of the four-cam engines, he bought the tools and rebuilt it himself. Then he built a few engines for other people. "After the 550, I got an RS60," Bill notes. "It was the ex–Peter Ryan car from Canada. It was a gentleman's car, very easy to drive ... that is, if you could get it started on a cold morning. But it couldn't keep up with the big boys."

Next was a Maserati 200S, bought from Briggs Cunningham. "The Maserati Corporation of America was right there in Glen Cove, Long Island. Their main business was machine tools. I used to go over there and have coffee once in awhile." But Bill had an incident at Lime Rock in which the flywheel flew off and came up through the dash. So he repaired the car and sold it. "I used to fly in to San Francisco," says pilot Bill, "so I knew about the Genie cars and Huffaker's on Van Ness Blvd. I used to walk down there and talk with Joe Huffaker, so naturally I bought one. I put the engine in myself. I got it from the local Buick dealer, it was like the crate engines they sell now, and it was under a thousand dollars, from carburetor to oil pan. That was not enough power so I put in a 289 Ford. That still wasn't big enough so we made it a 325. That's how we got to know the Ford people.

"I bought a GT40 direct from Ford. It was the car that Ken Miles and Lloyd Ruby used to win Daytona in 1965. I bought it at the end of the season and ran the USRRC, which was the forerunner of the Can-Am Series. I ran it in FIA races at Daytona, Sebring and Watkins Glen. It was my first taste of the big time and I never looked back." So Bill had a number of interesting cars later, but that's another story for another time.

~ Doc and Peggy Wyllie ~

Five days before my call to Doc Wyllie for this profile, he died. But thanks to Don Baker of the Steel Cities Region SCCA, Dave Nicholas of Team Unlimited, and the Charlottesville, Virginia, newspaper, I can describe the man that I worked races for, at corner stations on the Nelson Ledges and Mid-Ohio road courses.

At about the time that Doc Wyllie was working to organize the Steel Cities Region of the Sports Car Club of America, with Dr. Benedict Skitarelic and Ed Hugus (1951), he was driving an MG-TD. But he didn't compete in the 'TD.

Shortly afterward he moved on to a Jaguar XK120 and began racing. Then his wife Peggy started racing, too, also in the Jag. These were really nice cars, with predictable handling, plenty of power and marginal brakes.

Doc's name was actually Malcolm Robert Jesse Wyllie, which no one knew until he died. He would put "M.R.J. Wyllie" on the entry forms but people would call him

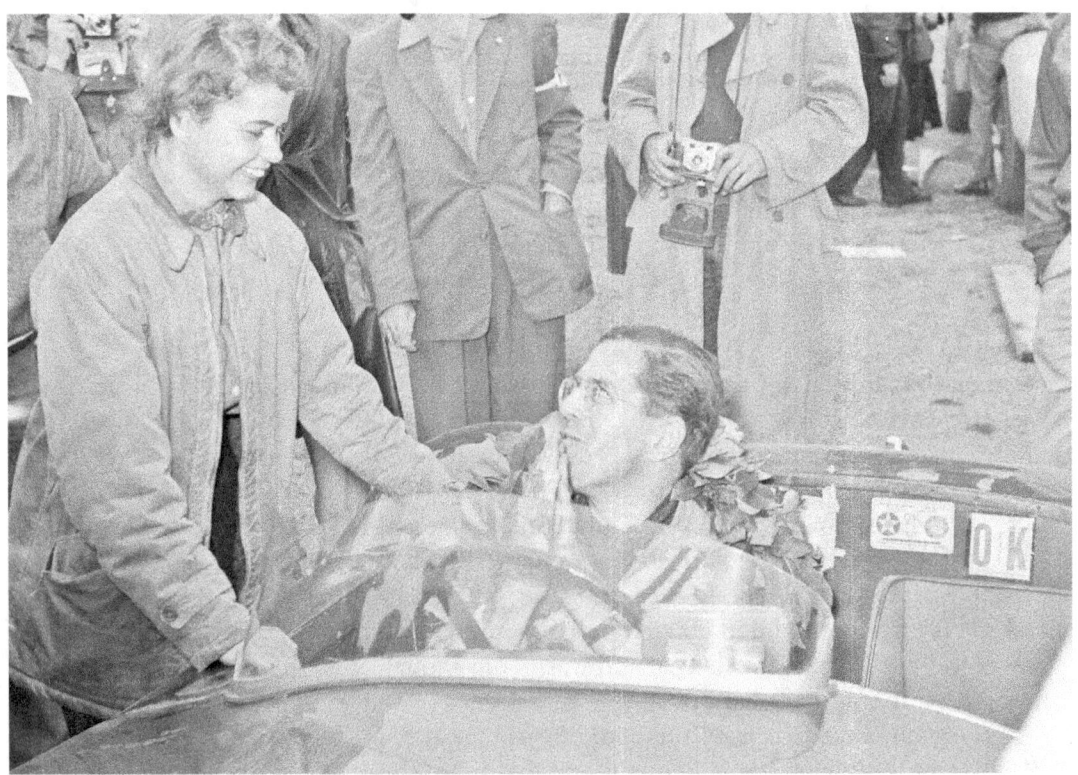

Peg and Jesse Wyllie with their C-Type Jaguar at Watkins Glen in 1954. Doc Wyllie won the Seneca Cup race that day (courtesy Alix Lafontant).

Enjoying a light moment after winning the race at Watkins Glen in 1961, Doc Wyllie and Peggy joke with race starter Tex Hopkins of the Lavender Hill Mob. Doc drove the same Lola Mark I to an SCCA national championship that year (courtesy Alix Lafontant).

"Doc" or Jesse, because it was more friendly. Here again, not everyone knew that, rather than being a physician, he was a doctor of chemistry, and he worked at Gulf Oil.

He was a very good chemist, according to the *Charlottesville* (Virginia) *Daily Progress*, and he held 72 U.S. and foreign patents on exploration and production in the oil industry. He was born in Cape Town, South Africa, in 1919, earned a bachelor of science degree in chemical engineering, and was a Rhodes Scholar at Oxford University in England (1942). During World War II, he joined the British Navy to work with the Department of Miscellaneous Weapons Development, reaching the rank of lieutenant commander. Right after World War II, he came to America as a research fellow at Johns Hopkins University, and he met his wife Peggy there. He joined Gulf Oil in 1947 and remained with them until his retirement in 1978. In 1961 he became a naturalized citizen of the United States of America.

Picking up from the Jaguar in 1953, he then got the competition model, a C-Type, in 1954. At Chanute AFB, he began the race in 7th place, had a flat tire, changed it and worked his way back up to 7th. At Cumberland in '54, Peggy Wyllie won the Ladies' Race over Suzy Dietrich in the supercharged TC and Doc Wyllie won the feature over

Jesse Wyllie buckles his helmet prior to the G-Modified race at Watkins Glen in 1961. Wyllie is driving his Lola Mark 1 (courtesy Alix Lafontant).

Bill Eager's Offenhauser-engined Aston Martin. In 1955, the Wyllies were driving a Jaguar XK-140 and Doc ran it at the Mt. Equinox Hill Climb, posting a 16th overall. The next year, Doc became aware of the new lightweight cars from England, particularly the Lotus. He met with Colin Chapman and bought the Lotus 9 that had raced at Le Mans. It was a special car that was lighter yet than the customer Mk9s. He had the 750cc engine removed and replaced with an 1100cc Coventry Climax, for competition in the G-Modified class.

He was immediately successful with this car and his main competitors were the owners of other lightweight British cars, including Chuck Dietrich in the Elva Mark I and Tom Hallock in the Cooper Bobtail. Wyllie was most closely associated with the car with the yellow and green badge — people would say, "Oh yes, the Lotus driver." He drove them from 1955 to 1970. Of the Le Mans Mark 9 he said, "It was an experimental car. You could see where tubes had been welded on and then cut off to reduce weight. It had Borrani alloy wire wheels [as opposed to the heavier Dunlop steel wire wheels], and even the knock-off hubs had been machined lighter. It was a small, nimble, fast car and it was the first Lotus to have disc brakes. I drove it from 1955 to '59 and then my wife took it over. Then I got the famous #58 Lotus 11 that won Le Mans in the 750 class. It was also very light. It was the first car to have the magnesium wobbly wheels. Colin put an 1100 in it. That was also a very successful car."

In 1960, Wyllie took a detour from Lotus, briefly, and bought a drum-brake Lola. None of the new disc-brake Lolas were available and he bought this one used in England. "The drum brakes were large and very good," he said. "The first time we raced, at the Road America 500 Enduro, we won our class. We raced with the same oil and water in the engine as it had in England. In 1962 I knew Eric Broadley pretty well and I bought a new Lola with disc brakes. The Lola was a good car. Nothing could beat it." That was the year Wyllie won the SCCA National Championship in the G-Modified class. The Lola Mark 1 was the last fast front-engined car in G-Modified. In 1961, an American rear-engine car named the Bobsy was developed, and in 1962, the Lotus 23 was introduced as a sports racing version of the Lotus 22 Formula Junior.

Of course Doc and Peggy Wyllie drove many different cars over the years. These included Bobsy, Porsche and Corvette. Their racing friends were Pittsburgh Region people like Don Baker, Ed Lowther and Donna Mae Mims. One time Grady Davis at Gulf Oil asked Doc to co-drive a Corvette with Don Yenko. Donna Mae asked him, "Well, how did you like the Corvette?" He replied, "It was sufficiently terrifying," and added, "When a Corvette is totally out of control, it's under control."

In addition to his role as a driver, Doc Wyllie also served the SCCA as a contest board member. At the controversial 1956 race at Watkins Glen, he wisely took a vote among competitors about who would like to race at the track that was experiencing problems with the breakup of its new paving. The Wyllies also organized rallies for the Steel Cities Region and hosted the post-event parties. You could always find Peggy in the paddock, wearing a baseball cap and sports jacket. Jesse was very proud of his membership in the exclusive Road Racing Drivers' Club and wore their emblem on his helmet.

Doc Wyllie retired from racing in 1970, when he accepted the Gulf Oil Company assignment in London, England, as vice-president, Eastern Hemisphere. He then moved on to become president and then chairman of the company in 1975. He returned to the U.S. in 1976 and became VP of Exploration and Production until his retirement.

∽ SHERRIE ZUCKERT ∽

Sherrie didn't do too much racing, to be honest, but we had to wrap up with someone whose last name began with "Z" and Ugo Zagato never drove an MG. According to Jim Sitz, Sherrie did — an MG-TD that she raced briefly in Long Island Sports Car Association events. We know that she raced at Windham Hillclimb, where she took a 3rd in the ladies' class, and she may have raced at Lime Rock but we can't be certain. According to Fred Stevenson of Lotus East, Sherri was a pretty young woman with a nice figure and popular with the racing teams ... and she had an ocelot, which stayed with her one time in a hotel at Thompson, Connecticut. She wrote articles for *Sports Car Graphic* (often confused with *Sports Cars Illustrated*, which later became *Car and Driver*), including a race report on VIR in 1963 and a road test of the Lotus Elan in 1964.

She was a friend of the late Connie Lovejoy, who was a Chowderhead (Madison Avenue Sports Car Driving and Chowder Society) and former historian at Lime Rock. She worked in timing & scoring at Lime Rock for announcer Art Peck, and she lived in Great Neck, Long Island. No pictures of her racing MG could be found or, for that matter, of Miss Zuckert.

Of course, a number of other MG drivers are missing. Bill Stroppe, the third driver of the MG V8-60 known as "2 Jr.," would be one of them. He drove it after Phil Hill and Richie Ginther. And what of the few early drivers who did not start in MGs? Phil Walters, considered the best of that era, started in midget racers before the war. After service as a glider pilot in the invasion of Holland, he came back and, despite serious injuries, was persuaded to return to racing. He had tremendous success in a Kurtis-

Offenhauser and then, when attendance at midget races waned, switched to stock cars, where the legendary #23 was almost unbeaten. He met Briggs Cunningham at a hill-climb and began a sports car career that included two Sebring wins, a 3rd at Le Mans and an offer to drive Formula One cars for Ferrari.

Some of the drivers coming into the sport in the early fifties found a greater variety of cars to choose from. Sherwood Johnston, for instance, decided to get a Jaguar when he started racing in 1951. And then there was Colorado racer Danny Collins, who got into it with a supercharged 1928 Alfa Romeo.

But the MG was a great car for the early racing driver. It was affordable, durable and easy to drive — no unexpected handling like the 1951 Porsches. In an era where few trailered their cars to races, TC owner Bob Watts reminds us, you could drive it from Columbus, Ohio, to McDill Air Force Base at Tampa, Florida — as his brother Harley and Bob Fergus did — drive it in the 6-hour race, taking a 1st in class, and drive it back to Columbus. In stock form, MGs offered even competition, although, as Ohio racer John Comey noted, "Some were more equal than others."

And it's true that MGs responded well to modification. Chuck Dietrich ground, polished, lightened, drilled and balanced every part of his supercharged MG-TC until it was almost as fast as a Porsche Spyder. Or maybe it was just Chuck's driving. Early racing grids were full of aspiring MG race drivers who were stockbrokers, car dealers, dentists and engineers during the week. These great little cars opened the door to a rewarding life in amateur racing for thousands of people. Today, unfortunately, with the exception of VSCCA races, few T-Series MGs are found on the grids of vintage racing events. But of course that could change. Say, do you have an MG? Ever thought about racing it?

Bibliography

While some of this book is based upon material from other sources, the vast majority of its content, approximately 95 percent, consists of conversations with the racing drivers featured, their friends, relatives, competitors, photographers, mechanics, racing officials and spectators.

Correspondence and Interviews

Adamson, Henry. Telephone interviews, December 19, 2009, and January 4, 2010.
Allison, Jeff. Email correspondence, October 21, 2002.
Argetsinger, Cameron. Telephone interview, August 19, 1998.
Argetsinger, Michael. Telephone interview, May 11, 2007.
Ash, David. Telephone interview, October 27, 2006.
Askew, Ken. Telephone interview, February 28, 2010.
Baker, Don. Email correspondence, February 10, 2010, and February 16, 2010.
Ballenger, Bob. Email correspondence January 15, 2010; telephone interview, January 16, 2010.
Becker, Hank. Personal interview, May 3, 2009.
Berman, Larry. Email correspondence, March 8, 2010, and March 12, 2010.
Brow, Art. Telephone interviews, July 17, 2007, January 27, 2009, and February 3, 2009; personal interviews, February 6, 2009, and July 2, 2010.
Brow, Dutch. Telephone interviews, January 27, 2009, and February 3, 2009; personal interview, July 2, 2010.
Brown, David. Email interview, March 18, 2010.
Brundage, Jan. Email correspondence, May 7, 2007.
Bryant, Tom. Email correspondence, January 29, 2008.
Cadwallader, Ralph. Telephone interview, March 7, 2003.
Carroll, Sally. Personal interview, January 30, 2008; email correspondence, February 9, 2008, and February 10, 2008.
Carroll, Tony. Telephone interview, March 8, 2007.
Chamberlain, Beverly. Telephone interview, February 15, 2010.
Collins, Danny. Letter correspondence, July 1, 2003.
Constant, Harry. Telephone interviews, April 20, 2007, and January 14, 2010.
Cornett, Denver. Telephone interview, May 9, 2007.
Countryman, Tom. Email correspondence, January 15, 2010.
Crane, Larry. Email correspondence, January 19, 2010.
Davis, David E. Jr. Email correspondence, March 6, 2010.
De Boer, John. Email correspondence, March 1, 2007.
Dickens, Bob. Letter correspondence, April 7, 2010.
Dietrich, Chuck. Personal interview, June 8, 2008.
Dietrich, Jane. Personal interview, June 8, 2008.

Dietrich, Suzy. Personal interviews, January 17, 2010, February 20, 2010, March 2, 2010, and March 4, 2010; letter correspondence March 4, 2010.
Dillard, Pat. Email correspondence, March 10, 2010, and March 11, 2010.
Dominianni, Frank. Telephone interviews, January 3, 2006, February 27, 2007, and September 7, 2007.
Donner, Bob. Telephone interviews, January 10, 2008, and March 12, 2009.
Eaton, Michael. Email correspondence, September 21, 2007, and April 14, 2008.
Egloff, Fred. Letter correspondence, January 13, 2010, January 21, 2010, March 12, 2010, and March 14, 2010; telephone interview, February 14, 2010.
Ehrman, Gus. Telephone interviews, January 8, 2007, and September 19, 2007.
Ellmers, Charlie. Personal interview, April 15, 2007.
Ellmers, Ruth. Telephone interviews, January 15, 2005, and January 19, 2009.
Evans, Art. Email correspondence, February 22, 2010.
Fitch, John. Telephone interviews, July 28, 2007, and April 18, 2010.
Gleason, Cal. Letter correspondence, March 10, 2010.
Gordon, John. Email correspondence, March 15, 2010.
Green, Bill. Telephone interview, March 8, 2007; letter correspondence, March 11, 2010, and March 12, 2010.
Hassan, John. Telephone interview, March 31, 2010.
Henry, Paul. Telephone interview, July 2, 2008.
Hill, Phil. Telephone interview, January 8, 2008.
Holbert, Bob. Telephone interview, February 2, 2006.
Hugus, Ed. Telephone interview, March 28, 2004.
Irish, Dick. Telephone interviews, November 6, 2006, and November 27, 2006; email correspondence, February 8, 2009.
Ivanyi, George. Letter correspondence, August 6, 2010.
James, Tom. Email correspondence, March 22, 2010.
Jarmain, Walter. Telephone interview, January 27, 2009.
Jasberg, George. Email correspondence, April 18, 2007, May 8, 2007, May 9, 2007, and May 19, 2007; telephone interview, March 22, 2007.
Jeffords, Jim. Telephone interview, April 4, 2004.
Keith, Rowland. Telephone interviews, November 5, 2006, November 14, 2006, and November 16, 2006.
Kovarick, Frank. Telephone interview, March 18, 2010.
Kramer, Lee. Telephone interview, March 25, 2010.
Ksayian, Haig. Telephone interview, January 10, 2010.
Lafontant, Alix. Letter correspondence, April 9, 2005.
Larson, Bob. Letter correspondence, January 16, 2010.
Licht, Ed. Telephone interviews, December 29, 2009, and March 15, 2010.
Linton, Otto. Letter correspondence, January 10, 2004; email correspondence, February 7, 2009.
Ludvigsen, Karl. Email correspondence, February 15, 2010, and March 13, 2010.
Lunken, E.B. Telephone interviews, January 25, 2010, and February 14, 2010.
Marsh, Don. Telephone interviews, March 28, 2007, and August 2, 2007.
McAfee, Jack. Telephone interview, January 8, 2008.
McAfee, Rex. Telephone interview, January 15, 2008.
McCluggage, Denise. Telephone interview, January 8, 2010.
Moran, Charles. Telephone interview, April 26, 2007.
Moran, David. Email correspondence, April 29, 2007.
Morrison, Bob. Telephone interview, September 9, 2007; email correspondence, September 11, 2007.
Moss, Al. Telephone interviews, May 21, 2007, and May 22, 2007.
Nicholas, Dave. Email correspondence, February 25, 2010, February 26, 2010, and March 22, 2010.
Parsons, Bob. Telephone interview, April 29, 2007.
Patterson, Alan. Telephone interviews, February 10, 2009, and March 25, 2010.
Pollack, Bill. Telephone interviews, May 16, 2007, and May 17, 2007.
Rye, Walter. Telephone interview, February 8, 2010.
Satava, Bob. Letter correspondence, April 4, 2009.
Schiemer, Paul. Email correspondence, April 28, 2007.
Schreyer, Cecilia Manney. Email correspondence, May 26, 2007.

Seielstad, David. Telephone interview, January 1, 2007.
Seyler, Art. Telephone interview, April 27, 2009.
Sitz, Jim. Letter correspondence, March 29, 2007, April 7, 2007, May 29, 2007, January 9, 2008, February 6, 2009, May 29, 2009, and February 3, 2010; telephone interviews, May 29, 2007 and January 9, 2008.
Staufer, Chris. Telephone interview, February 15, 2008.
Staufer, Pat. Telephone interview, January 14, 2008.
Steger, Gerry. Telephone interview, January 20, 2009.
Stevenson, Bruce. Telephone interview, April 12, 2005.
Stoddard, Chuck. Telephone interviews, February 27, 2009, and March 5, 2010; email correspondence, January 8, 2009.
Stone, Matt. Email interview, March 6, 2010.
Tame, John. Telephone and email, April 8, 2009; telephone interview, April 19, 2009.
Thompson, Dick. Telephone interview, July 28, 2007.
Tierno, Joe. Email correspondence, March 22, 2010.
Troyan, Fred. Telephone interview, January 4, 2009.
Underwood, Lake. Telephone interview, November 28, 2004.
Vack, Pete. Email correspondence, February 21, 2010, and March 14, 2010.
Victor, Bill. Telephone interview, March 23, 2007.
Walters, Phil. Personal interview, May 28, 1996.
Watts, Bob. Telephone and letter correspondence, March 11, 2010.
Wheat, Morris. Email correspondence, March 22, 2010.
Wonder, Bill. Telephone interviews, June 3, 2005, and December 12, 2008.

Books and Periodicals

Allison, Jeff. Chuck Dietrich profile, Mid-Ohio Racing Program, SVRA Vintage Race. Lexington, OH: Mid-Ohio, 1997.
Berman, Larry. *Chronology of the Cunningham Team*. Newton, MA: self-published, 2009.
Bochroch, Albert R. *American Automobile Racing: An Illustrated History*. New York: Viking, 1974.
Breslauer, Ken. *12 Hours of Sebring: The Complete Record Book of America's Greatest Sports Car Races*. St. Petersburg, FL: Auto Racing Memories, 1989.
Brown, Allen E. *The History of America's Speedways: Past & Present*. Comstock Park, MI: self-published, 1994.
Brown, Allen E., and Nancy L. Brown. *National Speedway Directory, 2003*. Comstock Park, MI: self-published, 2003.
Castle, John. *A History: Finger Lakes Region, SCCA*. Rochester, NY: Finger Lakes Region, SCCA, 1986.
Considine, Tim. *American Grand Prix Racing: A Century of Drivers & Cars*. Osceola, WI: MBI, 1997.
Defechereux, Philippe. *Watkins Glen 1948–1952: The Definitive Illustrated History*. Indianapolis, IN: Beeman Jorgensen, 1998.
Egloff, Fred. "Fifty Years Ago: The First Races." *Piston Patter*, the newsletter of the Chicago Region of the Sports Car Club of America (June 1999): 4–5.
Evans, Art. *Race Legends of the Fabulous Fifties*. Redondo Beach, CA: Photo Data Research, 2003.
Fitch, John. *Adventure on Wheels*. New York: G.P. Putnam's Sons, 1956.
Goodwin, Carl. "And Then the British Cars Came: The G-Modified Revolution." *Automobile Quarterly* 47, no. 1: 20–29.
_____. "Cameron Argetsinger." *Classic MG*, no. 33: 6.
_____. "The Cunningham Equipe." *Automobile Quarterly* 28, no. 1: 44–65.
_____. "Milan Hillclimb." *The MG Messenger*, newsletter of MG Car Club, Lake Erie Centre (September 1969): 2–4.
_____. "Tony Pompeo: The Etceterini Man." *Automobile Quarterly* 44, no. 3: 46–57.
Green, Bill, and J.J. O'Malley. *Watkins Glen from Griswold to Gordon: Fifty Years of Competition at the Home of American Road Racing*. Charlotte, NC: UMI, 1989.
Lyons Pete. *Can-Am*. Osceola, WI: Motorbooks International, 1995.
Marini, Mike. "Racing at Elkhart Lake, WI—Part I: The Early Years, 1950–1952." *MG Vintage Racers* (June 15, 2001): 1–6.
McCluggage, Denise. *By Brooks Too Broad for Leaping*. Santa Fe, NM: Fulcorte Press, 1994.
Nye, Doug. *Cooper Cars*. London: Osprey, 1991.

Pollack, Bill. *Red Wheels and White Sidewalls: Confessions of an Allard Racer.* Carpinteria, CA: Brown Fox Books, 2004.

Royce, Suzanne. *Detroit Region Sports Car Club of America Celebrates 50 Years 1948–1998.* Detroit: Detroit Region SCCA, 1998.

Schultz, Tom. *Road America: Five Decades of Racing at Elkhart Lake.* Indianapolis, IN: Beeman Jorgensen, 1999.

Stone, Matt. *McQueen's Machines: The Cars and Bikes of a Hollywood Icon.* Minneapolis, MN: MBI, 2007.

Taylor, Rich. *Lime Rock Park: 35 Years of Racing.* Sharon, CT: Sharon Mountain Press, 1992.

Van Der Feen, Dic, and Ray Boldt. "Road America 500: Hall Wins: Follmer USRRC." *Sports Car* (October 1965): 10–12.

Wyllie, M.R.J. "Competition at Cumberland." *Sports Car* (September/October 1953): 2–8.

Index

Abarth 35, 36, 65, 140
Ace Bristol 34, 208, 266
Adamson, Henry 184, 186
Akron Airport Race 28, 39, 77, 90, 124, 170, 182, 243
Akron Sports Car Club 232
Alfa GTZ 240, 241
Alfa Romeo 1, 28, 34, 46, 49, 52, 60, 87, 89, 111, 131, 151, 152, 240, 256
Alfa Romeo Giulietta 51, 91, 121, 139, 152, 189, 205, 214, 215, 238
Allard 30, 131, 132, 137, 146, 147, 179, 198, 210, 211
Allen, Fred 7
Ambrosini, Georgio 33
Ambrosini, Renato 33
America's Cup 50
Amey, Peggy 75
Amey, Ron 75
Andrews AFB 33, 87
Ardent Alligator 12
Argentine Grand Prix 120
Argetsinger, Cameron 9
Argetsinger, Michael 10
Arkus-Duntov, Zora 246
Arnolt, S.H. 13
Arnolt Bristol 14, 15, 16, 19, 20, 54, 87, 149
Arnolt MG 13, 114
Artemus Images 86
Arutunoff, Toly 121
Ash, David 16
Askew, Ken 87, 89, 90
Aston Martin 62, 178, 231, 272
Atterbury AFB 33, 87
Austin-Healey 54, 57, 87, 89
Austin-Healey 100S 8, 147, 148
Automobile Magazine 69
Automobile Racing Club of America 46, 60

Baker, Don 137, 270, 273
Bakersfield CA 84
Ballenger, Bob 19
Bandini 49, 72, 117, 118, 122, 124, 187

Barber, Charlie 225
Barlow, Roger 254, 255
Barri, Italy 120
Battle of the Bulge 224
Beach sports racer 36
Bear, Roger 122, 179, 180
Beasley, Ma 228
Becker, Hank 25
Behm, Herm 187
Behra, Jean 181, 215
Bellfontaine Hillclimb 261, 263
Bencker, Bill 39
Bendix Cup 178
Benett, John Gordon 31
Bentley, John 33
Bergstrom AFB 219
Berman, Larry 33, 62, 107, 140
Bertone 14, 20
Beverly, Mass. 133
Blackhawk Farms 57, 93
BMC 99
BMW 94, 95, 96
Bobsy 75, 272
Bonneville 18, 99, 107, 131
Bott, Frank 65, 160, 219
Boynton, Ted 15, 20, 22, 23, 182
Brabham, Jack 11
Brabham cars 65
Bradley, Bill 35
Brainerd 57
Brands Hatch 80
Brennan, Jay 156
Bridgehampton 33, 47, 53, 61, 83, 87, 97, 205, 235, 236, 237
British Leyland 99
British Motor Corporation 18
BRM 113
Broadley, Eric 272
Brocken, Karl 92
Brow, Art 37
Brow Dutch 37, 38, 42, 170, 223, 225, 226, 227, 228
Brown, David 251
Brown, Joe 13, 42, 48, 102, 103, 211 242,
Brumos Porsche 42

Brundage, Hubert 39
Brynfan Tyddyn 33, 46, 191, 211, 217
B.S. Cunningham Co. 62
Bucher, Bob 250
Budlong, Barry 239
Buell, Temple 84, 139
Bugatti Type 35 10, 26, 188, 202, 203, 206
Bugatti Type 54 205
Bu-Merc 59, 60
Burrell, Frank 246

C-47 aircraft 153
C-Type Jaguar 30, 220, 221, 262
Cabianca, Giulio 165
Cadillac 49
Cadwallader, Ralph 42
Cahier, Bernard 2
California Sports Car Club 254
Callicoon, NY 247
Camaro 39, 228
Campbell, Jack 130, 132
Campbell, Malcolm 130, 132
Campbell-Ewald 69, 70, 71, 246
Canaan, Bob 131, 192, 193, 215, 255
Car and Driver 70, 71
Caracas, Venezuela 120
Carrell Speedway 209
Carroll, Jim 43
Carroll, Sally 43
Carroll Shelby Children's Foundation 232
Carsten, Tom 213
Case Tech 243
Castrol R 28
Chamberlain, Beverly 195
Chamberlain, Jay 195
Chanute AFB 33, 54, 67, 71, 78
Chaparral 87
Chapman, Colin 211, 272
Charlottesville Daily Progress 270, 271
Cherryhomes, Roy 229
Chevron 220
Chicago-to-Mackinac 149

279

Chicago Tribune 252
Chinetti, Luigi 36, 62, 139, 143, 144, 179, 183
Chrysler Corp. 229, 232
Cincinnati Gang 122, 179, 180, 183
Cinema Center Films 198
Cisitalia 34, 44, 45, 217
Clark, Barney 69, 246
Clark, Jim 75, 113, 239
Cleveland Sport Car Club 43, 44, 243, 264
Cleveland Yacht Club 170, 266
Cobra 201
Cole, Ed 62
Cole, Tom 237
Coleman, Jesse 30
Colgate University 251
Collier, Miles 46
Collier, Sam 46
Collins, Danny 83, 193, 246, 274
Colorado Automobile Hall of Fame 87
Columbus Dispatch 263
Columbus Sports Car Co. 263
Comey, John 274
Competition Motors 255
Competition Press 201
Constant, Harry 49
Constantine, George 85
Continental Divide Raceways 85
Cooper 64, 65, 78, 139, 153, 196, 211, 222
Cooper, Charles 197
Cooper, Jackie 7
Cooper, John 197
Cooper Bobtail 34, 216, 272
Cooper FIII 145, 146
Cooper-Porsche 201, 256
Cord Phaeton 54, 57, 177
Cornell University 29, 159
Cornett, Denver 52
Corvair 116
Corvette 23, 24, 57, 81, 82, 83, 95, 117, 122, 139, 144, 158, 166, 183, 215, 216, 244, 245, 247, 273
Corvette Grand Sport 247
Corvette Hall of Fame 244
Countryman, Tom 54
Cracraft, Leach 126, 137
Crawford, Ed 65, 123,182, 183
Crosley Special 161
Crusoe, Jack 239
Cumberland Airport 33, 39, 67, 83
Cunningham 31, 33, 72, 208, 209
Cunningham, Briggs 59
Cunningham C-4R 31, 61, 105, 106, 208

D-Type Jaguar 30, 33, 62, 65
Daigh, Chuck 257
D'Arcy MacManus & Masius 70
Davis, David E., Jr. 65
Davis, Grady 244, 247, 273
Davis, Lucille 138
Davis, Newt 268
Davis, Pete 138
Daytona Beach record 220

Dean, James 195
Decker, Sherm 252
de Beaufort, Carel 138, 139
de Boer, John 187, 210
Deen, Dorothy 255
Deepwater Race 266
Deitz, Emil 192
de Portago, Marquis 126, 181, 183
de Tomaso, Alejandro 120, 138
Deutsche-Bonnet 36
Dick Irish 140
Dickens, Bob 71
Dickens, Ruth 71
Dickens, Sid 71, 73
Dietrich, Chuck 73
Dietrich, Suzy 76
Dobbins, Lefty 15, 20
Dolin, Irv 80
Dominianni, Frank 80
Donick, Jim 229
Donner, Bob 83
Donner, Bobby 87
Donner, David 87
Donner, Joan 85
Dreyfus, Rene' 16
Duckworth, Bill 42
Duesenberg 73
Duncan, Dale 23
Dunkirk, New York 9, 30, 243
Dunlop 175
Durbin, Ralph 87

Eaton, Michael 18
Ecurie Yankee 217
Edenvale, Ontario 7
Edgar, John 192, 193, 194, 213, 214, 231
Edgar, William 214
Egloff, Fred 91
Ehrman, Gus 96
Eichenlaub, Jim 228
Ekins, Bud 197
Elkhart Lake 14, 19, 20, 33, 49, 51, 52, 53, 72, 87, 89, 92
Ellmers, Charlie 100
El Paso Lawman 96
Elva 35, 75, 76, 77, 81, 162, 272
Enever, Sid 16, 177
England 31, 75
Equations of Motion 206
Erickson Ernie 16, 25, 92
EX-179 Record Car 18
EX-181 MG Streamliner 131
EX–219 Austin-Healey Streamliner 99

F4U Corsair 260, 266
Fangio, Juan Manuel 20, 24, 25, 181, 215
Fergus, Bob 103, 143
Ferguson, Alice 148
Ferguson, Jim 145
Ferrari 19, 21, 22, 44, 49, 60, 61, 62, 63, 112, 121, 124, 125, 126, 179, 182, 208, 215, 229, 231
Ferrari 4.4 231
Ferrari 166 63, 178, 179, 181

Ferrari 195 188
Ferrari 212 208
Ferrari 335S 257
Ferrari 412 257
Ferrari GTO 190
Ferrari Mexico 116
Ferrari Mondial 218
Ferrari Row 122
Ferrari Testa Rossa 125, 126, 183, 184, 256
Ferris Bueller's Day Off 92
The 1500cc Triple 219
Fina, Perry 173
Fitch, John 105
Floyd Bennett Field 266, 267
Flying Shingle 256
Flynn, Chet 139
Ford 66
Ford GT40 12, 201, 229, 232, 269
Ford Thunderbird 90
Formula Atlantic 157
Formula 5000 75
Formula Ford 157
Formula Junior 39, 63, 79, 83, 194, 197, 212
Formula Libre 206
Formula III 145
Formula Vee 38, 39, 57, 58, 228
Foster, Bill 17, 100, 244
Frazer Nash 96, 266, 268
Frick-Tappett Motors 62
Funny Face Auto Racing Team 108

Gary, Bob 23, 92
Gausti, Secondo 255
Gent, Dick 123
Ghia 120
Giants Despair Hillclimb 33, 46, 87, 208, 191
Giaur 185, 186
Ginther, Richie 111
Gleason, Cal 113
Glockler Porsche 83, 160
Goldich, Bob 16, 20, 24
Goldman, Max 16, 67, 90
Goleta Time Trials 213
Goodwin, Carl 6
Goodwin, Nancy 38
Gordon, Jack 36
Gough Industries 99, 199
Grand Island 114
Green, Bill 33, 87, 151, 161, 239, 249
Green, William — Motor Racing Library 10, 151
Greenacres, Ontario 49
Greenwood Raceway 57
Gregory, Masten 19, 20, 126, 135, 183, 220, 231
Grier, Bob 16
Grossman, Bob 37
Gulf Oil Company 271, 273
A Gullwing at Twilight 107
Gurney, Dan 11, 65, 206

Haas, Carl 92, 187
Hagerstown, MD Race 29, 33
Hall, Jim 75, 87

Index

Hallock, Tom 272
Hambro Automotive Corp. 18, 99
Hambro Distributors 99
Hanna, Howard 36
Hansgen, Walt 63, 64, 65
Harewood Acres 49, 73, 148, 243
Haskell, Isabelle 117
Hassan, Chuck 121
Hassan, Jane 121, 122, 123
Hassan, John 121, 122
Hawthorn Mike 181, 229
Healey Silverstone 11, 28, 33, 62
Healey Westland 188
Henry, Chuck 126
Hill, Alma 133
Hill, Derek 133
Hill, Graham 11
Hill, Phil 130
Hill & Vaughn 133
Hi-Speed Power Equipment 80
Hively, Howard 23, 122, 125, 179, 180, 183, 194
Hoffman, Max 255
Holbert, Bob 85, 133
Holder, Lorrain 228
Holder, Manny 26
Huffaker, Joe 269
Hugus, Ed 137
Huntoon, George 39, 46, 252

Indianapolis 206
International Motor Racing Research Center 12, 33, 96, 112, 161, 162, 239, 249
International Motors 254
Iowa City Race 19, 71
Ireland, Innes 11
Ivanyi, George 37
Iwo Jima 260

Jack Pry Motors 211
Jaguar Cleveland 232, 264
Jaguar XK-120 11, 19, 30, 33, 72, 123, 252
Jaguar XKSS 30, 196
James, Tom 249
Janesville, Wisc. 14, 87
Jarmain, Walter 223, 224, 228
Jasberg, George 81, 131, 208, 219, 229
Jazz and Reba 73
Jeep 266
Jeffords, Jim 183
Jennings, Bruce 246
Jerome, John 70
Johnston, Jim 21, 122, 184
Johnston, Sherwood 64, 65, 231, 274
J.S. Inskip 16, 17, 18, 31, 99, 137, 151, 169, 211, 265
June Sprints 85, 123, 181

Kansas City Races 20
Keift 26, 28, 222
Keift-Norton 140
Keikhaefer, Carl 187
Keith, Rowland 145

Kendall, Bob 239
Kennedy, Dick 52
Kenyon & Eckhardt 69, 70
Kilborn, John 23
Kimberly, Jim 30, 178, 179, 180, 183, 184, 231, 243, 257
Kimes, Beverly Rae 96
Kincheloe, Bill 244
Kirschoffer, Charlie 140, 141, 143, 144
Kleen, John 188
Kovarick, Frank 251
Kramer, LeRoy, Jr. 148
Krasberg, Bob 92, 156
Ksayian, Haig 150

Lafontant, Alix Cover, 8, 9,12, 31,32, 33, 60, 61, 63, 64,113, 118, 119, 120, 133, 134, 135, 139, 163, 167, 189, 191, 202, 207, 208, 230, 231, 245, 250, 251, 259, 270, 271
Lafontant, Nicole 162
La Junta Airport 84
Lake Forest College 185
Lamport, Richard 123
Lancia Aurelia 188
Larson, Bill 156, 157
Larson, Bob 153
Larson, Verna 156
Lawrenceville, IL 71, 180
Le Mans 33, 34, 36, 49, 57, 64, 131, 206, 208, 231
LeMans (movie) 198
Leonard, Elmore 70
Leonidis MG 46, 48, 59, 149
Lester, Harry 109
Lester MG 34, 73, 190
Lewis, Marsh 65
Licht, Ed 158
Linden Field 83, 217
Linsay's Tavern 44, 228, 243
Linton, Otto 163
Lister Jaguar 65, 81
Lloyd, Bill 167
Lockbourne AFB 26, 33, 49, 67, 74, 87, 119, 120, 191
Lola 271, 272
Long Island Sports Car Association 273
Lossman, Bob 168
Lossman MG 223, 234, 235
Lotus 34, 65, 78, 79, 162, 194, 195, 208, 211, 228, 272
Lotus East 211, 212, 273, 273
Lotus Elite 36
Lovely, Pete 201
Lowther, Ed 37, 273
Ludvigsen, Karl 171
Lunken, E.B. 177, 181, 183
Lunken, Ebby 177
Lunken Airport 177
Lyndale Farms 57, 93
Lyons, Charlie 83

MacArthur, Sandy 184
Madison Avenue Sports Car Driving and Chowder Society 273

Manney, Annie 188, 189
Manney, Cecilia 188, 189
Manney, Henry, III 188
Manting, Jack 259
Marlboro 39, 166
Marsh, Don 190
Martini Formula Atlantic 76
Maserati 24, 31, 36, 52, 54, 117, 120, 182, 215
Maserati Corporation of America 269
Massachusetts Institute of Technology 171, 175, 238, 239
McAfee, Ernie 188, 193, 214
McAfee, Jack 192
McAfee, Rex 192, 194
McCluggage, Denise 59, 65, 96
McDill AFB 105, 117, 165, 254, 264
McDonald, Dave 137, 202
McGee, Jim 235
McLaren, Bruce 65
McLaren 4B 75
McQueen, Steve 195
McQueens Machines 195, 197
Meadowdale 57
Mentor Harbor Yachting Club 30, 243, 266
Mercedes Benz 300SL 34, 54, 107, 252
Mercedes Benz W196 67, 68
Merhar, Ed 241
Merlyn 35
Merriman-Holbrook 30
Metropolitan Museum of Art 45
Meyer Drake 68
Meyer Special 235
MG Car Club 13, 18, 19, 44, 61, 67, 156, 171, 172, 220, 235
The MG Guide 176
MG J2, J4 14, 163
MG Magnette 1, 2, 59, 163
MG Specials 111, 131, 161, 192, 193, 199
MG YB 46
MG-TC 10, 30, 33, 37, 42, 43, 44, 47, 52, 53, 54, 60, 61, 69, 71, 72, 73, 74, 77, 97 78, 83, 92, 113,114, 122, 129, 171, 190, 202, 229, 235
MG-TD 19, 26, 27, 30, 31, 32, 37, 39, 44, 49, 66, 67, 83, 84, 97, 98, 115, 159, 169, 208, 264
MG-TF 67, 87, 88, 116, 241
MGA 46, 54
MGB 46
Mid-Ohio 39, 75
Mid-Ohio Sports Car Club 227, 270
Midwest Sports Car Council 72
Milan Hillclimb 127, 128
Miles, Ken 199
Mille Miglia 107, 189
Milliken, Bill 202
Milliken's Corner 204
Milwaukee Fairgrounds 185, 187
Mims, Donna Mae 273
Mitchell, Bill 247
Moffet, George 211, 219

Index

Momo, Alfred 62, 63, 64, 151, 208
Monise, Frank 195
Monkey Stable 109, 191
Moran, Charles 206
Moretti 34, 186
Morgan 43, 51, 52, 99, 100, 249
Morgan, Gary 161
Morris 46
Morris, Gordy 160, 252
Morris Garage 252
Morrison, Bob 102
Moss, Al 209
Moss, Stirling 11, 20, 24, 167, 168, 183, 197, 231
Moss Motors 209, 210
Motor Trend 177, 196, 198
Motto MG 7, 8, 16, 17, 99, 115
Mouatt, Bob 244
Mt. Equinox Hillclimb 33, 167, 208
Mulholland Drive 196
Musso, Luigi 181

Nakagawa, Jack 265
Nardi 14, 39, 40, 80
Nash Healey 244
Nassau Speed Week 9, 126, 168
Nelson Ledges 39, 220, 228, 270
Nicholas, Dave 270
Nichols, Frank 212
Northern Ohio Region of PCA 265
Nuvolari, Tazio 255

Offutt AFB 15, 155, 188, 193
Ogilvie, Reggie 263
Okinawa 260
Oliver, Barbara 153
Oliver, Hemp 150, 152, 153
Olson, Warren 254
Origin of the Checker Flag 96
OSCA 26, 33, 34, 36, 117, 121, 140, 160, 165, 166, 167
O'Shea, Paul 34, 134, 135, 138

P-40 aircraft 177, 235
P-47 aircraft 180, 235
P-51 aircraft 2, 105, 177, 178, 180, 184
Pabst, Augie 95, 139, 184
Packard 12, 177
Palm Beach Shores 39, 97
Pan American Airways 266
Panamerican Road Race 83, 144
Paravano, Tony 192, 193, 215, 229
Parks, John 16
Parsons, Bob 239
Patterson, Alan 211
Payne, Tom 16, 26, 52, 67, 89
Pebble Beach 132, 201
Peck, Art 273
Penske, Roger 65, 85, 100, 135, 137, 228
Perona, John 143
Pervo, Chuck 43
Pete Lovely 256
Peterson, Jim 15, 20, 23, 24
Pfabe, Edsel 188
Philippine Islands 110, 185

Pick 65
Pikes Peak 85, 86, 87, 132, 203
Pirelli 175
Piston Patter 13, 92, 149
Polak, Vasek 194
Pollack, Bill 213
Pomona CA 84
Pompeo, Tony 83, 117, 137, 138, 140, 160, 162, 163, 195, 238
Pontiac GTO 70
Porsche 19, 20, 22, 23, 25, 26, 35, 37, 54, 55, 56, 57, 58, 65, 8, 115, 198
Porsche 904 58, 249
Porsche 906 249
Porsche 908 198
Porsche Club of America 265
Porsche Speedster 19, 22, 23, 55, 57, 58, 78, 129, 193, 249
Porsche Spyder 23, 25, 30, 37, 58, 78, 84, 85, 86, 87, 102, 112, 135, 138, 166, 182, 193, 194,195, 240, 248, 264, 266
Pratt Institute 172
Put-in-Bay 13, 15, 26, 28, 37, 42, 43, 44, 73, 88, 115, 127, 129, 139, 169, 170, 211, 220, 223, 227, 234, 235, 238, 242

Quackenbush, John 122, 179

Race Car Vehicle Dynamics 206
Race Communications Association 29, 158
Racing in the rain 187
Racing Safety 184
Rand, George 46, 61, 63
The Red Car 174
Redman, Brian 198
Reinhart, Johnny 110
Reventlow, Lance 24, 215, 216, 257
Revson, Peter 198
Richards, Paul 65
Riley 46, 47, 62
Ripley, Millard 240, 251
Riverside Raceway 83
Road America 20, 21, 22, 23, 25, 56, 57, 71, 94, 95, 123, 231, 257
Road & Track 33, 67, 69, 189, 190
Road Racing Drivers Club 76, 168, 273
Rodriguez, Pedro 113, 196
Rose, Maury 66
Rosenthal, Stanley 81
Ross 162
Rouen 219
Rubirosa, Porfirio 122, 255
Rudd, Tony 113
Russell, Jim — Driving School 157
Ryan, Peter 269
Rye, Walter 122, 180, 181

Saal, Tom 153
SAC Base Races 64
Said, Bob 217
Sailing 25, 30, 59, 149, 157
Sam Collier accident 205

Satava, Bob 227
Scarab 257
SCCA 7, 12, 19, 20, 33, 37, 39, 46, 49, 60, 64, 67, 68, 75, 87, 95. 131, 139, 153, 155, 165, 171, 202, 205, 206, 220, 243
SCCA Glen Region 162
SCCA NEOhio Region 228, 243
SCCA Ohio Valley Region 264
SCCA St. Louis Region 125
SCCA Steel Cities Region 270, 273
Scher, Doctor Sam 205
Scuderia Bear 36
Seaverns, Bud 57, 92
Sebring 15, 26, 34, 36, 49, 64, 99, 118, 119, 131, 181, 211, 215, 245, 266
Sesslar, Don 85, 125, 135, 182
71st Eagle Squadron 180
Seyler, Art 220
S.H. Arnolt Corporation 13, 156, 265
Shea, Bob 222
Sheffer, Hector 140
Shelby, Carroll 229
Shelby Cobra 36, 82, 137, 140, 229, 231
Shelby Mustang 201, 232
Shell Oil movies 243
Siata 17, 26, 33, 34, 44, 45, 46, 49, 72, 74, 117, 118, 137, 138, 140, 144, 160, 163, 165, 189, 193, 238, 264
Siffert, Jo 198
Sikorsky S39B amphibian 59
Sitz, Jim 112, 120, 130, 133, 135, 144, 168, 188, 189, 192, 199, 200, 201, 213, 215, 254, 255, 257, 273
Smalley, Les 161
Smith, George 39
Smith, Spankey 250
Smith, Steve 70
Snavely, B. Roy 225
Snelbaker, Don 14, 17, 18, 34, 46, 47, 53, 203, 204, 236
Soderstrom, Bengt 247
Solar Productions 198
Solomon Islands 184
Sparkman & Stephens 244
Spear, Bill 64, 65, 178
Spitfire aircraft 96. 97, 153, 180
Sports Car Graphic 92, 273
Sports Car magazine 3, 92, 165, 239
Sports Cars Illustrated 70
Sports Cars Limited 44, 45
Sports Cars of Ypsilanti 67
Sprint cars 192
Stablimenti Farina 165
Stains, Emmett 25
Stanford, Donald K. 174
Stanguellini 31, 32, 63, 65, 187
Star Class 235
Staufer, Bill 232
Staufer, Chris 233, 234, 235
Staufer, Pat 232, 234, 235
Steger, Fred 110
Steger, Gerry 110
Stevenson, Bruce 235

Stevenson, Fred 211, 212, 273
Stewart, Phil 15, 16, 19, 20
Stewarts Photo 85, 131
Stoddard, Chuck 238
Stoddard Imported Cars 240
Stone, Matt 195, 196
The Story of the MG Sports Car 163
Stout Field 190
Stroppe, Bill 273
Sugarman, Stan 194
Sunbeam Tiger 36
Super Vee 157
Surtees, John 75
Swan, Herb 136
Swedo, Chris 107

Tame, John 241
Targa Florio 11
Terhune, Walter 265
Thistle Class 243
Thompson, Dick 244
Thompson Products 264
Thompson Raceway 14, 61, 80, 171, 173, 175, 238, 268
Thornley, John 16, 177
356 Registry 138
Tierno, Joe 250
Trego, Ed 19
Triumph TR2, TR3 30, 58, 93, 95, 176, 211, 225
Troyan, Fred 223, 224, 225
Trullo d'Oro 218, 219
Tufte, Clif 23, 95

Turner AFB 54, 87
Tweety Bird 238

Uhr, Jack 37, 170, 227
Uihlein, Dave 92
Ullrich, Hal 114
Underwood, Lake 247
United States Grand Prix 11, 206
U.S. Marine Corps 195
University of Miami 211
University of Michigan 185
USRRC 76, 220, 269

Vack, Pete 33, 137, 139, 140
Valentine, George 249
Veloce Today 33
Vero Beach 12-Hour 33, 146, 147
Victor, Bill 252
Victor Gasket 253
Vignale 120
Vineland 166
Vintage Sportscar Club 96
Volkswagen 29, 39, 41, 73, 257
von Hanstein, Huschke 57, 85
von Neumann, Eleanor 112, 257
von Neumann, John 254
von Neumann, Josie 112, 256

Wacker, Fred 257
Wallace, Charlie 33, 229
Walters, Phil 31, 61, 63, 64, 65, 72, 106, 108, 188, 229, 273
Wangers, Jim 70

Watkins Glen 9, 10, 11, 33, 39, 46, 47, 48, 49, 53, 54, 61, 62, 73, 83, 88, 96, 97, 115, 203
Watts, Bob 260, 262, 274
Watts, Harley 260
Weaver, George 46
Webb, Norm 239
Weitz, John 23
Westhampton Airport 83
Westover AFB Race 33
Weyer, Gerry 138
Wheat, Morris 249
Whiting, Herb 264
Whiting, Larry 92
Wilkens, Ed 229
Willow Springs 201
Wilmot Hills 25, 72, 93, 157
Wisdom, Tommy 18
Wittenburg University 126
Wonder, Bill 266
Wonder, Lillian 268
Wyer, John 202
Wyllie, Doc 270
Wyllie, Peggy 270

Yates, Brock 70
Yenko, Don 244, 273

Zagato 36, 152, 273
Zandvoort 218
Zuckert, Sherrie 273

www.ingramcontent.com/pod-product-compliance
Lightning Source LLC
Chambersburg PA
CBHW081544300426
44116CB00015B/2744